acce *studies*

Accession no.
01081377

LIBRARY

Tel: 01244 375444   Ext: 3301

This book is to be returned on or before the last date stamped below. Overdue charges will be incurred by the late return of books.

Chester

A College of the
University of Liverpool

KT-500-781

UCC LIBRARY
0 5 DEC 2002
CANCELLED

WITHDRAWN

WITHDRAWN

Hodder & Stoughton

A MEMBER OF THE HODDER HEADLINE GROUP

OCR

RECOGNISING ACHIEVEMENT

Acknowledgements

The front cover illustration shows 'Twelve Apostles' rock formation, reproduced courtesy of © Australian Picture Library/Corbis.

The publishers would like to thank the following individuals, institutions and companies for permission to reproduce copyright illustrations in this book: AKG London/Jean Louis Nou, page 139; © Dean Conger/Corbis, page 159.

The publishers would also like to thank the following for permission to reproduce material in this book: Amana Publications for the extracts from *The Meaning of the Holy Qur'an* translated by 'Abdullah Yusuf 'Ali, published by Amana Publications, Beltsville, Marland 20705, USA (ISBN 0915957760/0915957329/0915957779); the extracts reproduced from *The Stone Edition Tanach* edited by Rabbi Nosson Scherman with permission from the copyright holders Artscroll/Mesorah Publications, Ltd; the extracts from *Hindu Scriptures* translated by Zaehner, Everyman, 1992, reprinted by permission of Everyman Publishers, Plc., Gloucester Mansions, 140a Shaftesbury Avenure, London WC2H 8HD.

Every effort has been made to trace and acknowledge ownership of copyright. The publishers will be glad to make suitable arrangements with any copyright holders whom it has not been possible to contact.

Orders: please contact Bookpoint Ltd, 130 Milton Park, Abingdon, Oxon OX14 4SB. Telephone: (44) 01235 827720, Fax: (44) 01235 400454. Lines are open from 9.00–6.00, Monday to Saturday, with a 24 hour message answering service. Email address: orders@bookpoint.co.uk

British Library Cataloguing in Publication Data
A catalogue for this title is available from The British Library

ISBN 0 340 79959 5

First published 2001

Impression number	10	9	8	7	6	5	4	3	2
Year		2007	2006	2005	2004	2003	2002		

Copyright © 2001 Libby Ahluwalia

All rights reserved. This work is copyright. Permission is given for copies to be made of pages provided they are used exclusively within the institution for which this work has been purchased. For reproduction for any other purpose, permission must first be obtained in writing from the publishers.

Typeset by Transet Limited, Coventry, England
Printed in Great Britain for Hodder & Stoughton Educational, a division of Hodder Headline Plc, 338 Euston Road, London NW1 3BH by The Bath Press, Bath.

Contents

Preface

To the reader

Access books are written mainly for students studying for examinations at higher level, particularly GCE Advanced Subsidiary (AS) level and Advanced (A) level as well as the Scottish National Qualification in RMPS at Intermediate 2 and Higher Levels.

To use this book most effectively, you should be aware of the following features.

- The Contents list gives a breakdown of the main sections in each chapter.
- Within each chapter, the material is broken down into subheadings and bullet points to make it easier to use.
- The Key Words at the beginning of each chapter are for easy reference and to help you become more familiar with the technical language of the subject.
- There are suggestions for further reading at the end of each chapter.
- There are also Summary lists of the main points at the end of each section. It can form the outline of your study notes on the topic. It is also a quick revision tool.
- There is also help with answering examination questions, and a list of typical questions is given. Do tackle the specimen questions, just planning your answers to some of them and writing others in full.

General advice on answering essay questions
Structured questions will tell you what to include.

- Make sure that you are aware of the number of marks available for each part question, and plan your time accordingly, so that you spend more time on the parts for which more marks are available.
- Before you choose your questions, make sure that you have read both parts and are confident about both.
- The first part of the question is aimed to assess your knowledge and understanding of the topic, and your skills in presenting a description. Try to keep to what is relevant, and use technical terms correctly where you can. Aim to provide some evidence of your background reading, by referring to the author or the title of the book, or by contrasting one thinker with another.
- The second part is designed to assess your evaluative skills. This is not the place to present a lot more description, but to weigh the evidence. Often, these questions consist of a statement followed by 'Discuss.' Try and explain why some people would agree with the statement, while others disagree. Aim to give supported reasons for your own position, rather than just saying 'I feel' without any justification.

Introduction

1 About this book

This book is written primarily to support students beginning an AS in Religious Studies. There are different chapters which correspond to different sections of the specification, and you will not need all of them; you will be studying two options, for example Philosophy of Religion and Religious Ethics, or Islam and Developments in Christian Thought, and so these are the chapters which apply to you. Some of the chapters are longer than others; this does not mean that some of the topics require more knowledge than others for the examination. However, some options are more popular than others, and the book is weighted so that the majority of students have the most material. There are also some areas where there is a wide variety of suitable reading matter for this level, and others where there is very little, and this book aims to 'fill the gaps', dwelling at greater length on the topics where most other material is written with a different readership in mind.

2 Background reading

Each section or chapter of this book contains suggestions for background reading. At AS and A level, it is important that candidates read widely, rather than depend exclusively on the teacher's notes or on just one text book. One of the characteristics that distinguish achievement of a higher standard in the examination is that a candidate shows evidence of background reading. This does not mean that students are expected to learn long quotations verbatim, but they should be able to refer with confidence to different views. When examination candidates have read widely, this is apparent from their work; they do not merely repeat remembered material, but have learned and adopted different ways of expressing ideas and the ability to question different writers, especially when the views of one are not consistent with the views of another. Although this book is written to support students through the Foundation Unit of AS, it is not meant to be used exclusively. Further reading will always help, and it will establish good study skills in preparation for University.

The books suggested are just some of many possible sources. If other books are more easily available, it might be preferable to use those instead. Books are not all written for the same kind of level of knowledge and understanding, and a book which one person finds fascinating might leave another completely bemused; the suggestions usually provide a range of possibilities from which to choose, according to the abilities and tastes of the student.

The Internet can provide some very useful source material. Those studying Hinduism, for example, might benefit from visiting the websites of archaeological investigations in Harappa and Mohenjo-Daro. There are many excellent sites dealing with philosophical and ethical issues, and for world religions. However, there is also a lot of complete rubbish on the Internet, and students should make sure that they do enough reading from reputable books to be able to distinguish good material from bad. The Internet is a useful supplement to background reading, but is not a good substitute for it.

3 Essay questions

The essay questions are separated into two parts, and the first part is worth effectively twice as many marks as the second. The first part tests skills in knowledge and description; time is limited, and therefore it is essential to read exactly what is being required to ensure that irrelevancy is kept to a minimum. For example, in the first question in the section on Islam, the revelation of the Qur'an to Muhammad ﷺ is required, and details about his life afterwards are not relevant. For higher marks, you should aim for accuracy, detail, relevance to the question and clarity of expression. You might find it useful in an examination to jot down a quick list of bullet points, but avoid writing long and detailed essay plans, as you will run out of time.

In the second part, an evaluation is required. Aim to explain the point of view being expressed, and then why some people might agree with it while others would disagree. Your own opinion is valuable, but for the highest marks you should consider why other people might not think in the same way. Try to justify views with reasons, rather than just saying 'This is how I feel'. The opening and closing sentences of your answer are particularly important; you want to give the examiner a good impression as you begin, and reinforce that at the end. Make sure that you open and close by showing that you understand exactly what the question is about.

Note

In this book, CE is used for Common Era, and BCE is used for Before Common Era. CE means the same as AD, but it is preferred because AD translates as Anno Domini (the year of our Lord) and it cannot be assumed that everyone is a Christian.

In the sections on Judaism G-d is used.

Whenever Muhammad ﷺ is used it is followed by the symbol for 'Peace be upon him' (ﷺ).

1 Philosophy of Religion

KEYWORDS

Hellenistic – an adjective relating to Greek culture, language, history and concepts, of the period between the fourth and first centuries BCE

philosopher – someone who is engaged in the study of philosophy

philosophy – Philosophy itself is difficult to define; some people have called it 'thinking about thinking', reflective thought about the nature of the world and the concepts used to understand it. It is literally the love of wisdom, from the Greek words 'philos', love, and 'sophia', wisdom.

teleological – a word based on the Greek 'telos', which means 'tail' or 'end'. Something is teleological if it looks at the end result; a teleological argument for the existence of God considers the end result of creation, the world, in order to argue for the cause of this result. A teleological system of ethics judges whether actions are right by the results the actions bring about.

transcendent – existing apart from the material world; surpassing and excelling other things

1 Introduction

Philosophy is a tradition in which people have tried to make sense of the world through the use of their reason, rather than through experimentation or through asking another authority for answers. It involves questioning the concepts we use to understand the world, and asking ourselves what we really mean when we use particular words or ideas. It also includes the consideration of whether it makes sense to hold particular beliefs and opinions, analysing the reasoning behind them and asking whether they are coherent.

Two of the most important thinkers in the history of philosophy are Plato and his pupil Aristotle. Although they lived before Jesus, they have been hugely influential in the shaping of Christian thought and doctrines; Augustine (354–430 CE), for example, owed many of his ideas to Plato, and Aquinas (1224–1274 CE) was very much inspired by Aristotle. A study of Christian beliefs about God and about the world shows very clearly two different strands of thought woven together; the thinking of the ancient Greek philosophers, and the ideas and imagery of the Bible.

2 Plato (c.428–347 BCE)

a) Biographical note

Plato is probably the best known of all the ancient Greek philosophers; it has been said that all of philosophy is simply 'footnotes to Plato' (A.N. Whitehead), adding to and discussing issues that Plato raised. Many of the world's greatest philosophers, including philosophers of religion, developed their systems of thought by agreeing or disagreeing with aspects of Platonism. Bertrand Russell, in his *History of Western Philosophy*, writes:

> Plato and Aristotle were the most influential of all philosophers, ancient, medieval, or modern; and of the two, it was Plato who had the greater effect on subsequent ages.

The written works of Greek philosophy begin with Plato; his are the earliest writings that have survived. He was a pupil of Socrates, but as far as we know Socrates taught only by word of mouth; if he did write anything, it was lost long ago. Most of what we know about the thinking of Socrates comes from Plato's writing.

Plato was born into an aristocratic Athenian family, in about 428 BCE. Because of his birth, he might have been expected to become a politician of Athens; but he came under the influence of the great teacher Socrates, and he was filled with enthusiasm for philosophy. Socrates is renowned for many things, but particularly for his method of teaching by questioning, encouraging his pupils to examine their own ideas; and sometimes making people who were over-confident about their own expertise look foolish in the process. The government of Athens was democratic, but Socrates made no secret of the fact that he preferred a form of government where a single wise individual ruled. He also did not believe in the accepted gods, but claimed to hear 'divine inner voices'.

Because of his outspokenness and his readiness to challenge the beliefs and opinions of the leaders of Athens, Socrates made himself very popular with some, notably the young including Plato, but also very unpopular with others. He was arrested on charges of corrupting the young (by his antidemocratic teaching) and of introducing new gods, was found guilty by a slender majority, and was condemned to death by poison. Socrates could, perhaps, have appealed for leniency, or agreed to leave Athens for ever, but he decided to make a stand. He would not back down – the search for the truth, including challenging the accepted opinions of the day, was more important than loyalty to the state, or even life itself. Socrates drank the poisonous hemlock, and died, in 399 BCE, when Plato was about thirty.

Plato was present in the court throughout the trial and conviction of Socrates. He was horrified and disgusted at the treatment given to the teacher he admired so much, and he left Athens soon after, perhaps in disgust, or perhaps because he was afraid for his own safety. It is believed that he travelled extensively, possibly including a visit to Egypt, and then on to Italy and Sicily before returning to Athens.

Some time after Socrates' death, Plato began to produce and circulate a series of philosophical writings, presented in the form of dialogues, where the main character was always Socrates. The Socrates of the dialogues is presented with various moral, political and philosophical questions. The other person in the dialogue is someone who at first appears wise, and to know all the answers, and Socrates pretends to be ignorant, asking questions to clarify his own understanding. But as the dialogues progress, it becomes clear that Socrates' opponents have not really thought through their positions, and Socrates himself is the wiser man – not because he knows everything, but because he recognises the limitations of his own knowledge and is prepared to question generally accepted ideas. People take it for granted that they know the meaning of 'justice', or 'friendship' or 'courage', but they are made to look again and to realise that there are problems in the concepts that they hold.

In this way, Plato was able to keep alive Socrates' ideas and reputation. In Plato's early dialogues, there is probably a fairly accurate portrait of the real Socrates, and a record of the kinds of things he said. Plato defends Socrates, and protests about the manner of his death, by showing a figure who was not corrupt but a great educator, a man who thought for himself and encouraged others to do the same. Plato's early dialogues include *Laches* (a discussion of the meaning of courage) *Euthyphro* (a consideration of the meaning of piety) and *Book 1* of the *Republic* (a discussion of justice).

However, as Plato's writing developed and was enthusiastically received, he began to include more of his own ideas. The quality of his work was superb; many believe that his writing stands among the greatest in world literature. He still used dialogues, with Socrates as his main character, but he introduced more and more of his own philosophy, so that today, it is difficult to tell where the ideas of the original Socrates end, and the ideas of Plato begin. The scope of Plato's interests was vast, including not only philosophy, ethics and politics, but also mathematics and physics, which he believed were vital for an understanding of the natural world. However, he was hostile to the arts because believed that they are representations, and illusions. The search for reality and truth, he thought, should not be obscured by things which are only pretences, designed to appeal to the senses rather than the reason.

In 387 BCE, Plato founded the Academy in Athens, an institution which is often regarded as the first of the European Universities, and which was to last for nine hundred years, until it was closed by Justinian. It provided a wide curriculum, including astronomy, politics, mathematics, biology, and of course philosophy. The most famous student of the Academy was Aristotle.

Plato was eager to put his ideas about politics and philosophy into practice, and so he went to Sicily for a while to tutor Dionysius the Younger, the new ruler. This did not work, and Plato returned to the Academy, to spend the rest of his life teaching and writing. He died at the age of about eighty, in 348 or 347 BCE.

b) The allegory of the cave

The *Republic* is the work in which Plato discusses the nature of justice, the ideal society, and who should rule it. He considers the kind of person who would be fit to rule, and the kind of education that he would need in order to do the job properly.

Plato's *Allegory of the Cave* is possibly the most famous passage in all of his writings. As an allegory, the story has meanings on several different levels; there is not just one 'moral to the story', but a variety of linked points are made in order to express Plato's understanding of the progress of the mind from its lowest stages to an enlightened knowledge of the Good. Using the allegory, Plato expresses something of his beliefs about learning, and his beliefs about the relation between the world of appearances and the world of Reality. He suggests that the body is a kind of prison in which the soul is trapped; and he also suggests that Socrates was killed because of the stupidity of people who did not recognise the value of enlightenment.

Plato believed that there was a difference between intellectual knowledge, gained through reason, and the knowledge gained through using the senses. He thought that knowledge gained through the senses was no more than opinion, because the senses can be mistaken; but knowledge gained through philosophical reasoning was certain. The allegory of the cave makes a contrast between people who see only appearances, but mistake them for the truth, and those who really do see the truth.

> And now, I said, let me show in a figure how far our nature is enlightened or unenlightened: Behold! human beings living in an underground den, which has a mouth open toward the light and reaching all along the den; here they have been from their childhood, and have their legs and necks chained so that they cannot move, and can only see before them, being prevented by the chains from turning round their heads. Above and behind them a fire is blazing at a distance, and between the fire and the prisoners there is a raised way; and you will see, if you look, a low wall built along the way, like the screen which marionette-players have in front of them, over which they show the puppets.
> I see.

And do you see, I said, men passing along the wall carrying all sorts of vessels, and statues and figures of animals made of wood and stone and various materials, which appear over the wall? Some of them are talking, others silent.

You have shown me a strange image, and they are strange prisoners.

Like ourselves, I replied; and they see only their own shadows, or the shadows of one another, which the fire throws on the opposite wall of the cave?

True, he said; how could they see anything but the shadows if they were never allowed to move their heads?

And of the objects which are being carried in like manner they would only see the shadows?

Yes, he said.

And if they were able to converse with one another, would they not suppose that they were naming what was actually before them?

Very true.

And suppose further that the prison had an echo which came from the other side, would they not be sure to fancy when one of the passers-by spoke that the voice which they heard came from the passing shadow?

No question, he replied.

To them, I said, the truth would be literally nothing but the shadows of the images.

That is certain.

And now look again, and see what will naturally follow if the prisoners are released and disabused of their error. At first, when any of them is liberated and compelled suddenly to stand up and turn his neck round and walk and look toward the light, he will suffer sharp pains; the glare will distress him, and he will be unable to see the realities of which in his former state he had seen the shadows; and then conceive someone saying to him, that what he saw before was an illusion, but that now, when he is approaching nearer to being and his eye is turned toward more real existence, he has a clearer vision—what will be his reply? And you may further imagine that his instructor is pointing to the objects as they pass and requiring him to name them—will he not be perplexed? Will he not fancy that the shadows which he formerly saw are truer than the objects which are now shown to him?

Far truer.

And if he is compelled to look straight at the light, will he not have a pain in his eyes which will make him turn away to take refuge in the objects of vision which he can see, and which he will conceive to be in reality clearer than the things which are now being shown to him?

True, he said.

And suppose once more, that he is reluctantly dragged up a steep and rugged ascent, and held fast until he is forced into the presence of the sun himself, is he not likely to be pained and irritated? When he approaches the light his eyes will be dazzled, and he will not be able to see anything at all of what are now called realities.

Not all in a moment, he said.

He will require to grow accustomed to the sight of the upper world. And first he will see the shadows best, next the reflections of men and other objects in the water, and then the objects themselves; then he will gaze upon the light of the moon and the stars and the spangled heaven; and he will see the sky and the stars by night better than the sun or the light of the sun by day?

Certainly.

Last of all he will be able to see the sun, and not mere reflections of him in the water, but he will see him in his own proper place, and not in another; and he will contemplate him as he is.

Certainly.

He will then proceed to argue that this is he who gives the season and the years, and is the guardian of all that is in the visible world, and in a certain way the cause of all things which he and his fellows have been accustomed to behold?

Clearly, he said, he would first see the sun and then reason about him.

And when he remembered his old habitation, and the wisdom of the den and his fellow-prisoners, do you not suppose that he would felicitate himself on the change, and pity him?

Certainly, he would.

And if they were in the habit of conferring honours among themselves on those who were quickest to observe the passing shadows and to remark which of them went before, and which followed after, and which were together; and who were therefore best able to draw conclusions as to the future, do you think that he would care for such honors and glories, or envy the possessors of them? Would he not say with Homer, "Better to be the poor servant of a poor master,"

and to endure anything, rather than think as they do and live after their manner?

Yes, he said, I think that he would rather suffer anything than entertain these false notions and live in this miserable manner.

Imagine once more, I said, such a one coming suddenly out of the sun to be replaced in his old situation; would he not be certain to have his eyes full of darkness?

To be sure, he said.

And if there were a contest, and he had to compete in measuring the shadows with the prisoners who had never moved out of the den, while his sight was still weak, and before his eyes had become steady (and the time which would be needed to acquire this new habit of sight might be very considerable), would he not be ridiculous? Men would say of him that up he went and down he came without his eyes; and that it was better not even to think of ascending; and if anyone tried to loose another and lead him up to the light, let them only catch the offender, and they would put him to death.

No question, he said.

This entire allegory, I said, you may now append, dear Glaucon, to the previous argument; the prison-house is the world of sight, the light of the fire is the sun, and you will not misapprehend me if you interpret the journey upward to be the ascent of the soul into the intellectual world according to my poor belief, which, at your desire, I have expressed—whether rightly or wrongly, God knows. But, whether true or false, my opinion is that in the world of knowledge the idea of good appears last of all, and is seen only with an effort; and, when seen, is also inferred to be the universal author of all things beautiful and right, parent of light and of the lord of light in this visible world, and the immediate source of reason and truth in the intellectual; and that this is the power upon which he who would act rationally either in public or private life must have his eye fixed.

I agree, he said, as far as I am able to understand you.

Moreover, I said, you must not wonder that those who attain to this beatific vision are unwilling to descend to human affairs; for their souls are ever hastening into the upper world where they desire to dwell; which desire of theirs is very natural, if our allegory may be trusted.

Yes, very natural.

And is there anything surprising in one who passes from divine contemplations to the evil state of man, misbehaving himself in a ridiculous manner; if, while his eyes are blinking and before he has become accustomed to the surrounding darkness, he is compelled to fight in courts of law, or in other places, about the images or the shadows of images of justice, and is endeavoring to meet the conceptions of those who have never yet seen absolute justice?

Anything but surprising, he replied.

Plato *Republic, Book VII 514A –521B*

The allegory begins with a description of prisoners in a cave, who are only able to look straight ahead of themselves because they are chained. They have a fire behind them, and a wall in front, and the cave has a long tunnel entrance so that there is no natural daylight in the cave, only the firelight.

The imagery of a cave was a familiar one to Plato's audiences. In a poem by an earlier philosopher, Empedocles, for example, the powers that trap a soul in its human body say, 'We have come under this cavern's roof'; the cave conveys the sense of being trapped, in a different world, away from light, and away from reality. Cornford, in his translation of Plato's *Republic*, mentions the use of caves in so-called 'mystery' religions, where the person who was being initiated into the religion would be led through a series of caves and tunnels, representing the underworld, to a sudden blaze of light revealing sacred objects. The scene set in a cave, then, emphasises that the prisoners were trapped, away from 'real life'.

The prisoners have been in the cave since childhood; it is important for the allegory that they have never known anything different from their present situation. Behind the prisoners, where they cannot see, between them and the fire, is a kind of track, with a parapet in front of it, rather like the stage of a puppet show. People carry a variety of artificial objects along the track, making them move, and sometimes giving them voices, making them seem as though they are talking. The prisoners, then, have an experience of something rather like being in an underground cinema. They cannot see the objects that are being carried, only the shadows of the objects cast by the firelight onto the wall they are facing. The shadows are not very good shadows, because they are caused by flickering firelight; and they are not even the shadows of real objects, but are the images of artificial things made out of wood or stone. The sounds that they make are not real, they are only echoes, and they are echoes of people who are only pretending to be the objects they carry.

So the prisoners in the cave have an experience of reality that is as far removed as possible from the everyday world. They see only poorly formed shadows of artificial objects pretending to move, and they hear only echoed sound that does not really come from the objects they see at all; but as far as they know, using the evidence of their senses, this is the only reality. Their language reflects this experience.

This is a state of mind which Plato called 'eikasia' in chapter VI of the *Republic*. It is a word which cannot be translated, and comes from 'eikon' – an image or likeness. The word has connotations of likeness (representation), likening (making a comparison) and likelihood (probability). When the word is used by Plato to describe this state of mind, the lowest level of understanding, it carries all these different meanings, of artificiality, guesswork and opinion. The prisoners in the cave see only images of images, and yet they take these at face value, without questioning whether there is any other, greater reality or truth. They are, in Plato's view, comparable to people whose lives and minds are empty of philosophy, and who accept everything they see and hear without question, never thinking about it or challenging the accepted ideas and morals of their society.

In the cave, at last one of the prisoners is set free. He can stand up and turn around. At first he finds movement painful, and is too dazzled by the new light to see anything properly at all. (Plato shows here that the first response to philosophical questioning is puzzlement.) But as he becomes more used to the light, he begins to realise that his former view of reality was not accurate; he begins to question his own previously held beliefs. Looking at the fire makes him uncomfortable, and he wants to go back to looking at the shadows again, when he was happy with his interpretation of the world. But the released prisoner is forced outside – the journey is described as steep and rough – into the daylight.

Again, the former prisoner at first finds it impossible to see anything at all, because he is so dazzled by the sunlight. However, gradually his sight adjusts to the daylight; he sees the objects around him, first as shapes and reflections, and then he is able to focus on real objects. The more his eyes get used to the world outside the cave, the more he is able to perceive. Having looked at the world around him, he is then able to look into the sky – at night-time first, seeing the moon and stars, and eventually in the day-time. He is able to see the real world, and draw conclusions from it which are true. He begins to understand that the world depends for its existence on the sun, the source of all the light, reflections and shadows. He also is very much aware that his earlier understanding of reality was wrong, and that skills which had been prized by the prisoners were worthless. Plato suggests that the prisoners might have made up a game, where they observe the passing shadows and remember the order in which they appear, so that they can make good guesses about which object will come next – but this requires no philosophical insight, just a skill at guesswork. The person who has real knowledge can see that this skill has no true value when it is compared with a genuine understanding of reality.

The former prisoner feels sorry for the others who are still in the cave, and so he decides to go down again. When he finds himself suddenly in darkness after having adjusted to the light, his ability to see the shadows on the wall is worse than it was before his release. The people who are still in chains laugh at him, and say that the journey up into the light is a waste of time, because it has spoiled his ability to see clearly. They do not want to try to find the light for themselves; and if someone ever tries to come and set them free, they will kill him.

c) Plato's Theory of Forms

At the heart of all of Plato's philosophy is his Theory of Forms, sometimes called the Theory of Ideas. He believed that, as well as the material world in which we live and which we experience, there is also another, eternal world of concepts or Forms. This eternal world is more real than the world we experience through the senses, and it is the object of knowledge, not opinion.

The world of sense experience is subject to constant change, and this was a popular topic for discussion in Greek philosophy; how can the truth be known, if the world never stays the same from one moment to the next? Heraclitus, a philosopher who lived about two hundred years before Plato, had considered this idea. He was famous for the saying 'It is not possible to step into the same river twice'. According to Heraclitus, everything in the world is in a constant state of flux. Things come into the world, they change all the time that they are here, and they go away again. The objects we perceive are not eternal 'things', they are processes. Heraclitus believed that there is nothing in the world that is reliable and unchanging, and nothing that we can hold up as a certain, unchanging truth.

Plato had a different view. He believed that the answer to this question was that there is certain truth, but that this material world cannot reveal it. It can only present appearances, which lead us to form opinions, rather than knowledge. The truth is to be found elsewhere, on a different plane, in the non-material world of Ideas or Forms. For Plato, in order for something to be real, it had to be permanent and unchanging. Reality and perfection for Plato were closely related.

When Socrates asked 'What is justice?' or 'What is beauty?', he was not just trying to find a good definition of the words. He was asking about the nature, or essence, of these qualities. Plato believed that the qualities had a sort of universal existence, a reality of their own. When we see examples of justice in the world, we recognise them as such because we see that they reflect the nature of True Justice, or the Form of Justice. When we call something beautiful, it is because we have an innate knowledge of True Beauty, or the Form of Beauty. The justice or the beauty that we see in the world around us is always imperfect, but even though we have never seen perfect justice or beauty, we know what they are, according to Plato, because knowledge is a kind of recollection. We have an instinctive understanding of the Forms; so we can say to each other 'Her eyes are too close together' and know that this means that she falls short of true beauty, which we understand as a concept even though we have never seen a perfect example of it.

According to Plato's thinking, because we have concepts of the Ideal Forms, without having experienced them, our souls must have known the Forms before we were born. This leads him to the belief that people must therefore have immortal souls.

Plato argued that when we use words and apply them to particular objects, we make reference to the world of Forms. To use Bertrand Russell's example:

> There are many individual animals of whom we can truly say 'this is a cat'. What do we mean by the word 'cat'? Obviously something different from each particular cat. An animal is a cat, it would seem, because it participates in a general nature common to all cats. Language cannot get on without general words such as 'cat', and such words are evidently not meaningless. But if the word 'cat' means anything, it means something which is not this or that cat, but some kind of universal cattiness. This is not born when a particular cat is born, and does not die when it dies. In fact, it has no position in space or time, it is 'eternal'.

Bertrand Russell, *History of Western Philosophy*

Plato believed, then, that when we use a word such as 'cat' to describe the particular animal we see, we are not just classifying it. We are referring to some particular quality or essence that it shares with all other animals that also are described as 'cat'; they all share something of the Form of Cat. Plato went further than this: he also claimed that, in the world of Forms, there is an Ideal Cat, created by God. The cats we see as we go about our daily lives are inferior instances of this Ideal Cat. They are constantly changing, they are born, and they die; but the Ideal Cat is eternal, depending on nothing for its existence, and is the object of knowledge, not opinion.

Another way of understanding the theory of Forms might be to consider them in terms of mathematics. For example, a circle is a two-dimensional figure made up of an infinite series of points, all the same distance from a given centre. This is not a matter of opinion, but something that we know. No one has ever actually seen a perfect circle, however. What they have actually seen are imperfect copies, reasonable approximations of a perfect circle. A perfect circle could not be seen; the infinite points which make up its circumference do not take up any space, they exist in logic rather than in a physical form. As soon as someone tries to draw it, even if he uses the most sophisticated computerised equipment, it becomes imperfect. But although the Ideal Form of a circle has never been seen, and never could be seen, people do know what a circle is, they can define it while at the same time accepting that it cannot be translated into the material world without losing its perfection.

For Plato, therefore, the Form of a Circle exists, but not in the physical world of space and time. It exists as a changeless object in the world of Forms or Ideas, which can be known only by reason. Forms have greater reality than objects in the physical world both because of their perfection and unchangingness, and because they are models. As Ideals, they give ordinary physical objects whatever reality they have, because of the ways in which the physical objects resemble the Forms; just as the shadows, in the Allegory of the Cave, only had any kind of existence because of their resemblance to their corresponding physical objects. Circularity, squareness, and triangularity are excellent examples, then, of what Plato meant by Forms. An object existing in the physical world may be called a circle or a square or a triangle only to the extent that it resembles ('participates in' is Plato's phrase) the Form 'circularity' or 'squareness' or 'triangularity'.

Plato believed that the Forms were interconnected, and arranged in a hierarchy. The most important Form is the Form of the Good, which is the ultimate principle. Like the Sun in the Allegory of the Cave, the Good illuminates the other Forms. We can see that Justice, for example, is an aspect of Goodness. And again, we know that we have never seen, with our senses, any examples of perfect goodness, but we have seen plenty of particular examples which approximate goodness, and we recognise them as 'good' when we see them because of the way in which they correspond to our innate notion of the Form of the Good. By Plato's logic, real knowledge becomes, in the end, a knowledge of goodness; and this is why philosophers are in the best position to rule.

Plato developed his Theory of Forms to the point where he divided existence into two realms. There is the world of sense experience (the 'empirical' world), where nothing ever stays the same but is always in the process of change. Experience of it gives rise to opinions. There is also a world which is outside space and time, which is not perceived through the senses, and in which everything is permanent and perfect or Ideal – the realm of the Forms. The empirical world shows only shadows and poor copies of these Forms, and so is less real than the world of the Forms themselves, because the Forms are eternal and immutable (unchanging), the proper objects of knowledge.

d) Plato's understanding of body and soul

Plato's understanding of the relationship between the soul and the body is closely related to his other ideas about duality; he thought of existence in terms of two levels. His discussion of the theory of Forms showed the differences between appearance and reality, between experience of the senses and reason, between opinion and knowledge, between physical objects and their Ideal Forms. In the same way, he believed that the human person also has different elements: the physical body, the mind, and the immortal soul. The body, like everything else physical, is in a constant state of change, and as such, cannot be the source or the object of reliable truth, because it is never the same from one moment to the next. The soul, in contrast, is immortal and unchanging, and therefore can both know and be known.

According to Plato, the body is the physical component of each person. The body is the part of a person that others can see and hear, the part that presents an appearance. It is through the body that we receive our sense experiences, so that our minds are able to form our opinions. Our minds are also able to achieve an awareness of the eternal truths beyond the physical world, in the realm of Ideas, or Forms.

Plato believed that the mind and the body are often in opposition. The mind wants to understand ideas, to gain real knowledge of the Forms; but the body is interested in sense pleasures, and it has needs such as eating and sleeping which are constantly getting in the way of intellectual pursuits, because they keep interrupting. Often the demands of the body are so great that they take over completely, cluttering the mind with thoughts of what might be for lunch, or whether we are looking our best, or whether we are too hot or too cold. Plato writes:

> The body is the source of endless trouble to us by reason of the mere requirement of food; and is liable also to diseases which overtake and impede us in the search after true being: it fills us full of loves, and lusts, and fears, and fancies of all kinds, and endless foolery, and in fact, as men say, takes away from us all power of thinking at all.

Plato, then, saw the body as a nuisance and a bind. It is not the real person. This way of thinking is often reflected in the way that we speak of our bodies. If we say 'I have a cat', we mean something entirely different from 'I am a cat'; 'I have a cat' means that I am not the cat itself, I am separate, distinct, the cat is something I own but it is not me. We say 'I have a body', not 'I am a body'; this hints at Plato's idea that the real person is separate and distinct from the body it inhabits.

The soul, according to Plato, is the directing force of the body. Plato compares the soul to a charioteer, in charge of two horses, the mind and the body. The soul tries to guide the two together, rather than allowing them to contradict and be pulled in opposite directions. Many people never achieve this direction; they allow their lives to be completely dominated by bodily needs and sense pleasures. They have no time left for intellectual pursuits, are satisfied with the world of appearances, and mistake their opinions for true knowledge. They are like the prisoners in the cave, who do not want to be released and who value shadows and the skill of guesswork. The philosophers, in contrast, try to minimise their interest in bodily needs. They only eat and drink what is necessary, they only wear simple clothes and cannot be bothered with decoration; they are far more interested in the soul.

Plato believed that the soul is immortal. It exists before, during and after it is trapped in a human body. It has to pre-exist the body, because it is unchanging, and part of being unchanging means that it cannot come into existence or go away again, it has to stay the same. This concept is connected with Plato's view that all real knowledge is remembering, recollection. He thought that we have ideas such as the meaning of 'perfect circle', or 'absolute equality', not because we have ever seen any examples of them but because these ideas were already with us, from a previous existence. As a person discovers different elements of the physical world, this begins a process of remembering. The soul, or psyche, begins to remember the world of Forms which it once inhabited, and it longs to return to this unchanging world; it becomes dissatisfied with the limitations of the body and the world of appearances.

The differences between the real knowledge grasped by the soul and the confused opinions gained by sense perception are explained by Plato using the metaphor of sight. He argues that sight needs not only the eye and an object to look at, but also light. Without the light, the object cannot be clearly seen. The light is compared to the Form of the Good; a knowledge of true, essential goodness allows the soul (the eye) to gain real understanding, clarity of vision. Without any light, with no perception of the Form of the Good, the eye cannot see very much at all, and has to be satisfied with poor appearances.

In Plato's dialogue *Phaedo*, Socrates claims that doing philosophy is a rehearsal for death. Death separates the soul from the body, and philosophy is about trying to concentrate on the real truth rather than appearances; so Plato is arguing that, in causing the death of Socrates, his opponents did not win at all, because they released his soul from the trap of the body and enabled it to re-enter the world of Forms and renew its knowledge of the Form of the Good.

In Plato's earlier dialogues, he gives a fairly simple account of the duality between the body and the soul. As his thought develops, and he follows his own recommendation to challenge his previously-held beliefs, it becomes more complex. The soul is divided into three different parts, roughly translated as reason, emotion, and desire, and Plato becomes less certain about which parts of the soul are immortal.

e) Plato's justification of the existence of the soul

Plato clearly believed that each person has a soul which lives on after the body dies; he also wanted to show that (in his view) this belief is reasonable and can be justified through logical argument. His dialogue *Phaedo* is mainly concerned with these arguments; Cebes, the person who is in dialogue with Socrates, suggests that perhaps the soul just disappears, like smoke, into nothingness when the body dies, and he asks for some kind of persuasive argument to justify Socrates' belief in the immortality of the soul.

i) The Argument from the Cycle of Opposites

Plato's first argument relies on the idea that every quality comes into being from its own opposite. It depends on the existence of its opposite, or it would not exist at all. He argues that big things would not be bigger or small things smaller without their opposites; they depend on their opposites for their existence. In the same way, people who are awake are just people who were asleep but then woke up, while people who are asleep are just people who were once awake. This idea very much influenced Augustine in his understanding of evil, as a quality that is the absence of goodness rather than a real power in its own right.

> Are not all things which have opposites generated out of their opposites? I mean such things as good and evil, just and unjust.

Plato argued that it follows that death must come from life, and life from death. That is, people who are dead are just people who were in the past alive but then experienced the change we call dying, and people who are alive are just people who were among the dead but then experienced the change we call being born. Plato's thought suggests an endless chain of birth, death and rebirth.

ii) The Argument from Knowledge

As we have already seen, Plato thought that the most important kinds of human knowledge are really remembering, 'leading out' things which we already knew. For example, according to Plato, we have our knowledge of equality even though we have never seen any two things that are perfectly equal, because there will always be some minute difference; and yet we know what true equality (or the Form of Equality) must be.

Plato thought that the same was true of many other abstract concepts: even though we only ever experience imperfect examples, we have genuine knowledge of truth, goodness, and beauty, just as we have true knowledge of equality and circularity. Plato distinguished this kind of knowledge from the sort of inferior, temporary, unreliable 'knowledge' that we might gain through the senses but which is merely opinion. Plato believed that this knowledge of the Forms must be innate, and must have been gained by our souls before we were born. When we come to understand something that is the object of true knowledge, such as the square root of 81, which is not available to the senses but is true for all time, we have a sense of recognition. For Plato, this was evidence that the soul pre-existed the body.

f) Criticisms of Plato

Plato's thought is complex. It works on many different levels, and interrelates, and his ideas change as he challenges his own beliefs and follows his own quest for knowledge. However, the key elements of his thought have been challenged, by Aristotle his pupil, and by many others who have come after him, who recognise his greatness as an original thinker but who nevertheless cannot accept many of his conclusions. Some points that might be raised include:

● The existence of the Forms Plato describes is not necessarily the obvious conclusion of logical reasoning, or the only conclusion. He does not seem to provide any convincing argument in favour of the belief that there is a realm of ideas, more real than the world of appearances. We might agree with him that we need to have concepts of perfect equality, or perfect circularity, or even perfect goodness, as tools to understand the world, but this does not mean that they must have a kind of independent existence, any more than language has any sort of independent reality beyond the world to which it refers. Plato, however, believes this higher level of reality in the realm of the Forms to be self-evident. We might argue that it is not self-evident to us; the 'appearance' of a wall or a parking meter is real enough when you accidentally walk into one, whereas the Ideal Form of a Cat does not seem to have much reality even as a concept. What colour is the Ideal Cat? Does it have long or short hair? How large is it? Some concepts fit Plato's system of thinking better than others. We can appreciate what he says about the Form of a Circle, or the Form of Equality, because these are mathematical concepts that we put into use, but it is difficult to imagine an ideal Form of something unpleasant such as Dirt or Disease, or even of something mundane such as Train Tickets.

● Another related problem with Plato's ideas is that he is not very clear about how far the Forms relate to specific items in the 'world of appearances'. Is there an Ideal Form of Animal, to which all animals relate, ourselves included? Or do Forms have to relate to specific animal species? Is there a Form of Pig, in general, or a separate Form for each variety of pig? Perhaps the Tamworth Pig has its own Form; perhaps there is a distinct Form of Male Tamworth Pig, and another for Female Tamworth Pig; and if the argument is taken to its logical conclusion, we might need a Form of Female Short-Sighted Pregnant Tamworth Pig, and so on, until every creature in the world is considered to have its own Form. The Forms stop being 'universals' and degenerate into something which has little meaning or use.

● Plato's ideas about the immortality of the soul are dependent on our acceptance of his other ideas about the existence of Forms and about knowledge being recollection or re-cognition of things we already know. We might not accept Plato's view that knowledge gained through sense experience is not valuable, even if we can agree that it is temporary. We need, for our survival, to use the knowledge given to us by our senses. The idea that bodily survival is not really important goes against our instincts. If our senses and our past physical experiences tell us that we are about to get hurt, we want to avoid it; and we need our knowledge of the physical world if we are going to be able to help other people. Plato's concerns about politics and ethics do not fit very logically with his view of the body as an encumbrance. If physical needs, and the physical world, are only appearances, then it should not matter too much who rules, or whether the people who live in the Republic have a decent quality of life.

● Plato believes that the highest of all forms of knowledge is an understanding of the Form of the Good, which he holds to be an absolute. However, this raises many of the problems which occur in the study of ethics; how are we to know what goodness is? How can two people, equally intelligent and equally sincere (or as nearly equal as the physical world allows), come to completely different conclusions about right and wrong? Plato appears to hold that the Form of the Good keeps in existence the whole world of Forms, and appearances too, just as the sun gives light and casts shadows; but if asked, we will all point to the same sun, whereas we cannot agree about what true Goodness is or how it should be shown to other people.

In Plato's thought, then, we can see the seeds of many of the concepts which have had a profound influence in shaping Christian philosophy:

- A person's appearance is not the most important thing about them. The 'real person' is far more important.
- Bodily pleasures should not be the main object of a person's existence; there is another, better focus of attention which is unchanging, enduring and far more worthwhile.
- The acquisition of physical objects is tempting, but misleading and shallow.
- This world is not the only world. There is another realm where we will live eternally after death.
- When the body dies, the soul is released.
- The concept of the Form of the Good has helped to shape the way in which Christians understand God, as a perfect being, beyond space and time, eternal and unchanging, the source of all goodness and the proper focus of all thought and pursuits.

3 Aristotle

a) Biographical notes

Aristotle was a pupil of Plato, just as Plato had been a pupil of Socrates. He lived from 384 to 322 BCE; he became known as Aristotle of Stagira, because he was born in the city of Stagira in Macedonia. His father was court physician to the King Amyntas of Macedonia, and his mother was rich in her own right; later, Aristotle was to become tutor to Amyntas' grandson, Alexander, known as Alexander the Great. Aristotle was brought up by a guardian, because when he was still a child his father died. At the age of seventeen, he was sent to school at Plato's Academy in Athens, where he was recognised as a brilliant student. He remained at the Academy for about twenty years, and hoped to succeed Plato as its director; but when Plato died, a nephew took over instead as his heir. This was partly because by right he inherited from Plato, and partly because although Aristotle was greatly admired, he was not an Athenian and some people were suspicious of his links with Macedonia, as relations between Athens and Macedonia were not particularly good. Because he had not been given the post he was expecting, Aristotle left Athens in 347 BCE.

After this, he travelled, developing a great interest in animals and plants, married Pythias, and accepted the post of tutor to the thirteen-year-old Alexander. Alexander and Aristotle are reputed to have been friends, but it was an uneasy relationship, and they had very different ideas about the importance of Greek culture and its place in the world. Unfortunately, everything we might really like to know about the relationship between the two is impossible to discover, as many legends were soon invented on the subject which have obscured the truth beyond recovery. Eventually, when Alexander came of age at sixteen, Aristotle left him, and after a while returned to Athens to lecture in a school called the Lyceum. He had a habit of teaching while walking about under the covered walkways, and became known as 'peripatetic' (walking about) because of this.

Aristotle directed and lectured at the Lyceum for twelve years. During this time he produced the treatises (lecture notes) which form his surviving works. His writings covered an amazing range of topics including logic, physics, biology, zoology, ethics, politics, economics, psychology and metaphysics. He developed a theory of matter, and of the relationship between ethics and politics; he began the notion of categories and classification of species; he invented meteorology. Aristotle set the agenda for intellectual pursuit for the next two thousand years, achieving so much that it is almost impossible to believe that it all came from the mind of one man. Jonathan Barnes, one of the world's leading experts on Aristotle, writes:

> Choose a field of research, and Aristotle laboured in it; pick an area of human endeavour, and Aristotle discoursed upon it. His range is astonishing.

Alexander the Great died in 323 BCE, possibly by poison. In Athens, the anti-Macedonian mood began again, and it was remembered that Aristotle was not an Athenian and that he had once tutored Alexander. The public mood turned against him; an inscription in his praise, dating from about 330 BCE, has been discovered torn up at the bottom of a well in Delphi. He was charged with 'impiety', disbelief in the established Greek gods, just as Socrates had been, but rather than stay and face going the same way as Socrates, he left Athens with his second wife Herpyllis, and he died the following year, at the age of 63.

It is difficult to know very much about the personality of Aristotle, because he lived so long ago. He had many admirers, but also many enemies. From his admirers, we learn that he was a good speaker, a generous man, and an inspiring teacher; his enemies tell us that he was 'spindle-shanked', arrogant and rather too fond of fashion.

b) Aristotle's writings

Only about a fifth of Aristotle's writings has survived. The major part of his life's work is lost, and what we have left is mostly in the form of notes and jottings which were almost certainly never meant to be read as continuous prose. Much of Aristotle's work was forgotten in Europe after the decline of Rome, during the Dark Ages, but it was kept and studied by the Arabs, in Arabic translation. The twelfth-century scholar Averröes is the best known of the Arabic scholars who commented on the work of Aristotle. When the Europeans began to make contact with the East in the Middle Ages, Aristotle was rediscovered and greeted with great enthusiasm by many, who were stunned by the range of his thought, just as if they had uncovered a whole new continent. Others, however, particularly within the Christian church, were worried that Aristotle's system of reason and logic might lead people away from faith, by providing them with a way of understanding the world that worked quite well on its own, without any reference to or dependence on God. Was there any way in which the obvious greatness of Aristotle could be reconciled with Christian faith?

Thomas Aquinas, in the thirteenth century, was convinced that there was, and his logical, systematic defences of Christian beliefs helped to support the structure of Christian philosophy, based on his interpretation of Aristotle's thought.

Aristotle is not an easy writer to read. His works do not often have the same kind of polish that characterises Plato. He does not bother with the well-chosen adjective, or with making clear the connections between one passage and the next. He does not often give clear examples, or repeat his ideas in two or three different ways in order to ease understanding. The poet Thomas Gray once described reading Aristotle as being 'like eating dried hay', which is not an experience many of us would want to try, or to repeat if we had tried it once. The usual explanation for the difficulty of Aristotle's writing is that what we have available to us are working drafts, rather than finished pieces of writing. Many scholars have concluded that the surviving works are lecture notes, rather than books, because there is evidence that Aristotle could write organised, coherent prose when he wanted to. The writings may have been lecture notes used many times, and over-written where Aristotle's thinking changed during the course of his lecturing career, or perhaps where a student contributed a useful point or a criticism. Perhaps the writings which have survived were not all written by Aristotle himself, but are notes which were taken by the students during the lectures, revealing their own occasional misunderstandings, and this could account for the abbreviated, terse form and occasional lapses into confusion.

Whatever the truth might be, the fact remains that Aristotle is difficult. Some find him almost impossibly frustrating, while others (such as Jonathan Barnes) prefer to call him 'challenging', and enjoy the ways in which speculating on what Aristotle might have meant can lead to all sorts of interesting trains of thought.

c) Aristotle and Plato

Aristotle loved Plato, and thought him a genius, but he did not agree with him. In particular, he rejected Plato's theory of Forms. Aristotle did not believe that there were these two different realms, and he refused to accept that true knowledge does not belong in the empirical world. He took the view that we can have real knowledge of the world in which we live; in fact, this is the only area where we can have true knowledge, because it is through our experience that we come to understand things. Aristotle argues that an abstract world of concepts, beyond space and time, gives us nothing to talk about or learn about. There is no evidence for its existence. All we can really know is here, in the world around us, and our experience through our senses is the only way in which we can get reliable facts. Plato and Aristotle represent two of the major streams in philosophy. There are philosophers who believe, with Plato, that reason comes first when we are seeking true knowledge; and there are those who follow Aristotle, saying that we must start with our experience.

The physical world presented Aristotle with endless fascination. He wanted to know everything, about everything, and rather than accepting that this was impossible, he threw himself into discovery with enormous energy. The rest of us, when writing or reading about Aristotle, have to be content with looking at just a few aspects of his thought.

d) Aristotle and Cause

Some of the questions that Aristotle wanted to answer were to do with the nature of things, their substance. What does it mean, for something to 'exist'? What gives particular objects their characteristics? What is it about, for example, a table, that gives it its tableness, and what makes it *this* table, rather than any other one? For Aristotle, the 'form' of something was not some kind of abstract Ideal, as Plato had believed, but was found within the item itself. Its form was its structure, and its characteristics, the 'form' of an object can be readily perceived with the senses. Aristotle used the word 'substance' in many different ways, making it one of his most difficult concepts, but one of the ways in which he used it was to express the material of which things are made. So the substance of a table is the wood and the nails and the glue; the 'form' of the table is that it has four legs (usually), a flat horizontal surface, and so on.

Aristotle also used the word 'matter' to mean the stuff of which something was made. So a chair's matter is wood, and its form is the structure of the chair itself; not Plato's universal 'Form of Chair', but the structure of that particular chair. Aristotle also wondered whether something could have matter, but no form, and he concluded that it could. There can be prime matter, or 'stuff', that has no particular form, it is not organised into any particular structure. He also raised the question if there could be a substance with form but no matter, and he concluded that this is God.

What causes something to be what it is, to have the characteristics that it has, or to change in the way that it does? Small children often wonder about this. Sometimes they go through a phase of asking 'why?' about anything and everything. For each answer they are given, they want to know the reason for this answer, and the cause of something can be traced back, showing not just one reason but a whole chain, going from the immediate to a final 'because it just is', or 'because I say so' or 'because it's just made that way'. Aristotle thought about this; he concluded that the explanation of things could be seen in four different ways, at four different levels: the four causes. 'Cause' is the best translation we have of the word he used – 'aition', which is a responsible, explanatory factor.

1. Firstly, there is the **material cause**. This answers the question, what is it made of? His examples included that the cause of a statue could be the bronze, or of a goblet, the silver. The material cause of a chair is the wood. But this material is not enough, on its own, to make the object whatever it is. We could not, for example, understand a great painting just by knowing which colours of paint had been used and which type of canvas. Material is necessary, but it does not give us the whole answer.

2. Secondly, there is the **efficient cause**. This is the agent which brings something about, for example, in the case of a statue, it is the person chiselling away, and the act of chiselling, that causes the statue. This answers the question, how does it happen? It is the sort of answer we usually expect when we ask about cause; the thing which happened to bring about certain results.

3. Then, there is the **formal cause**, the characteristics that make the object fit into whatever category it fits into. The formal cause provides the form. So the 'formal cause' of the statue might be that it has the characteristics of a statue. It is not just a lump of marble that someone is idly chiselling; it looks like a particular person perhaps, or a mythical beast. This answers the question, what are its characteristics?

4. Lastly, there is the **final cause**, and this is the most important aspect of Aristotle's thinking on the subject for an understanding of his contribution to the philosophy of religion. Aristotle believed that all objects have an ultimate reason for their existence. The final cause of the statue is that the sculptor wants to make a beautiful object for decorative or commemorative reasons; he or she set out with a particular aim in mind. The question here is, what is it for?

For Aristotle, then, the essence of an object was not just its material component parts, or its particular shape or characteristics; it also had a purpose, a function to perform. When he studied the world and the objects in it, he did not just ask what is it made from, or how can it be classified according to its characteristics, but also, what is it for, what purpose does it serve, why is it here at all?

It is this fourth, final cause which is the most important, and which in Aristotle's view gives the best explanation of an object. The final end, or purpose, or 'teleology' of a thing, when realised, gives that thing its full perfection and reality. When something is doing what it was meant to do, or has developed into whatever it was supposed to develop into, it has achieved goodness. The purpose of an object, for Aristotle, is part of the object itself, and not something which we might choose to impose on it – it is intrinsic.

All the different elements of nature have a purpose, according to Aristotle, and nothing is superfluous. We might not know what a slug is for, but nevertheless it still has its own intrinsic purpose. But that is not all; the universe as a whole has a purpose too.

e) The Prime Mover, or Unmoved Mover

Aristotle believed that all movement depends on there being a mover. By 'movement', he did not just mean motion, but also all kinds of change, such as growth or change in quality (such as 'melting', 'cooling', 'darkening' and so on). Like other thinkers before him, he recognised that everything in the world is transient, constantly changing.

If nothing acted on A, then it would stay the same and not move. So if A is moving, it must be being moved by B, which in turn is being moved by C, and so on. Aristotle argued that this chain must eventually lead to something which moves, but is itself unmoved or motionless: the Unmoved Mover, or Prime Mover. (We might ask at this point: why must it? Why could there not be an everlasting chain of cause and effect, with no beginning? Or why could each separate mover not be motionless itself, while causing movement in something else?)

Aristotle was not talking simply about a sequence of events in time. His ideas about the Prime Mover are not simply that it started everything off in motion in the first place. It is more subtle (and more difficult) than that. Change, in Aristotle's view, is eternal; there cannot have been a first change, because something would have to have happened just before that change which set it off, and this itself would have been a change, and so on. (Just as children might ask: and who made God?) Aristotle goes on to say that certain things (i.e. the planets and the stars) that we see 'in the heavens' are always moving, in circles, without any apparent beginning or end, and this is clear to our observation. We can therefore conclude that, because there is eternal movement,

> There must be a mover which moves them without being moved, eternal and a substance and actual.

In his book *Metaphysics* (literally, after physics), Aristotle calls this source of all movement the Prime Mover. The Prime Mover to Aristotle is the first of all substances, the necessary first source of movement which is itself unmoved. It is a being with everlasting life, and in *Metaphysics* Aristotle also calls this being 'God'.

The Prime Mover causes the movement of other things, not as an *efficient* cause, but as a *final* cause. In other words, it does not start off the movement by giving it some kind of push, but it is the purpose, or the end, or the teleology, of the movement. This is important for Aristotle, because he thought that an efficient cause, giving a push, would be affected itself by the act of pushing (the same conclusion that Isaac Newton came to in his Third Law of Motion, when he said that 'action and reaction are equal and opposite'). Aristotle was keen to establish that the Prime Mover is itself Unmoved, or unaffected, otherwise the whole concept would break down.

So the Prime Unmoved Mover is not an efficient cause, it is a final cause, or even The Final Cause. This is because ultimately, it is the object of everything. It causes movement **as the object of desire and love**. This part of the argument seems strange to modern people; it appears that Aristotle crosses over from a consideration of physics and the movements of the planets to his concept of God, which today we might think of as being an entirely different area of discussion. If God caused motion by efficient physical means – pushing, or the equivalent depending on the kind of 'moving' – he himself would be changed, so he must instead move by drawing things towards himself, while remaining unaffected. (The 'heavenly spheres', in Aristotle's understanding of astronomy, desire to imitate God in their spirituality, but as they cannot do this, they do the best they can by moving in eternal circles. They are all moved by their own 'unmoved movers', the number of which Aristotle thought was 'either 55 or 47'; but these unmoved movers are not the same as the Prime Mover. In understanding Aristotle's concept of the Unmoved Mover, this is something of a red herring. Perhaps, somewhere along the line, Aristotle's cosmology and astronomy became muddled together.) The final cause of movement, according to Aristotle, is a love of and desire for God. God is perfection, and everything wants to imitate perfection and is drawn towards it.

Aristotle held that God exists necessarily, which means that God does not depend on anything else for existence. He never changes or has any potential to change, never begins and never ends, and so is eternal. Eternal things, Aristotle claimed, must be good; there can be no defect in something that exists necessarily, because badness is connected with some kind of lack, a not-being of something which ought to be there, an absence of the 'actuality' that Aristotle thought God most perfectly has.

The Prime Mover, argued Aristotle, had to be immaterial. It could not be made of any kind of stuff, because matter is capable of being acted upon, it has potential to change. As it is immaterial, it cannot perform any kind of physical, bodily action. Therefore, Aristotle thought, the activity of the Prime Mover, God, must be purely spiritual and intellectual. The activity of God is **thought**.

But what does God think about? It must be the best of all possible things to think about, because God is perfectly good. God could not think about anything which caused him to change in any way; nothing which could affect him, or make him react, or even change him from not-knowing to knowing. Aristotle concludes that God thinks about himself only. Nothing else is a fit subject. He even defines God as 'thought of thought', or 'thinking about thinking'. At the end of this line of argument, Aristotle comes to the conclusion that God knows only himself; so he does not know this physical world that we inhabit, he does not have a plan for us, and he is not affected by us.

f) Aristotle on the body and soul

Aristotle's understanding of the relationship between the body and the soul is found in Chapter 1 of Book II of his work *de Anima.* According to Aristotle, a living creature is a 'substance'. He saw the body as being the matter of a living thing, and the soul as its 'form', understood as its characteristics and covering every function of living things, including sensation, movement, and reproduction. The soul (psyche) is a much broader concept than the mind, or the 'soul' in the way in which we usually use the word. A living being is a composite whole – the body is the matter, and the soul is its form.

The soul, in Aristotle's understanding, is the structure of the body, its function, and its organisation. The particular nature of any soul will depend on the kind of living thing that it is, and these are arranged in a kind of hierarchy. Plants, for example, have only a vegetative sort of soul, with the powers of nutrition, growth and reproduction appropriate for their kind. Animals are above plants on the scale of things, and their souls have appetites as well as the powers found in plants, so that animals can have desires and feelings, which in turn gives them the ability to move. Even the human soul is nothing more than the organisation of the body, but it has a special quality in addition to plant and animal qualities; the power of reason. Through the working of the soul, people develop their intellects and their ethical characters.

Aristotle tries to make his point about the nature of the soul clearer by giving illustrations. One is the example of an axe; if it were a living thing, he says, then the matter from which it is made is its 'body', the wood and the metal. Its soul would be the things that make it an axe, rather than just wood and metal: its capacity to chop. He goes on to give another example, this time of an eye:

> Suppose then that the eye were an animal – sight would have been its soul…when seeing is removed the eye is no longer an eye, except in name – it is no more a real eye than the eye of a statue or of a painted figure.

Elsewhere, he claims that a dead animal is an animal in name only; it has its body, its matter, but it no longer has its soul. When it is dead, it has lost its capacity to do all the things that animals of its kind usually do.

For Aristotle, the body and soul are not two separate elements, but are one thing:

> We can dismiss as wholly unnecessary the question whether the body and soul are one: it is as meaningless as to ask whether the wax and the shape given to it by the stamp are one.

The soul and the body are not, as Plato would have it, two distinct entities, but are different parts or aspects of the same thing.

In general, then, Aristotle's concept of the soul does not allow for the possibility that it is immortal. It is not separable from the body, if it is that which makes the body a person rather than just material. Therefore, without the body, it cannot exist, just as the characteristics and functions of a dog cannot exist on their own, without any material dog.

However, Aristotle did not stop at this point, with a clear view that the soul dies along with the body. He made an exception to the rule. All the faculties of the soul are inseparable from the body, he thought, with the exception of reason. Aristotle's discussion of the different aspects of reason, and the extent to which they are dependent on the physical body, are among the most obscure and most debated of all of his writings. It is not at all clear whether the reason was believed to be immortal, but perhaps Aristotle said that it was. If the reason lives on after a person dies, however, it does not seem to be in a personal, individual kind of way; we could not say that *this person* is immortal, with a recognisable identity.

g) Criticisms of Aristotle

The problems of understanding what Aristotle meant can sometimes make it difficult to criticise him. However, there are points which could be raised in objection to his thought, including:

● Aristotle criticises Plato for his belief in the world of Forms, when he has no concrete evidence of their existence. But we could also say the same to Aristotle himself; he has no concrete evidence for believing that this material world is the source of true knowledge. There could be other ways in which knowledge can be gained, apart from through sense experience or reason; religious believers might argue, for example, that faith and revelation from God are a source of true knowledge.

● Many people would not agree with Aristotle's assumption that everything which exists in nature does so for a reason, and has a 'final cause'. There are many who would say that there is no reason, and that things happen by blind chance. The French writer Albert Camus, for example, described the universe as 'absurd', and Sartre said that it was 'gratuitous'; they thought that it was ridiculous to suppose that the universe had any meaning or purpose beyond the simple fact of its existence.

● Aristotle's concept of the Prime, Unmoved Mover raises problems. Some have criticised the idea of God as an uncaused causer, saying that the argument depends on the idea nothing can cause itself, but then contradicts itself by saying that God does exactly what it just claimed was impossible.

● Aristotle does not successfully explain how his concept of God as 'thinking about thinking' could be responsible for causing movement. He stressed that real knowledge begins with sense experience, and yet none of us have ever experienced something being moved just through the agency of thought, outside the world of fiction.

h) Aristotle's influence on Christian thought

Aristotle, like Plato, has had an enormous influence on Christian thinking. Many of his concepts have been woven into the fabric of the Christian understanding of God:

● God is understood as eternal, beyond time and space, and incapable of change.

● The universe and everything in it is believed to exist for a reason, with a function to perform.

● God is seen as the cause of the existence of the universe; the cosmological argument for the existence of God is based on Aristotle's concept of the Unmoved Mover.

● Looking at the world around us can give us real insights; this provides the basis for teleological, or Design, arguments for the existence of God, where the world is believed to reveal a pattern or design which only God could have produced.

4 The Judaeo-Christian understanding of God

Introduction

Plato and Aristotle base their understandings of the causes of existence, of goodness, and of the soul, on philosophical argument. But in the traditions of Judaism and Christianity, questions about these issues are not answered by the use of human reason, but by faith, in the teachings of the Bible and in the powers of personal religious experience.

For the ancient Greeks, the concepts of a creator of the world, or a source of all goodness, are almost like the solution to a mathematical problem. Using reasoned argument, God (or something like the concept of God) is postulated as a way of making an explanation hold together coherently, rather in the way that modern scientists postulate the existence of black holes, or the curvature of space, in order to understand the rest of their knowledge.

For Plato and Aristotle, the Form of the Good or the Unmoved Mover do not interact with the world. They have characteristics, but nothing that could be described as personality. The Form of the Good is an ideal, and the Unmoved Mover is an explanation, but these concepts are not themselves affected by the way in which we behave. They do not have a relationship with us; they are, by their very nature, changeless and eternal, incapable of emotion and unaffected by anything else. They are not involved with the world any more than a prime number cares about or is affected by whatever we choose to do in our mathematics.

The ways in which God is described in the Bible give a very different picture, and it does not begin at the same starting-point. In the Bible, the existence of God is barely questioned. It is accepted as self-evident. The Bible, for the most part, is not a philosophical book, but a response of believers who want to share their faith. God is not explained, and belief in God is not justified with reasoned argument; it is an object of faith. There are many different Biblical understandings of the nature of God, often based on reported personal religious experience, and in order to express what is, fundamentally, inexpressible, the Biblical writers tend to use imagery and myth, rather than logic. Biblical understandings of truth are expressed through stories and symbols, not argument.

The differences of approach between the ancient Greeks and the writers of the Old Testament, in particular, are marked. In the Bible, God is shown as the creator and the source of goodness, but not as a sterile concept on a separate plane; he does things on purpose, he interacts with people, he cares about what they do and makes demands of them, and he is affected by the ways in which they respond to him. The Old Testament and the New are rather different; by the time the New Testament was written, Greek ideas were well established in Palestine, because it was being ruled by the Romans who had adopted many Greek ideas into their culture. An outlook which incorporates Greek ideas is known as **Hellenistic**, and the New Testament was written in a Hellenistic context.

a) The concept of God as creator

In the Bible, the belief that the world was created by God is assumed. There is no attempt made to justify this belief, or to argue against people with different opinions. The Biblical writers, instead, show in different ways how they understand the creation to have happened, and they explore the relationship between God and humanity which has developed because of this creation.

The most obvious place to look for Biblical views about creation is Genesis. In Genesis, it is usually agreed, there are two creation stories. One begins at the start of chapter 1, and the next in chapter 2. The Biblical accounts of creation usually deal with questions of the origins of humanity, rather than of the universe as a whole; they do not tend to look for reasons why anything exists at all, but they explore why humanity, in particular, exists. This is done in the context of the rest of the Biblical story; God, the creator of the world, calls the patriarchs and promises them a land, and they make covenants with him, and disobey him, and he controls history in order to bring about his plans for them. The creation stories, therefore, are not just explanations of how we came to be here, but set the scene for the rest of the Bible, showing who God is and who we are in relation to him.

At the beginning of the Genesis story, God is introduced. He is not one of many gods, and not one of the forces of nature or Nature-itself, but is separate. He stands apart from the universe and is transcendent. It is not clear, in Genesis, whether God creates everything out of nothing at all (*creatio ex nihilo*), or whether God gives shape and structure to a chaos of matter which already existed. Usually, Jewish and Christian doctrine has taken the view that God did not only fashion new shapes from material which already existed, but that he did indeed create everything out of nothing, bringing the universe into existence where before there was only the existence of God himself. This has given rise to some conflicts between science and religion, where some scientists hold that matter cannot have been brought into existence when there was no matter before. **Augustine** tackled this problem by suggesting that time itself is an aspect of the created world, so that the ideas of 'in the beginning' and 'creation out of nothing' do not refer to some particular moment. The universe of time and space as we know it could be eternal on its own terms, while also being created, sustained and dependent upon God.

Scholars have drawn attention to the similarities of Genesis and Babylonian creation myths, where there were dark and swirling waters before the beginning of the world. Perhaps the writers of Genesis believed that theirs was scientifically and historically accurate as an account of how the world came to be, or perhaps they borrowed the imagery in order to express something that is fundamentally inexpressible.

In Genesis, humanity is the pinnacle of creation. In the first creation story, God sets everything in place, producing the perfect setting, and then finally adds people, as the finishing touch. In the second story, humanity comes first, followed by the animals who are brought in to act as possible companions. But both stories strongly suggest that the world was created for humanity, and not that people happened by accident or chance once the world had become established and evolution set in motion.

God creates all the different components of the universe by his word: he says 'Let there be…' and there is. The will of God is all that is required to make physical matter exist and take the shape that God wants it to take. Everything made by God is 'very good', and made deliberately; nothing exists by chance, or is of inferior quality, or is by nature bad. God is responsible for the existence of everything that there is in the world. This immediately raises questions about the existence of evil, of ugliness, and of things which appear to be less than perfect such as creatures with diseases or disabilities; were these planned by God, and put into the world because of God's word?

The second creation story in Genesis begins to address these questions; it tells the story of Adam and Eve falling away from God and destroying the perfection that he has given them, by disobeying him through their own free choice and succumbing to the temptation presented to them by the serpent. But many questions are still left unanswered; did God deliberately, purposefully create the serpent and give it its craftiness, and was this considered to be 'very good'? Did God know, in advance of the creation of humanity, that they would disobey him in this way? Did God intend that the world should be perfect, containing only goodness, or was the existence of the possibility of evil part of the plan?

Genesis is not the only part of the Bible where God's nature as creator is described. Elsewhere, too, there are poetic descriptions of the ways in which God gives the world its shape and adds its details, with all the care and skill of a master craftsman. For example, in the book of Job, the description of the creation of the world compares God with an expert builder:

> "Where were you when I laid the foundation of the earth?
> Tell me, if you have understanding.
> Who determined its measurements—surely you know!
> Or who stretched the line upon it?
> On what were its bases sunk,
> or who laid its cornerstone?"
>
> *Job 38:4–6*

The creativity of the God of the Bible contrasts noticeably with the Unmoved Mover used by Aristotle as an explanation of movement and change. In the Judaeo-Christian concept, God is not at all unmoved, but takes an interest and a pride in the things that he has made. He does not just indifferently set them off, without caring which direction they take, but fashions them, according to a plan, just as the craftsman works the materials in order to achieve a desired result. For Aristotle, the Unmoved Mover creates motion by attracting everything towards itself; it is the objects in motion that are attracted, and that 'choose' to move, while the Unmoved Mover itself remains immutable. In the Judaeo-Christian concept, in contrast, the will to move and to create comes from God. He does not think only about himself, but purposefully calls the world into existence, desiring a loving relationship with creation, a relationship that works both ways.

Summary

- The creativity of God is described in the Bible as being deliberate; God has a mind and purposes, and the creation of the world is done in accordance with these.
- The traditional Christian and Jewish view is that God creates 'ex nihilo', out of nothing. Matter comes into existence where there was no matter before.
- God is believed to be the creator of everything that exists, which raises problems when people try to account for the existence of evil and suffering in the world.
- God's creation of the world is ongoing and continual. God did not just set the world off in motion and then go away; he created the world as the beginning of a process and a relationship.

b) The goodness of God

The goodness of God, as described in the Bible, is very different from the sterile Ideal of Plato, and to some extent Aristotle. God provides an interactive sort of goodness; it is a goodness which makes demands of humanity. God is not merely an ideal to follow, which remains unaffected and does not care whether or not anyone attempts to live up to it. God, in the Bible, is more than a concept; he exists as a personality, reacting to people and caring about the way they behave. 'Goodness', as a quality, does not actually do anything, but the God of the Bible very definitely does things. 'Goodness' as a scale against which things are measured is not interested in the results of the measuring, because qualities do not have the capacity for taking an interest, but the God of the Bible is far more than just a measuring tool.

The goodness of the Biblical God sets a standard for the people to follow, and then watches over the way that they respond to the guidance and laws they are given. For example, in Exodus 20, the Hebrew people, who have been led out of slavery by Moses and into the wilderness, are given laws directly from God which they are to follow as part of their covenant relationship with him. Some of the laws relate to their behaviour towards God, and others to their treatment of one another, for example in the Ten Commandments:

> You shall not make wrongful use of the name of the LORD your God... Honour your father and your mother... You shall not murder... You shall not steal.

from *Exodus 20*

The main characteristic of God's relationship with the people is that they are to respond to his goodness with obedience to his commands. They do not have to guess what goodness means, or try to work it out intellectually, through the use of their reason. It is revealed to them directly, and they are meant to respond to it with faith. It does not matter whether or not the people understand why they are meant to behave in certain ways and not in others; God's goodness is revealed to faith, not reason. Some of the characters in the Bible who are singled out for special commendation are those who, through faith, continued to obey God's commands even though they obviously did not understand the reasons for them. In Genesis, for example, Abraham was prepared to sacrifice his beloved son Isaac because of his faith in the goodness of God; and Job continued to praise God and be obedient to him even when he felt he was being unjustly punished:

> I hold fast my righteousness, and will not let it go; my heart does not reproach me for any of my days.
>
> *Job 27:6*

The goodness of God, then, demands that people respond with faith. They should accept that their reason alone is not necessarily going to lead them to the right choices, because God defines what goodness is, even if it might sometimes appear unreasonable or incomprehensible. People are meant to accept that they can approach the goodness of God, but that they will never fully comprehend it.

The concept of God's goodness also includes the idea of 'righteous indignation'. He does not remain implacable and unaffected, but becomes angered at injustice, and calls prophets to make the people aware that they are failing him. Throughout the Bible, God is shown to have a particular concern for the poor and the weak; his goodness, often described as 'righteousness', involves a desire that people should treat one another fairly, recognising each other's equal value as creations of God (see pages 123–5). When people treat the poor with contempt and exploit the weak, God is determined to teach them a lesson; for example, the prophet Jeremiah claims to speak the words of God when he tells his hearers:

> You have rejected me, says the LORD,
>   you are going backward;
>   so I have stretched out my hand against you and destroyed you—
> I am weary of relenting.
>
> *Jeremiah 15:6*

God's words and actions change, in response to the behaviour of the people. He is not an Unmoved Mover, but is made angry and is hurt when the people refuse to recognise and respond to goodness:

> I thought
>> how I would set you among my children,
> and give you a pleasant land,
>> the most beautiful heritage of all the nations.
> And I thought you would call me, My Father,
>> and would not turn from following me.
> Instead, as a faithless wife leaves her husband,
>> so you have been faithless to me, O house of Israel,
>>> says the LORD.
>
> *Jeremiah 3:19–20*

Anger is not the only response of God to the people; he can also be moved to pity, and displays his goodness in compassionate responses to prayer. For example, at the beginning of I Samuel, Hannah was distraught because she had no children:

> She was deeply distressed and prayed to the LORD, and wept bitterly. She made this vow: "O LORD of hosts, if only you will look on the misery of your servant, and remember me, and not forget your servant, but will give to your servant a male child, then I will set him before you as a nazirite until the day of his death… In due time Hannah conceived and bore a son. She named him Samuel, for she said, "I have asked him of the LORD."
>
> *I Samuel I: 10–11, 20*

For the writers of the Bible, then, perfect goodness does not have to mean a completely static, unchanging being who remains unaffected by his relationship with the world. On the contrary, the God of the Bible is very much affected by the ways in which people respond to him. For example, the prophet Hosea, in the eighth century BCE, spoke movingly of God's love for the people and goodness to them, using the imagery of an adult with a small child:

> Yet it was I who taught Ephraim to walk,
>> I took them up in my arms;
>> but they did not know that I healed them.
> I led them with cords of human kindness,
>> with bands of love.
>> I was to them like those
>> who lift infants to their cheeks.
> I bent down to them and fed them.
>
> *Hosea 11:3–4*

Here, Hosea shows how God cares for the people in a way that can be likened to the love and pride of a parent when a baby is taking its first steps; God's goodness is compared with the reins used to steady a toddler. The language used shows a God who feels deep tenderness for his creation, and whose relationship with them is of the utmost importance. In many parts of the Bible, the goodness of God is seen to be synonymous with his love; and it is the love of God which demands that people become the best that they have the potential to be, by obeying his commands as they are revealed.

God's goodness, then, is not just concerned with the people as a whole, but with individuals. This contrasts sharply with the universal Form of the Good, which is the same for everyone and takes no interest in personal circumstances. The writer of the famous Psalm 23 explains how he experiences the goodness of God not just as an abstract concept but as a personal presence in his own life:

> The LORD is my shepherd, I shall not want.
>> He makes me lie down in green pastures;
>> he leads me beside still waters;
>>> he restores my soul.
>> He leads me in right paths
>>> for his name's sake.
>
> Even though I walk through the darkest valley,
>> I fear no evil;
>> for you are with me;
>>> your rod and your staff—
>>> they comfort me.
>
> You prepare a table before me
>> in the presence of my enemies;
>> you anoint my head with oil;
>>> my cup overflows.
> Surely goodness and mercy shall follow me
>> all the days of my life,
>> and I shall dwell in the house of the Lord
> my whole life long.

Psalm 23

Although God's goodness is very much interactive, it is also described as perfect:

> The Rock, his work is perfect,
>> and all his ways are just.
> A faithful God, without deceit,
>> just and upright is he;
> yet his degenerate children have dealt falsely with him,
> a perverse and crooked generation.

Deuteronomy 32:4–5

> This God—his way is perfect;
>> the promise of the LORD proves true;
> he is a shield for all who take refuge in him.

2 Samuel 22:31

> The law of the LORD is perfect,
> reviving the soul.
>
> *Psalm 19:7*

Some philosophers have found difficulties in combining the concept of a personal and interactive God with the idea that God is perfect. It is sometimes argued that a God who can have relationships must be capable of change and response, but perfection, by its very nature, is always the same. Therefore, for some philosophers, it is impossible to hold that God is both perfectly good and at the same time capable of having relationships with his creation. The question of whether God can suffer, or be affected in any way, is one of the areas which is debated in the philosophy of religion, and different scholars have suggested different conclusions.

In the New Testament, the goodness of God and his interaction with the world is shown in the person of Jesus, and this is the primary, most important concept in Christianity. According to the New Testament writers, God came into the world as a man in order to demonstrate his love for humanity:

> For God so loved the world that he gave his only Son, so that everyone who believes in him may not perish but may have eternal life.
>
> *John 3:16*

This whole concept, too, raises many philosophical questions, for example: how, if at all, could God have been in human form, when part of the nature of God is that he does not have a body? How does time work for God; is he outside time and space, and if so, how could he come into the world at a fixed point in history, and grow and develop as a human being? When God was in the world, was he also in heaven at the same time, and what does this say about the unity of God? Discussions of these and many other questions have occupied Christian philosophy for centuries.

Christian belief is that the goodness of God can be seen in the words and actions of Christ. His moral teachings, healings, miracles and self-sacrifice all reveal God's goodness as active and interactive, part of this world as well as part of the world of spiritual reality. In some mysterious way, the material, physical world and the supernatural world are brought together. Although ancient Greek ideas can clearly be seen woven into the text of the New Testament, especially in John's gospel, this is a point at which Christianity and Platonism have very different approaches. Goodness-Itself, for the Christian, does not only inhabit a separate plane unavailable to the senses but 'the Word became flesh and lived among us, and we have seen his glory' (John 1:14).

Summary

- In the Bible, the goodness of God sets a moral standard for people, and demands a response from them.
- God's goodness is perfect.
- God rewards and punishes people according to the extent to which they take notice of his goodness.
- God's goodness involves a personal care and concern for individuals. Their prayers are answered, their needs are met, and their behaviour is judged according to the extent to which they show concern for each other.
- For Christians, the goodness of God is revealed most completely in the person and work of Christ.
- According to Christian teaching, the Holy Spirit is the means by which Christians can share in and demonstrate to others the goodness of God.

c) God's activity in the world: the concept of miracle

In the Bible, God is portrayed as being **transcendent**: separate from and superior to the physical, material world. He has no body (is incorporeal) and exists outside time and space in eternity. This creates some problems for philosophers: if God is so different and separated from the world in which we live, then how can God be said to act in the world or have a relationship with humanity and personal relationships with individuals? The ancient Greek idea was that God had no interaction with the world, but the Biblical picture is very different.

One of the ways in which people have understood God to work in the world is through miracles. Belief in miracles is an important feature of the Judaeo-Christian framework; throughout the Old Testament and the New, stories are presented of miraculous events, in which the laws of nature are suspended in order for God to bring about a particular course of events.

For example, the natural properties of water are changed when God chooses: the Egyptian rivers turn to blood as a plague in an effort to coerce the Pharaoh into letting the Hebrew people go (Exodus 7:20–21); the Red Sea parts for the Hebrews to escape from slavery in Egypt (Exodus 14:21–23); water has miraculous healing properties for Naaman who was suffering from leprosy (2 Kings 5:1–14); Jesus walks on water (Matthew 14:22–33), turns it into wine (John 2:1–12) and calms a storm at sea (Mark 4:35–41).

The story in the book of **Joshua 10:1–15** is a typical example. It tells of the miraculous intervention by God in a war between the Israelites, led by Joshua, against the Amorites. According to the story, the Israelites were greatly outnumbered by the Amorites, but Joshua was told by God to stand up against them because he would be helped to win. God intervened in the battle by sending hailstones which killed many of the enemy, and also by causing the sun to stand still in the sky so that the battle could be finished and the men could return to their camp in safety. This story, like many other miracle stories, shows that God intervenes in history, according to his plans. It is important for God's intentions for the future of the Jews that the Israelites win the battle, and so God guides the course of history, suspending the laws of nature where necessary to ensure that events unfold in the right way for God's purposes to be fulfilled.

There are three main issues that arise in the discussion of miracles:

1. the problem of definition; what we mean when we use the word 'miracle' to describe an event
2. the issue of whether miracles actually happen, whether it is reasonable to believe in miracles
3. the implications of the idea of miracle for an understanding of the nature of God.

Some people claim that any event that excites wonder, such as the birth of a baby, or a beautiful sunset, can be considered to be miraculous. However, many others argue that in order for something to be classified as a miracle, it must be an unexpected and supernatural event, done for a religious purpose and revealing God to people in some way. Some scholars, such as **David Hume**, have argued that by definition, miracles are such unlikely explanations of events that it is unreasonable to believe in them.

Many religious people believe that the idea of miracle is important in their faith. In Christianity, for example, the fact that there are many reported incidents of miracle in the Bible is, for some, enough reason to believe that miracles happen. If the Bible is, in some sense, the Word of God, a special and holy book given by God for our help, and if the Bible says that miracles happened, then this is in itself a sound justification for believing in them. These Christians would argue that the Bible is a source of truth, and that we should be able to test other experiences against the Bible, rather than testing the Bible to see whether it matches other views. The Bible is quite clear that miracles do happen. If we want to disagree with this, then we have to abandon the idea that the Bible is a divinely inspired source of truth.

An argument which is linked to this view is that the idea of miracle is inextricably linked with Christianity. It is woven into the whole structure of Christian belief in such a way that without it, if we try to take out the notion of miracle, then we remove almost all of the central elements of the faith. The doctrine of Jesus as God Incarnate depends on miracle, as does the Virgin Birth and the Resurrection. The idea of the creation of the world could be seen as miracle. A large part of the Christian creed has to be abandoned, or at least rewritten, if the notion of miracle is rejected.

Also, it is argued that we limit the nature of God if we claim that although he exists, miracles do not happen. If God is capable of doing anything, and if God gave the universe its order in the first place, then it is up to God whether sometimes he decides to suspend those rules for his own purposes. A God who can create and sustain the world is also capable of acting in more individual ways. We may not understand why God performs miracles in some circumstances and not others, but we should not expect to understand the reasoning of God, who can see the whole picture. We need to accept that our understanding is of the limited, human kind, and that God knows what he is doing even if we do not.

Some people argue that although there are plenty of miracle stories in the Bible, placing too much emphasis on the miraculous element goes against the teaching and example of Jesus. In the story of the temptations of Jesus, he rejected throwing himself off the pinnacle of the Temple and being saved by angels; he wanted nothing to do with displays of magic and 'signs'. Luke 16:31 has Jesus saying that the people who took no notice of Moses and the prophets would take no notice of someone rising from the dead, showing that miracles are not meant to convince the unbeliever but to have a subjective meaning, brought in by the interpretation of the person with faith. According to the theologian **John Macquarrie**, the mythological elements of the stories have been ways of expressing the beliefs of the faithful. Macquarrie also points out that even if something publicly observable happened which suspended the laws of nature for everyone to see, there would still be some who saw it as an act of God and others who refused to.

One theologian who has argued strongly that stories of miracles are damaging to faith, is **Maurice Wiles**, who is a modern philosopher of religion. According to Wiles, God does not intervene in the world in occasional, individual ways, but the whole world should be seen as an act of God in its entirety. His argument against the more traditional view of miracle is that miracles, by definition, have to be unlikely and therefore not happen very often, otherwise we would have no rules of nature at all. This leaves us with a picture of a God who only intervenes in the world occasionally, and then at apparently strange and arbitrary times. People are being asked to believe in an all-loving, all-powerful God, who fed five thousand people in the first century but did nothing about the Irish potato famine and still does nothing about those starving in Sudan; a God who parted the Red Sea for the Hebrews but did nothing about the plight of the Jews in the Holocaust; a God who did nothing to prevent Hiroshima but who was prepared to step in and help in the comparatively trivial emergency of wine running out at a wedding. Wiles argues that this picture debases the whole idea of God, and that it presents us with a God who is not worthy of worship.

Another thinker, from earlier in the twentieth century, called **Rudolf Bultmann**, was of the opinion that the mythological view of the world found in the Bible is no longer acceptable in the twentieth century. Our knowledge of science is such that we can no longer believe that these things happen, and we should work at 'demythologising' both the Old and the New Testaments. This means taking out the superstitious, mythical elements which have been woven into the story, while keeping the essential truths. Bultmann's argument, then, included the view that miracle stories get in the way of faith for the modern, scientifically minded thinker.

A further problem with the idea that miracles happen is that belief in miracles contradicts other popular Christian arguments. It might be seen to contradict the teleological (Design) arguments for the existence of God, for example; because if we are meant to be able to see that the world has been designed, then why would God sometimes want to break his own rules and perform miracles, unless it was not really the best possible design in the first place? This implies that God sometimes made mistakes; that God wished, for example, that he had not designed water to work in the way that it does and had to step in and modify it for the crossing of the Red Sea.

Sometimes it is argued that the concept of miracle does not fit with traditional arguments justifying the existence of evil and suffering in the world alongside belief in an all-loving, all-powerful God. People are asked to believe that this is the 'best of all possible worlds', and that free will is essential for us to be fully human, and that sometimes this necessitates our suffering; and yet, at the same time, God sometimes steps in and changes the rules, and allows some people (though not many) to escape from the consequences of evil. If God does these things sometimes, why not always?

Summary

- The concept of miracle is closely woven into the fabric of the Judaeo-Christian understanding of the nature of God.
- Defining the nature of a miracle gives rise to different opinions, but many agree that they are a suspension of the laws of nature by God for a religious purpose.
- Some people argue that it is impossible for modern people to believe in miracles at all.
- Others argue that the suggestion that God sometimes suspends the laws of nature gives a picture of an uncaring and arbitrary God, not a God of love.

1. a) Explain Plato's Theory of Forms. (33 marks)
  b) How convincing is this theory? (17 marks)

Guide

In part (a), you need to concentrate on showing your knowledge and understanding. Time is short, so stick closely to what is relevant to the question itself; you should be explaining the Theory of Forms, not giving biographical detail, for example. Make a short list of the ideas you need to mention: the distinction between the Forms and the material world, the reasons Plato gave for suggesting that there are Forms, and some of the ways in which he illustrated this idea, perhaps using the cave analogy. In part (b), you need to make some evaluation, by saying what the strengths and weaknesses are of Plato's way of looking at reality. Remember to give your own view, rather than just listing arguments for and against, and justify it with reasons.

2. a) Explain what Aristotle meant by the 'final cause'. (33 marks)
  b) 'Aristotle was wrong to imagine that everything has a purpose.' Discuss. (17 marks)

Guide

In part (a), you need to concentrate on the subject matter of the question, rather than writing generally about Aristotle. You could concentrate only on the final cause, or you could give an outline of all the causes in order to show how the final cause differs from the others. For high marks, aim to write with clarity and in a way that addresses the question directly. For part (b), you need to assess Aristotle's view that everything has a purpose. Perhaps you could quote from Sartre or Camus, or you might have read another writer such as Russell defending the view that the universe has no purpose. Remember to give your own view as well, rather than simply outlining the views of others, and defend your view with your own reasons.

3. a) Explain, with examples, what people might mean when they describe something as a 'miracle'. (33 marks)
  b) 'Belief in miracles is essential for the Jewish and Christian faiths.' Discuss. (17 marks)

Guide

In part (a), you could use examples from the Bible or from other sources, such as reports from Lourdes. Try to show that you realise that the definition of miracle is an area of debate, and that the word means different things to different people. For high marks, you could relate these different ideas to particular thinkers, such as David Hume. For part (b), you need to consider whether a Jew or a Christian must believe in miracles. Perhaps it is possible to follow the religion while rejecting the idea that God works in the world in this way, or perhaps miracles are such an essential part of faith that they cannot be ignored. You might consider that the answer depends on the definition of what makes something miraculous.

Suggestions for further reading

On Plato:
Bryan Magee, *The Story of Philosophy* (Dorling Kindersley, 1998), pp.24–6
Mel Thompson, *Philosophy: an Introduction* (Hodder & Stoughton, 1995), p.13
Encarta 'Plato' article
Jostein Gaarder, *Sophie's World* (Phoenix House, 1995), chapters on Socrates, Athens, and Plato
Raeper and Smith, *A Beginner's Guide to Ideas* (Lion, 1991), chapters 2 and 3

On Aristotle:
Bryan Magee, *The Story of Philosophy*, pp.32–9
Jostein Gaarder, *Sophie's World*
Jonathan Barnes, *Aristotle* (Oxford University Press, 1996), chapters 1, 2, 11 and 12
Encarta 'Aristotle' article
Raeper and Smith, *A Beginner's Guide to Ideas*, pp.14–16, 21–2

On the nature of God:
Genesis 1–3, Job 38, Psalm 104, with commentaries, and some examples of miracle stories from the Bible, such as Joshua 10:1–15, 2 Kings 5:1–15, Luke 18:35–43
John Hick, *Philosophy of Religion* (Prentice Hall, 1989)
Mel Thompson, *Philosophy of Religion* (Hodder & Stoughton, 1997), p.155f
Peter Vardy, *The Puzzle of God* (Fount, 1999), chapter 17
Stephen Evans, *Philosophy of Religion* (Inter-Varsity, 1985), chapter 5
Brian Davies, *An Introduction to the Philosophy of Religion* (Oxford University Press, 1993), chapter 10

2 Religious ethics

KEYWORDS

ethical – an adjective used to describe something which is morally right

meta-ethics – the branch of moral philosophy which looks at the ways in which people use the language of morals, asking questions about what we mean when we call something 'good' or 'wrong'

1 Meta-ethics

Many students, when writing worthy but dull essays, begin by defining their terms: 'Before we can discuss this question, we must first explain what is meant by…'. Although this is a less than inspiring start to a piece of writing, it is often considered to be important, because, unless we agree, before we begin, that we are all talking about the same thing and using words in the same way, communication will be difficult. Perhaps, then, before we begin a discussion of ethics, we must first explain how we intend to use our terms.

Normative ethics is the term used to describe different moral codes of behaviour; the principles we might put into action, the rules by which we might live, the criteria we might use when making a moral judgement. Utilitarianism, Kantian ethics, religious ethics, situation ethics, virtue ethics and Natural Law are all examples of normative theories of ethics; they try to show us how we should behave.

Meta-ethics is a term used to describe the presuppositions and language of morality. What are we doing when we use words such as 'good'? Are we expressing our feelings of approval? Are we recommending a course of action to other people? Are we, perhaps, referring to some real, factual, objective goodness and saying that we have found an example of it? Meta-ethical philosophers try to work out what we are doing when we use moral language, because if there is no agreement about the meaning of ethical language (some argue that it has no real meaning at all), then ethical debate is pointless and will never achieve anything.

Philosophers of ethics, particularly in the twentieth century, have concentrated a lot of attention on meta-ethics, trying to define what our moral language actually means. In the past, moral philosophers wrote about how we might work out the right way to behave (normative ethics). They talked about which things are right, and which are wrong. However, more recently, people have suggested that this discussion is pointless unless we can first agree on the ways in which the language of morals actually works. We all use ethical language when we talk about right and wrong, but are we all using these words in the same way? What do we really mean, when we call some action or person 'right', or 'good', or say that someone 'ought' to do something? This question is more difficult to answer than it first appears.

Part of the problem is that we use these words in our ordinary conversation in other contexts, as well as when we are talking about morals. For example, we might say that we want to buy a 'good' pair of walking boots; we might think that we have found the 'right' answer to a mathematical problem; we might wonder whether we 'ought' to take an umbrella when we go out. However, these are non-moral uses of the words. In a moral context, the meanings are perhaps rather different, even though the words themselves are the same and the sentence structures are very similar.

Compare, for example, the use of the word 'ought' in the following pair of sentences: 'You ought to wear that colour more often' and 'You ought to be faithful to your wife.' In the first sentence, the speaker is clearly expressing an opinion; in his view, that colour suits you and, working on the assumption that you like to look your best, the speaker recommends that you wear it more often. You are, of course, free to disagree with the opinion that it suits you, and if you choose never to wear it again or to wear something that he does not think suits you at all, you are not behaving immorally. 'Ought' is being used in a non-moral context, and everyone recognises that the speaker is expressing an opinion and recommending that you share it.

But in the second sentence, 'You ought to be faithful to your wife', 'ought' is being used in a moral context, and perhaps the meaning of the word is different. Is the speaker merely expressing her opinion, which you need not share? Or is the speaker perhaps making reference to some actual fact, that it is wrong to be unfaithful to your wife and right to be faithful; and where can the evidence be found to support this fact? Does the speaker have any right to condemn you if you do not share this view?

One of the best eccentrics of the nineteenth century, William Morris, once said: 'Have nothing in your house which you do not know to be useful, or believe to be beautiful.' He makes a careful distinction here in his choice of verbs – we know for a fact whether or not something is useful, because we either use it often, or we do not (but even this 'fact' is relative to the individual and the kinds of objects he or she normally uses). But whether or not we believe something is beautiful depends on our making an evaluation, using our own judgement that we recognise to be subjective, a matter of personal opinion and preference. If usefulness is a matter of fact, but beauty is a matter of opinion (and not everyone would agree with this), then in which category might we place goodness? Do we know something to be good, or do we believe that it is good while recognising that our belief is subjective? Are we talking about facts, or values, when we use the language of morals?

These are questions that philosophers of meta-ethics try to answer, and they have taken a variety of different approaches, which can be categorised in a variety of ways. Sometimes, the approaches are divided into **cognitivist** and **non-cognitivist** views.

People who hold **cognitivist** views about moral language believe that moral statements are about facts, things that are true or false. Moral statements, according to cognitivists, are **propositions** – they make a proposal that some situation is, or is not, the case. Propositions are statements such as 'The cat is black' or 'The tide has gone out' or 'We went on holiday to Portugal'; we can ask questions about whether these are true or false statements, and the questions will make sense. If someone has a cognitivist view of moral language, then he or she believes that statements such as 'Stealing is wrong' are propositional, and their truth or falsity can be known. If something can be known, then it is available to cognition (knowledge), which is why this approach is called cognitivist.

Non-cognitivists believe that moral statements are not propositions at all, but perform some other, different function in language. Non-propositional language is the name for the kinds of sayings that are neither true nor false, and do not propose anything. Some examples of non-propositional uses of language might include questions ('How are you today?'), expressing feelings ('Happy birthday!') performative sayings ('I baptise you in the name of the Lord') or giving commands ('Hand your essay in next week'). These uses of language still make sense, but they are not sayings that could be followed by the question: true or false? A non-cognitivist view of moral language holds that moral statements are non-propositional; the truth or falsity of a statement such as 'Abortion is wrong' cannot be known. 'Abortion is wrong' is not a statement about facts, but is some other kind of saying. Moral language is not the subject of cognition, and therefore this approach is called non-cognitivist.

a) Ethical naturalism

Naturalist approaches to ethical language treat moral statements as propositions, in the same way as other, non-moral statements. If we make non-moral statements or assertions, such as 'Acid turns litmus paper red', we can find out whether this is true by looking at the evidence, and seeing by experiment whether the litmus paper turns red or not when in contact with acid. Ethical naturalists believe that it is equally possible to establish moral facts, by looking at the evidence. If we want to establish whether stealing is right or wrong,

CHESTER COLLEGE LIBRARY

for example, we look at the evidence of what happens when people do it: stealing causes people unhappiness; therefore stealing is wrong. The ethical naturalist, then, believes that moral statements are *verifiable*; they can be tested to find out whether they are true or false, and the fact of the matter can be shown. The main principles of ethical naturalism are that:

● ethical terms can be defined using non-ethical, natural terms – we can show what we mean by moral words, using information available to ordinary observation, for example we might say that something is right if it makes the majority of people happy, or if it helps societies to exist peacefully.
● ethical conclusions can be drawn from non-ethical statements – for example, we could say, 'Abortion ends the life of a foetus, therefore abortion is wrong', or 'Kindness makes other people happy, therefore kindness is good.'

b) G. E. Moore, the Naturalistic Fallacy, and Intuitionism

In 1903, the philosopher **G. E. Moore** published a book called *Principia Ethica*, which was hugely influential, shaping ethical debate for the next century. In this book, he argued that ethical naturalism makes a mistake, and that moral statements cannot be verified simply by looking at the evidence available to the five senses (empirical evidence). The mistake is known as the 'Naturalistic Fallacy'.

Moore's criticism is based on the work of **David Hume**, the eighteenth-century Scottish philosopher. David Hume was a very important thinker who was keen to show the possibilities and limitations of logical argument. He was able to see immediately and with great clarity when a line of argument disobeyed the rules of logic and, instead of moving from one step to the next, made a great leap in an unacceptable direction and claimed to have proved a point; and he called a halt to the argument, rather as the umpire of a chess match might stop someone who tried to move a knight the length of the board and claim a checkmate.

The principle of Hume's which was taken up by Moore is often explained in the following terms: *an 'ought' cannot be derived from an 'is'*. In other words, a statement of evaluation, or value, cannot be derived directly from a statement of fact. In *Principia Ethica*, Moore argues that no matter how 'good' is defined (whether as the greatest happiness for the greatest number of people, or as obedience to the will of God, or whatever), it can always be asked 'But is that good?' The question always remains open, and is not trivial. We can look at examples of people we believe to be good, and say things like 'Mother Teresa rescued abandoned babies' or 'Nelson Mandela spoke out against apartheid'; but it is still legitimate to ask 'And were those actions good?' There is still room for people to have different opinions, without there being any logical contradiction. Moving from an objective statement of fact to a subjective statement of value does not work, because it leaves open questions which have not been answered.

Goodness, according to Moore, resists definition. All attempts to give it some kind of absolute, definite content commit, according to Moore, the 'naturalistic fallacy'. Moore, however, was concerned that it should be possible to make judgements about what *things* are good. We need, in the end, to be able to make moral judgements. As he believed that this could not be done with reference to natural properties (or factual evidence), he proposed that goodness must have 'non-natural' properties instead, which are available to the intuition rather than the senses – which is how he came to arrive at his **intuitionist** approach to meta-ethical questions.

Moore believed that it is still possible for us to decide whether a moral statement is true or false, even if we cannot use our powers of observation to give us the answers. According to Moore, we cannot use our five senses to tell whether something is good, but we can use our 'moral intuition'. Although we cannot explain how we know when something is good, we do still recognise goodness when we see it – we just know it. Moore called this a 'simple notion'; it is impossible to analyse. He explained that it was rather like trying to define the colour yellow. There is no way that we can explain yellow, especially to someone who has never seen it, and if we try to say what it is like, we end up giving examples of yellow things rather than defining yellow itself; but we still know what yellow is when we see it. We cannot describe it to other people who have never seen it, but can only show them examples of it so that they too can have the same recognition. In the same way, we recognise goodness intuitively. It cannot be defined or described, but only known and demonstrated to other people. Moore's conclusion was:

> If I am asked 'what is good?' my answer is that good is good, and that is the end of the matter.

This 'moral intuition' could be compared, perhaps, to the feelings some people have when they meet someone and fall in love, and want to spend the rest of their lives with that person; they might not be able to justify their choice, but will say 'I just knew' that this was the right person, and they will be prepared to make important decisions on the basis of this knowledge.

The intuitionist, then, like the ethical naturalist, believes that goodness can be known. It is not just a matter of opinion, but something about which we can be certain. However, not everyone would agree with this, and there is plenty of evidence to suggest that we do not all recognise goodness intuitively in the same ways as each other. Intelligent, thoughtful people do not all vote the same way, or have the same opinions about ethical issues, even if they are all sincerely trying to follow what is good; they are far more likely to agree about whether or not something is yellow, and so perhaps the analogy cannot be stretched too far.

c) Ethical non-cognitivism

Ethical non-cognitivists reject the idea that we can have certain knowledge about good and bad, and make factual statements about them. Non-cognitivists argue that moral language is not objective; it does not refer to any actual facts, but goes no further than, for example, expressing the preferences and feelings of the person making the statement, or recommending that other people follow advice.

According to a group of philosophers known as Logical Positivists, a statement only has any meaning if it can be tested, using the real world of sense experience. If it can be tested, then it can be established firmly as true or false. However, if the statement cannot be tested, then no-one can know with certainty whether it is true or false; in fact, according to this way of thinking, it is meaningless. Moore's idea of knowing the nature of goodness just through intuition was rejected by ethical non-cognitivists such as **A. J. Ayer** in his book *Language, Truth and Logic*, in 1936. Ayer believed that moral language does not deal with objective, knowable facts, but with opinions. His own theory of meta-ethics is known as **emotivism**.

d) Emotivism

Emotivism, as expressed by Ayer, is the view that when we make moral statements, such as 'stealing is wrong', we are not talking about any objective facts which can be known, but are expressing our emotions or feelings about the issue. All we are saying is that we disapprove of stealing. The statement is only 'true' or 'false' insofar as it is an accurate or inaccurate reflection of the speaker's feelings and opinions. This view is sometimes described as the 'Boo-Hurrah theory'. All we are saying is 'Boo to stealing' or 'Hurrah to respect for other people's property', but these are non-propositional statements; we are not making any factual statement about some objective, knowable reality.

Emotivism can be a useful way of looking at the uses of moral language, because it draws attention to the ways in which the moral statements we make depend upon our own attitudes, feelings and upbringing. However, many people have criticised this approach because it does not seem to have enough substance to it. Our uses of ethical language, according to emotivism, could change from one day to the next, according to our feelings, and there would be no real reason for us to express one opinion rather than another. A statement such as 'murder is wrong' becomes no more important than children telling each other which sweets they prefer: 'I like the red ones', 'My favourites are the orange'. According to emotivism, if we say 'The murder of Jews during the Holocaust was evil', we are merely expressing our own feelings and not making reference to actual fact. Many would want to argue that moral statements go much further than just expressing our own approval or disapproval; they have a more justifiable basis than this. Also, in ordinary life we tend to give moral language more weight than this, whether or not we are right to do so. For example, if there is a difficult decision to be made in medical ethics, such as whether to allow someone to be assisted to die, or whether to separate Siamese twins, we expect more of the judge than that he or she just expresses personal feelings on the subject. Many of us do not want to agree with emotivist theories of moral language.

C. L. Stevenson, in his book *Ethics and Language*, modified Ayer's emotivist ideas. He took a similar non-cognitivist view and agreed that ethical statements are expressions of attitude or opinion, but he went on to argue that these attitudes are not just arbitrary, based on the mood of the day, but are based on beliefs about the world and the ways that it should work. Stevenson's views leave the way open for a possible compromise; moral statements can be expressions of emotion, but these emotions could themselves have a firmer basis than mere arbitrariness. Our attitudes are based on our experiences of the world and the way we want it to be; we disapprove of the Holocaust murders not just because they are not to our taste but because we have firm, justifiable beliefs about human dignity and worth.

e) Prescriptivism

Prescriptivism is another approach which is related to emotivism. It was developed by **R. M. Hare**, in a book called *The Language of Morals*, in which he agreed with Ayer that moral statements are fundamentally expressions of opinion rather than fact; so Hare, too, presented a non-cognitivist theory. He went further than Ayer, however; his view claimed that when we make moral statements, we are not only expressing our feelings but are encouraging others to share our attitudes. We are 'prescribing' our opinions, recommending that our listeners adopt our approach, and making it clear that we plan to follow a particular pattern of behaviour ourselves. Rather than being propositional, ethical statements give imperatives, similar to 'Come here for a moment'. Hare, then, saw that moral statements have a guiding role. When a headteacher tells the schoolchildren at assembly that they should be kind to each other and not bully, this is meant to guide them, not just make them aware of the headteacher's personal preferences. We become heated during moral debates because we hope that other people will share our views, and we try to persuade them by the use of argument. So, for Hare, this is the main function of moral language, to prescribe courses of action that the speaker intends to follow and wants other people to adopt as well. When people say 'Murder is wrong', what they are really saying is 'You ought not to murder, and neither will I'. Moral judgements are imperatives, like 'Come here' or 'Be quiet'. Prescriptivism holds that if we are to be consistent in our moral judgements, then when we say that someone else ought to do something, we need to accept that we ought to do it too. Also, in order to be consistent, if we think that something ought to be done to someone else, then we must accept that, in the same situation, the same thing should be done to us. So, according to prescriptivism, we can go further than to say 'Boo to the Holocaust murders'; we can say that they were wrong, because we would not prescribe them for ourselves.

Although prescriptivism offers some important insights, it might also be criticised, because it argues that moral judgements are founded on prescriptions, or imperatives, and do not have any claim to objective truth. It denies the possibility of moral knowledge, and does not help people to understand why they should follow one person's prescriptions rather than another's.

Summary

- Meta-ethics is about the ways in which people understand how moral language is used, rather than about finding answers to moral issues.
- Normative ethics is about making systems to help people know how to behave.
- People disagree about whether ethical language is about actual facts, or whether it is about values or opinions.
- Discussions of meta-ethics, rather than normative ethics, dominated moral philosophy in the twentieth century.

2 Moral relativism

Moral relativism is the belief that morality does not relate to any absolute standards of right and wrong, but that 'good' and 'bad' are dependent on culture and circumstance. It is the opposite of moral absolutism, which claims that there are universal standards of right and wrong, whether or not people agree with them, and independent of individual circumstances. **Immanuel Kant** (1724–1804), for example, was *not* a moral relativist. He held that there were absolute duties, or 'categorical imperatives', which were always right. He believed that we should consider whether we would be prepared for our own actions to become translated into universal laws before deciding what is right and wrong. If moral rules are right, according to absolutists, then it should be possible to apply them to everyone, without making allowances for different people or special circumstances; the laws should be 'universalisable'. In an absolute moral system, a rule that applies to, for example, a Muslim woman living in Afghanistan, is equally applicable to a Rastafarian living in London or to a farmer in rural Canada.

According to moral relativists, in contrast, there is nothing which is absolutely, invariably right or wrong, and there is no universal standard by which to measure our characters or our actions. A course of action, therefore, could be right for one person, but wrong for another, or right for one society and in one culture but wrong for another. When this is put into practice in normative ethics, it means that one group of people is never justified in judging another; everyone should be tolerant of other people's beliefs and behaviour.

This way of thinking has grown in popularity in recent years, particularly since the Second World War. The current emphasis on tolerance, on multi-culturalism, on freedom of speech and respect for the opinions and beliefs of others, implies that there are no 'real', absolute truths – or if there are, there are not nearly so many as was previously believed.

Today, unlike in the past, it is often accepted that different individuals can choose their own codes of behaviour, provided they keep within the laws of the society in which they wish to live, and need not fit in with any real or imagined absolute set of rules. For example, until relatively recently, most people considered it morally wrong for married women, particularly mothers, to work outside the home. This was considered to be a fact. It seemed obvious that it was wrong, and employers were well within their rights to terminate a woman's contract when she got married. Today, it is expected that women will make their own choices about whether to return to work after marriage or having a baby, and the choice which seems right for one woman will not necessarily be seen as right for another. The mood has shifted away from belief in a single set of rules that apply to everyone ('absolutism' or 'universalism'), to the belief that different codes could be equally valid for different people.

There has been a movement, too, away from religious absolutism, towards a feeling that everyone is entitled to his or her personal religious beliefs, if any, and it is no longer legal to discriminate against people because of their religion. In Victorian times it was accepted and admired for Christians from Britain to go and work overseas as missionaries, showing people from other countries how wrong non-Christian beliefs were and attempting to persuade them to adopt Christianity instead. Today, although there are still missionaries, their approach is regarded by many people as arrogant and intolerant; how can the missionaries be so convinced that their religion is right and that the beliefs of other cultures are wrong? What gives them the right to impose their beliefs and morality on another culture, which already has its own social structure and religious and moral codes? Relativists would argue that they have no right at all; but absolutists would argue that some beliefs and principles are always right, and the people who recognise them have a duty to try and make other people conform to them.

Cultural relativism encompasses morality and other areas too, such as religious belief and social behaviour. It is the sort of approach which leads people to say things like: 'When in Rome, do as the Romans do'. Other people's customs are different from our own, and, the theory is, we should respect this. Men should take off their hats if they go into a church, whether or not they are Christian, and they should cover their heads in a synagogue, whether or not they are Jewish; different ways of behaving are right, depending on, or relative to, the circumstances in which we find ourselves. The cultural relativist might argue that good manners and morality are pretty much the same thing, and we should adapt our behaviour to conform to the norms of the society in which we live. We should recognise that our ideas about the right way to behave are not absolute, and therefore we have no right to try and impose them on other people. If, for example, one society believes that families should be able to choose that their elderly relatives spend the ends of their lives being cared for in nursing homes, while another society believes that families have a duty to care for elderly relatives themselves in their own homes, then they could both be right in their own ways, according to their own social codes.

A **moral relativist**, then, believes that our ideas about good and bad, right and wrong, are dependent on the culture in which we live, in just the same way as dress codes and table manners are different in different societies. A statement such as 'Murder is wrong' is not absolutely, universally true; it is 'true for me' or 'true within my society' only. It might be true in most societies, but if there is a society in which murder is acceptable, then 'Murder is wrong' is not true for them.

J. L. Mackie, in his book *Ethics: Inventing Right and Wrong*, argues that our moral beliefs do not seem to shape the societies we live in; it is the other way round, where our morality is shaped because of our society. He also claims that if we believe morality has some kind of objective, absolute value, then it is difficult to know what form this absolute standard must take. It seems that we are expected to believe in a kind of invisible, spirit-like universal measure against which other values can be judged (rather like Plato's Form of the Good, see pages 11–14), and for Mackie this is an incoherent concept. Mackie argues that many people want to believe that morality has some kind of objective reality (a view which echoes the thinking of **Feuerbach** in the nineteenth century). They have learned the behaviour expected of them by their societies, and they want to believe that this relates to some real objective truth, but this is just because of a psychological need to try and find some objective reality on which to base our views, to give ourselves confidence. There is no real ultimate standard of right and wrong 'out there' at all, according to Mackie, however much we might wish that there were.

Moral relativists, perhaps not surprisingly, do not all share the same views. Some of them believe that all moral systems are equally valid; but this is an extreme view, and is difficult to justify in practice. There seems little point in having morality at all if there are no restrictions on the views it is acceptable to hold and the ways that a person is allowed to behave. Most have a more modified view, often believing that it is impossible to know with certainty whether one system is better than another, but that there might be very persuasive arguments one way or the other. If people have different moral beliefs, there is no valid way of proving that one is right and the other is wrong; but this modified version of moral relativism still has room for people to argue that, even if we cannot know that certain types of behaviour are wrong, nevertheless it is justifiable to make laws for the protection of society, and to punish those people who choose to go against this 'social contract'. The definition of the word 'good' is no more than 'that which is socially acceptable'.

Moral relativists tend to express the view that the practical applications of 'right' and 'wrong' depend on the context in which they are used. Something could be right in one circumstance, but wrong in another; for example, lying might be right if it was done to deceive an aggressive enemy and save lives, but it could be wrong if it was done out of malice or greed. Abortion might be argued to be the right choice for a pregnant girl of twelve, but wrong for an adult woman using it as a method of contraception. The attitude that there are things which are right or wrong in most, but not all, circumstances, is a weak form of moral relativism; it is the view that there are some things which are usually right or wrong, but nothing which is absolutely so, because there is always the possibility of circumstances which call for exceptions to be made. In this view, there are still broad, general rules which can be made, and principles which should, in most circumstances, be followed; judgements about other people's morality can be justified, but never absolutely.

One issue raised by moral relativism is the question of whether differences in moral behaviour between one society and another are the result of different *applications* of the *same* moral rules, or whether the *rules themselves* are different. Do societies each create their own sets of moral rules, which have no firmer basis than custom? Or do societies each respond in different ways to rules and principles which are fundamentally the same, and universal? It could be argued that there are absolute and universal rules, such as the duty to protect the weak, but that it is impossible to agree on how these rules should be put into practice and impossible to prove that one way of trying to express the principles is any better than another.

a) Criticisms of moral relativism

● A criticism that is frequently made is that relativist approaches, whether extreme or moderate, allow for any kind of behaviour, without completely condemning anything. Is it really morally acceptable to say something like: 'In my society, we do not accept torture, but if it is the custom in your country, then we will not condemn you'? Some people would argue that morality makes much more sense if there is an absolute standard of right and wrong to which everyone is subject. With a relativist approach, there seems to be little point in behaving morally beyond wanting to be socially acceptable, and morality becomes not much more important than wearing appropriate clothes for formal occasions or using the right knife at the dinner table. Many people believe that morality matters more than this, and that good and evil have a reality which we can recognise and which goes beyond mere opinion.

● One criticism that can be made of an extreme relativist approach is that, when taken to its logical conclusions, it is self-contradictory. The claim is made that every society, even every individual, might have a different set of rules which are not based on anything absolute, and are true only to the extent that they work within their own contexts. However, at the same time, relativists are making apparently absolute rules: you must not judge other people's morality against your own; you must tolerate other people's beliefs; it is universally, absolutely wrong to assume that your own beliefs are universal and absolute. Relativism is forced into a corner; by its own logic, it has to accept that absolutism might be equally valid, which is a nonsense.

● Relativists run into difficulties when they are faced with the situation of trying to tolerate someone else's intolerant system. Tolerance and acceptance of a variety of different moral codes, all co-existing peacefully, rather depends on everyone being a relativist. Those who argue that we should all respect each other's beliefs can have difficulties when, for example, they are trying to tolerate a system which oppresses women or denies basic human rights to some groups.

● Moral relativism could also seem very impractical: will one person, who believes that stealing is wrong, happily tolerate a neighbour borrowing his lawnmower and then refusing to return it, just because his neighbour happens to have a different moral code?

● **James Rachels** argues that societies do not each have their own, independent set of moral rules which bear no relation to one another; in fact there are principles which all societies need in order to function, and which are common to every social group. All societies, he argues, hold that we should care for children, and that dishonesty and murder are wrong. Rachels argues that relativists over-emphasise the differences between one culture and another.

b) Relativist approaches to moral decision-making

Most moral systems are relativist, but not all in the same way, or to the same extent; they might even be described as relatively relative.

Social contract theory, for example, works on the assumption that morality is based entirely on the needs of society. There is no external, supernatural law-giver, or absolute right and wrong that never changes. One famous exponent of this view of ethics was **Thomas Hobbes**; he argued that right and wrong are determined by the need for people to curb their naturally selfish desires and work in the interests of the group. They make systems of ethics, and determine what they are going to call 'right' and 'wrong', according to what is necessary to minimise conflict and promote survival. In this view, right and wrong are relative to the needs and desires of the society forming the 'contract'.

Utilitarianism, a system of ethics proposed by **Jeremy Bentham** and **John Stuart Mill**, puts forward the view that 'good' can be defined as 'the greatest happiness for the greatest number'. According to utilitarianism in its various forms, there is no ultimate or absolute goodness, but the best thing to do in a given situation is to find a course of action that will provide the greatest happiness for the majority. Right and wrong, according to utilitarianism, are relative to the people involved and the things which give them pleasure. In a group of sado-masochists, for example, torture would be good and right, although it might be considered wrong by a different group of people who did not happen to find pain pleasurable.

c) Situation Ethics

The approach to morality known as 'Situation Ethics' is another example of a moral system where it is accepted that, in practice, the right moral behaviour can be different for different people, according to the circumstances in which they find themselves. Like many other relativist systems, it makes a conscious attempt to get away from a blind following of moral rules, and encourages people to think for themselves, putting moral principles into practice using their own reason and common sense.

The phrase 'Situation Ethics' is usually associated with an American writer called **Joseph Fletcher** because he used it as the title of a hotly-debated book, but he was not the first to propose this kind of approach to morality.

Thinkers such as **Søren Kierkegaard** in the nineteenth century, and **Dietrich Bonhoeffer** in the 1930s, had emphasised the importance of individual freedom of choice. During the twentieth century there was a movement away from accepting rules and moral codes just because things had always been done that way. People were looking for a greater autonomy, or freedom to think for themselves and make their own decisions, and so when Fletcher published his book in 1966, it was very much in keeping with the mood of the time. It seemed to show a way of making the right, Christian, moral choices, without being bound by rules which prevented adults from thinking for themselves.

Fletcher wrote from a Christian perspective. He thought that it was important that Christians should get away from the idea that morality was all about following rules, such as the Ten Commandments, and away from the idea that morality was about obedience rather than autonomy (taking responsibility for one's own behaviour, or 'self-rule'). In his book, he rejected an approach to ethics based on following laws ('legalism'), but he also rejected the opposite extreme, where there is no morality at all and no grounds for judging anything to be morally better than anything else ('antinomianism'). He proposed, instead, that Christians should base their morality on one single rule: the rule of agape, or Christian love. In any situation requiring a moral decision, the Christian should ask himself or herself: what would be the most loving thing to do in this situation?

Fletcher rejected legalism on the grounds that it too often led people to do the 'right' thing regardless of the consequences. He wrote, for example, of a woman who was mentally unstable and pregnant as the result of rape, saying that to follow rules forbidding abortion and to insist that the pregnancy went ahead regardless of the circumstances would, in these circumstances, be morally wrong. Another example he gives is of a mother with a promiscuous thirteen-year-old daughter. The mother does the right thing (in Fletcher's view) by breaking rules condemning under-age sex and insisting that her daughter use contraception. Using these examples, Fletcher tried to illustrate his view that the right thing to do is not necessarily the same in all circumstances; the right choice is the most loving choice, and this will depend on the situation. He based his thinking on that of **Augustine**, one of the great saints of early Christianity:

> Augustine was right again, as situationists see it, to reduce the whole Christian ethic to a single maxim, *Dilige et quod vis, fac* (Love with care, and then what you will, do).

Love, in the New Testament and for Augustine and Fletcher, is not to be understood as an emotion, caused by the admirable qualities another person might have. Christian love, or agape, involves doing what is best for the other person, unconditionally, and valuing them just because they are human beings, even if they are unattractive or complete strangers.

According to Fletcher's book, situation ethics depends on six fundamental principles:

1. Love (agape) is the only absolute good. Everything else is only relatively good, in some circumstances. Nothing else is intrinsically good, regardless of all other factors.

2. Agape is the principle taught by Jesus. It is a self-giving love, allowing people freedom and responsibility to choose the right thing for themselves.
3. Justice will automatically follow from love, because justice is 'love distributed'; if love is put into practice then it can only result in justice.
4. Love must have no favourites, and give no-one preferential treatment, but must treat everyone as equally valuable.
5. Love must be the final end that people seek. It must not be a means to some other end; people must choose what to do because the result will be love, not be loving in order to achieve some other result.
6. The loving thing to do will depend on the situation, and as no two situations are ever exactly alike, different courses of action might be right in some circumstances but wrong in others. Because of this, most people would regard situation ethics as being a relativist approach to morality.

Summary

- Situation ethics has just one moral rule: the rule of agape, or unconditional love.
- It is meant to encourage people to behave as adults and to use their own common sense when making moral decisions.
- Situation ethics accepts that different decisions might be right in different circumstances.

i) Advantages of situation ethics

- Situation ethics allows people to take responsibility for their own moral decision-making. It does not treat them like children, by giving them rules and restrictions which must be followed unthinkingly, but recognises that they have common sense and encourages them to use their reason and their freedom of choice. In the 1960s, it was admired as being an appropriate ethic for 'man come of age'; the right approach for people who were now too sophisticated to be told what to do.
- Situation ethics provides a way in which people can make Christian decisions about issues not addressed in the Bible, such as genetic engineering, euthanasia, nuclear warfare and animal testing. It can be constantly updated to allow for new situations as they arise.

ii) Criticisms of situation ethics

- Even before Fletcher's book was published, some people were condemning this kind of approach to morality. Pope Pius XII, in 1952, argued that it was wrong to appeal to individual circumstances in an attempt to justify decisions which clearly went against the teachings of the Church. Situation ethics suggested that the decision made by the individual was more important than the teachings of the Church and of the Bible.

● This kind of approach expects people to have greater insight than perhaps most of us possess. How can we know what is the most loving thing to do? How can we know whether the course of action we are thinking of taking is going to result in the most loving outcome for everyone concerned? We can only judge these things to the best of our knowledge, and we may not be aware of crucial factors. No-one can step outside a situation and look at it objectively, weighing up all the possible outcomes, before making a choice.

● Situation ethics gives people too much responsibility, which experience has shown they cannot cope with. People do not always want to have to make their own decisions; they want to be told what to do. For example, someone with a very ill child does not usually want the doctor to say, here are the possible treatments, you decide, and in the same way, someone with a very difficult moral decision to make might want to be told, by a set of established rules, do this. People have moral problems because they cannot see which solution is for the best. If it were obvious, there would not be a problem.

● If two people, both using this approach and claiming to be acting out of love, come to different decisions, it is impossible to judge which one is right. There is no other point of reference, and nothing else which is regarded as absolute.

3 Natural Law

All people with some kind of ability to reason know that there are laws which govern the way the world works. We can observe the law of gravity, for example; we know that the angles of a triangle will always add up to 180 degrees; we can predict when we see a full moon how long we will have to wait until the next one. We know these things, because we accept that there are certain rules, which are a part of the universe. We can observe objects behaving in the same way every time. We work out answers with our reason, and find that other people, too, have reached the same answer. We might believe that God put these rules into place, or we might believe that the rules just exist without a reason, but whatever our view of their origins, we expect that the rules will continue to apply to objects in the future, in the same way that they always have done in the past. We know that in other parts of the world, even those which we have never visited and probably never will, gravity and triangles and so on work in just exactly the same way as they do for us.

Some people believe that the same can be said of morality. They hold that right and wrong, good and evil, follow a 'natural law' which we can discover through our observations and our reason. Morality works in the same way for every nationality, and at every time in history. Natural Law could be imagined as a kind of invisible measure, which never changes. Even if everyone in the world believed a certain action to be right, it could still be wrong, as Natural Law is independent of public opinion – just as perhaps once, everyone believed the world to be flat, and they were all wrong. A Natural Law approach to ethics is therefore different from a relativist approach. It is absolutist, or universal.

This idea that there is a natural law of morality, just as there is a law of gravity and there are laws of motion, can be found in many different cultures – it would be an over-simplification to suggest that there is one single moral concept of Natural Law. For example, in Hinduism, there is believed to be a 'natural law' called dharma, which governs the rules for different kinds of people to follow in order to gain merit. Dharma is an eternal, unchanging part of the universe, and it sets the standards for the right ways to behave. This 'natural law' gives a code of conduct for wives, for example, and another for soldiers, another for road-sweepers and another for shop-keepers; dharma prescribes what is right, and it remains unchanged regardless of personal opinions and preferences. Even the gods are subject to dharma.

Within Christianity there has been a great deal of support for the view that there is a Natural Law of morality. The Christian understanding of this concept is based very largely (although not solely) upon the work of **Thomas Aquinas** in the thirteenth century, and Thomas Aquinas himself was profoundly influenced by the great Greek philosopher, Aristotle.

When the mediaeval Europeans came into contact with Islam, they also encountered Aristotelian thought. Aristotle had such a remarkable mind that his ideas were quickly seen to be of enormous importance, and they were read with a new interest and enthusiasm by the leading scholars of the time, among whom was Thomas Aquinas. There was considerable resistance from within the medieval church to Aristotle's thought, because it looked as though people were trying to replace faith with reason, and as though Aristotle's way of thinking might replace Christianity. However, Aquinas set out to show that, if human reason is acknowledged to come from God, both faith and reason together can provide people with the best tools for living. In matters of ethics, he thought, people should not have to choose between blindly following the commands of God revealed in the Bible, or using their common sense instead. Natural Law theory is an attempt to show how the two can be brought together to form a system which is both reasonable, appealing to rational, intelligent people, and faithful to God.

a) Aquinas and Natural Law

Thomas Aquinas was a Dominican priest who lived from about 1224–1275. Although he was a quiet and unassuming man and his life was short, by modern standards, he achieved a vast amount. His work showed how different ways of thinking could be brought together, and how Christian belief could be shown to be not just a matter of blind faith, but reasonable and logical, fit for intelligent people. The writings of Aquinas were so full of insight that they became adopted as the 'official' views of the Roman Catholic Church; although today Roman Catholics might find things to criticise in Thomas Aquinas, nevertheless his way of approaching religious questions is still the basis of much Catholic teaching.

Aristotle believed that everything in the universe had both an 'efficient cause' and a 'final cause' (see pages 22–4), and Aquinas readily adopted this view, combining it with his Christian belief in the concept that everything which exists does so for a reason; God brought everything into existence on purpose. Aristotle had believed that something could be called 'good' if it fitted its purpose; a good knife is one which cuts well, for example. Aquinas took this idea and put it into a Christian context: something is good if it does whatever God wanted it to do when he made it.

Aquinas' understanding of human morality, therefore, begins with this understanding of what goodness is. It is fundamental to the Christian understanding of Natural Law in ethics. He presupposed that humanity was created on purpose, by God. What people have to do is to work out what that purpose is, and then aim to fit it, to behave appropriately and do what we are put in the world to do. If we can achieve this, then we will be good.

Aquinas' view of Natural Law also used Aristotle's idea that all existing things have 'potentiality' and 'actuality'. 'Potentiality' refers to the possibilities of change within an existing thing, for example a tadpole has potentiality to become a frog and an acorn has potentiality to become an oak tree. 'Actuality' is existence, or the way something actually is; and for Aquinas, the more a thing's potentialities are realised, the better it is. So, for example, a fully developed oak tree is better than a stunted one, or an acorn or a sapling. A healthy, educated man who has developed his conscience is better than one who is sick, ignorant or vicious. Fulfilling purpose, or as Aquinas would put it, turning potentiality into actuality, is the essence of goodness.

Of course, this raises the problem of how we can find out what the purpose of our existence might be, without direct access to the mind of God. For Aquinas, this was not an entirely unanswerable problem. Not only can Christians look to the Bible and to the teachings of the Church to find out God's purposes in creation, but also, they can look at the ways in which the human body is made, and this will give an indication of what the Creator made it for. Aquinas once again combined his Christianity with the thinking of Aristotle; not only can Christians use their faith in the Bible to learn God's purposes, but they can also use their observation, their perceptions of the world around them, and apply reason to their experiences. The way in which Aquinas looked at the functions of the human body anticipated the work of Charles Darwin seven hundred years later, by suggesting that living things are suited to a purpose – but, of course, Darwin's ideas about how that suitability had come about were very different from those of Aquinas.

Aquinas believed that various purposes were obvious, if a reasonable person considered the design and functions of the human body and mind. People are designed to grow, to reproduce, to seek nutrition, to use their brains, to follow their consciences, to live together in social communities, to seek what is good and avoid what is harmful. We can tell straight away that men and women are meant to complement each other. Aquinas believed that it was also a natural instinct of people to do whatever makes humanity flourish, and to avoid what is harmful. In terms of meta-ethics, then, Aquinas could be described as an ethical naturalist; he believed that it was possible to look at the observable facts of the world around us and see what we ought to do as a result.

Aquinas believed that the whole idea of law works at four different levels:

1. **Eternal law** – this is the order which is in the mind of God, and which forms the whole structure of the universe with its purposes.
2. **Divine law** – this is the law which is given to people from God, through the Bible and through the teaching of the Church.
3. **Natural law** – this is our inborn sense of right and wrong, discovered through the conscience.
4. **Human law** – these are the rules made by human societies in order for them to work successfully.

Each level of law depends, according to Aquinas, on the levels above it, which are superior. There is, therefore, nothing on which eternal law depends, because it is part of the nature of God and self-sufficient. Divine law, revealed in the Bible and through Church teaching, depends on eternal law, and eternal law is superior. Natural law depends on eternal law and divine law, which means that people should not attempt to work out how to behave solely on the basis of what is natural, but also need to educate their consciences and make reference to holy scripture and Church teaching. Human law, at the lowest level, should be based on the other tiers; and if there is a contradiction between human law and other levels, then the other levels have priority. This means that it would be right for people to break the law of the land, if their consciences told them to do so or if the Bible or the Church gave different teaching.

Summary

This Natural Law approach to discovering what is good, then, has several basic presuppositions:

- God made the universe and everything in it, for a reason.
- Goodness involves being fit for a purpose.
- People, by nature, want to be good.
- The purpose for which people exist is self-evident, a 'natural law', which can be discovered using God's gift of reason.

b) Advantages of a Natural Law approach to ethics

- An appeal to Natural Law is not just an expression of an opinion, but a way of asserting that there is an absolute authoritative code of moral behaviour which applies to everyone: many people would consider it an **absolutist**, rather than a relative, approach to ethics. Therefore it is possible for one society to judge another, and for one set of standards to be morally superior to another. If a nation commits an act of terrorism, it can be condemned for it, if one group of people decide to wipe out another through 'ethnic cleansing', they can be called to account; whereas if morality is purely subjective there is no way in which one society's moral code can be said to be any better than another's.
- The Christian version of the theory of Natural Law is seen as a way of combining faith with reason. A desire to follow the will of God, and the commandments in the Bible, is combined with an appreciation of humanity's ability to reason. Morality, according to this theory, is not just obedience to the arbitrary will of God, but uses and respects human rationality as well.
- Natural Law theory appeals to many people's instinctive conviction that right and wrong depend on more than just personal opinion and social convention. The ways in which very different societies come to the same conclusions about the existence of a natural law of morality support the idea that it is part of human nature to recognise this law through both reason and intuition, and that it is self-evident. Our instincts from childhood often seem to tell us that there is absolute right and wrong. Children have a very strong sense of justice and will cry 'It's not fair' as soon as they suspect that they are being given unequal treatment, indicating a strong intuitive belief that the same rules should apply to everyone and that exceptions should not be made, even if the other child is younger or a guest.

c) Criticisms of a Natural Law approach to ethics

- Thomas Aquinas took it for granted that God created the world, for a purpose, but not everyone would agree with this. Many modern thinkers, including for example the writers Jean-Paul Sartre and Albert Camus, the philosopher Bertrand Russell and the scientist Richard Dawkins, claim that the universe is 'absurd' or 'gratuitous'; it does not have a reason, it is 'brute fact', it came about by chance and not because of any divine purpose. This belief does not allow for a Natural Law approach to ethics, because it rejects the initial premise, or starting-point, of the whole system.

- Even if humanity were created for a purpose, it is not self-evident what this purpose is. An appeal to the 'natural' begs the question of how we can determine what this means. Ideas about what is and is not natural change between generations, and are different in different cultures. It can sometimes be difficult to separate what is truly natural from what is just culturally acceptable. For example, it has been argued in the past that it is unnatural for women to be doctors, and unnatural for people from different races to marry, and natural for some people to work as slaves for others from a 'superior' race, but most people no longer accept these ideas. Natural Law has frequently been cited in condemnation of homosexuality, with the argument that it is unnatural for people of the same gender to have a sexual relationship. However, recent suggestions that sexuality could be genetically determined rather than a deliberate choice by the individual raise the possibility of homosexuality being, in fact, 'natural' as part of the way in which some people are made. If we cannot agree upon a definition of what is natural, then it becomes very difficult to appeal to nature in the making of moral decisions.

- The concept of actuality being better than potentiality is difficult to understand and apply to practical ethics. There are many things we have the potential to become, but we would not necessarily see them all as good. Most people have the potential for old age and death but do not feel that they are goals, for example, and although Aquinas was not arguing that everything for which we have potential is good, he did not expand on this idea in a way that provides much help with practical problems.

- If the principles of Natural Law are strictly applied, some of the rules that result are unacceptable to common sense. For example, human teeth include incisors, for nibbling vegetables, and canines, for eating meat; by the principles of Natural Law, this would mean that people therefore ought to eat meat as well as vegetables, and that choosing to be a vegetarian is morally wrong. Or, to use another example, the principles of Natural Law claim that sexual intercourse is for the purpose of procreation; therefore people who are infertile, perhaps because they have passed the menopause or because of some other condition, should not have sex with their husbands or wives.

- The idea that humanity has a purpose is not without its problems as a concept. We might wonder whether there is one universal purpose for the whole of humanity, and whether this therefore means that we should all adopt the same kinds of behaviour. Natural Law suggests that every human adult should marry and aim to have children. However, this would mean that Mother Teresa was wrong to become a nun and devote her life to the poor when she could have been at home raising a family, and that Thomas Aquinas himself should not have been a priest but should have been a husband and father instead. Aquinas recognised this difficulty, and answered it by saying that as long as humanity as a whole fulfilled its purpose, by producing the next generation, it was acceptable for some individuals to choose other ways of life. People today might answer this with the comment that, in that case, it should be morally acceptable for some people to adopt a homosexual lifestyle, as long as there are plenty of heterosexuals around as well. In fact, it should be acceptable for any few individuals to choose to do the 'unnatural', whatever form it takes, as long as the majority follow Natural Law; and this paves the way for injustice, where some people consider themselves exempt from the rules they wish to impose on others.

- The ideas that there is one common purpose which applies to everyone is not completely supported by the Bible. In the book of Jeremiah, for example, God tells Jeremiah that his purpose is to be a prophet, and that he had been selected for the role before birth. Mary, in Luke's gospel, receives a message from the angel Gabriel telling her that she has been chosen to be the mother of the Son of God. These examples, and others, indicate a Biblical view that God can have different plans and purposes for different individuals, and can set aside some people or groups of people (such as the Jews) for particular tasks. If it is accepted that there might be different purposes for different people (and Aquinas did accept this), then the application of Natural Law becomes much more difficult. It could be possible, for example, that God intends one woman to remain single and devote her time and energies to medical research, while another might be intended to be an excellent mother of many children; and how are people to know which purpose applies to them, without direct access to the mind of God? Aquinas argued that careful education of the conscience and emotional maturity was necessary in order for people to discern what is right. Although this might be true, it introduces an element of subjectivity, where people must use their own judgement and choose from a range of possibilities rather than there being one answer which is 'naturally' obvious.

- The concept of Natural Law suggests that humanity has several different purposes to fulfil, rather than just one. A follower of Natural Law would accept that reproduction is not the *sole* purpose of humanity – otherwise there would be no difference between a person and any other animal, or even plant – but would argue that people have other purposes too, such as to love God, to learn, to contribute to society and so on. However, if people have several different purposes to fulfil, this could lead to dilemmas, where in order to fulfil one purpose, another has to be sacrificed. An intelligent mother, for example, might have to choose between putting her good brain to the uses for which it was intended and fulfilling her intellectual potential, or following the purposes of her fertility and bearing and raising more children. The Natural Law approach does not give guidelines for judging what to do in such cases, beyond advising the use of reason.

- It could be argued that Thomas Aquinas was too optimistic in his view of human nature and human reason. There is plenty of evidence on the news every day to suggest that not everyone is naturally inclined towards the good, and not everyone has the powers of reason which are necessary for the right application of Natural Law. Thomas Aquinas himself was a man of great intellect and wisdom, but perhaps he rather generously assumed that the rest of us are like him, instead of recognising his own superiority. Aquinas believed that when people act immorally, they do so because they mistakenly think that they are doing the right thing, but this is not always the case. Most of us have done something which we knew at the time to be wrong, but we went ahead and did it anyway, without being in any way mistaken about the morality of our actions. Occasionally people set out to do the worst thing they can think of, perhaps as a means of achieving a notoriety which they know they will never get in any other way. Sometimes, when there has been an indiscriminate shooting in a public place, for example, the perpetrator's only reason for the crime is that he wanted to be famous. It is difficult to accept that the playground bully, the football hooligan, the drug dealer and the pornographer mistakenly believe that they are acting for the best.

- Darwinian evolutionary theory has presented problems for the concept of Natural Law. According to Darwin, living things are motivated by a desire for survival, and evolutionary change occurs through a process called natural selection, where the creatures which are most suited to their environments survive and reproduce and the weakest fail and die. Not only does Darwin's theory suggest that humanity exists through chance rather than through the deliberate will of God, but also, it implies that humans naturally seek their own survival and are fundamentally self-interested. This contrasts sharply with Aquinas' view that people are naturally inclined towards the good.

- Some of Aquinas' critics from within the church claim that he did not give enough attention to the doctrine of the Fall, which is the traditional Christian idea that humanity has become tainted and imperfect because of the sin of Adam and Eve. Sin has made it impossible for people to have a reliable understanding of God's intentions for us, the critics argue, therefore we need the Bible and God's revelation to us in order to know what is right and cannot depend upon our own powers of reasoning to the extent that Aquinas claimed. The great twentieth century theologian **Karl Barth** held this view, arguing that people should recognise and accept the revelation of God, which is the only source of truth, rather than depending on fallible human reason.

- The concept of Natural Law has been accused of being based on a mistake known as the 'naturalistic fallacy', outlined by G. E. Moore. One of the main points of Moore's argument, taken from the philosopher David Hume, was that it is not logically possible to look at facts and arrive at value judgements; an 'ought' cannot be derived from an 'is' (see page 46). This has serious implications for Natural Law, which is based on the idea that our observation of what people are like gives a clear indication of how people ought to behave. According to Aristotle and Aquinas, our experience of human nature makes the ways in which we ought to behave self-evident, but in Moore's view this is a step of logic that cannot legitimately be made. It is not logically legitimate to take the fact of our human nature, and derive from it the values that determine human conduct.

d) Conclusion

Natural Law has been profoundly influential in ethics, particularly in the teaching of the Catholic Church. Many people continue to base their understanding of right and wrong around the concept of what is 'natural'. However, problems arise when people try to define exactly what is 'natural', and those who do not believe that the universe has any kind of purpose will not accept the principles of Natural Law at all.

4 Virtue ethics

a) Introduction

Virtue ethics is a tradition which goes back to Plato and Aristotle; it is also known as **aretaic** ethics, from the Greek word *arete* which means excellence or virtue. However, although it is a very ancient way of looking at morality, it has only become popular again fairly recently.

According to virtue ethics, the heart of morality is not found in actions, or in duties, but in the person performing the actions, the 'agent'. In other words, morality should concentrate on the person, and not necessarily on the choices they make in their moral behaviour. Ethical questions, therefore, should not be about whether one or another choice is morally right, but whether the person himself or herself is a good person. The personal character of the agent is what matters; morality is involved with developing one's own virtues in order to become the right kind of person. Virtue ethics, then, does not ask 'What is the right thing to do?' but 'What sort of person should I aim to become?' It concentrates on being, rather than on doing, and in this way it contrasts with other forms of ethics, which aim to show how to discover the right course of action.

The concept of virtue should not be considered as completely separate from other ethical approaches: Immanuel Kant and Jeremy Bentham, for example, both tried to define virtues and wrote about how these characteristics could be encouraged. However, although they wrote about what it means to be virtuous, these and other thinkers largely concentrated on explaining the right ways to behave, rather than focussing on the most excellent way to be. Modern revivals of virtue ethics have returned to concentrate on the agent, rather than the action, largely because the views of ethicists such as Kant and Bentham are seen to have serious and possibly insurmountable weaknesses.

b) The concept of virtue in the thinking of Aristotle

Aristotle, who lived in the fourth century BCE, is one of the most influential of all philosophers, and his thinking is the main source of inspiration for modern followers of virtue ethics. Aristotle was a pupil of Plato, and went on to become a teacher of Alexander the Great; the amount that he achieved in all kinds of areas of knowledge has probably never been surpassed (see pages 19–28).

Aristotle's main work about morality is called the *Nicomachean Ethics*. In this book, he started out from the assumption that what everyone wants most is a full and happy life: this all-round well-being is known as *eudaimonia*. Some people have translated *eudaimonia* as 'happiness', but it has a wider meaning than this: it involves both being happy and also living well, not only achieving happiness but also deserving it. It is a word which does not have a really adequate English counterpart. Perhaps the phrase 'good living' or 'a good life' might serve as a translation.

Aristotle argues that *eudaimonia* is the highest good because we desire it for its own sake, and not as a means to anything else at all. Other good things, such as justice, are desired because they lead to a good life, whereas good living itself is not wanted for anything which it might lead to; it is inherently worth having. He believed that there were three main forms of happiness: happiness as a life of enjoyment of pleasure, happiness as a free member of society, and happiness as a philosopher. *Eudaimonia* involves the combination of all three, rather than concentrating on just the first.

The best and happiest life for people, according to Aristotle, involves living well in a community or society, being able to exist alongside other people with due regard for their interests as well as one's own, and with the appropriate concern for the development of the society and the education of future generations. For Aristotle, then, ethics was very closely linked with politics.

Aristotle believed that the best way for people to achieve *eudaimonia* was for them to develop and exercise those qualities that are most productive for living in a society. Extremes of behaviour and of character are unhelpful in a society; for example, very timid people at one extreme, and very assertive people at the other, can both cause problems. For Aristotle, then, virtue could be found in what he called the 'Golden Mean': striking the right balance between extremes. Each of the extremes he called a 'vice', and the midway point where the right balance is struck he called a 'virtue'. Aristotle used the example of courage, as a virtue, lying in-between foolhardiness and cowardice, both of which are vices. What is morally right, for Aristotle, is to develop in oneself the virtues that will result in living in moderation, according to the Golden Mean.

In the same way as an athlete would adopt a fitness routine in order to develop his or her skills in sport, every person should work to develop his or her own character, trying to make a habit out of the virtues so that they become less of an effort and more a part of the personality. Right actions will automatically follow, once the agent acquires the virtues: an excellent person will automatically behave in the right way. Future generations can be taught goodness from the example of those who have gone before; it is argued that we learn more about morality from the living examples of virtuous people, than we do from learning a set of rules or principles. Someone might have been taught the principle 'Be kind to other people', but the principle on its own is less likely to have an influence on character than seeing real examples of kind people in action.

Aristotle was careful to point out that there are differences between a moral virtue and an intellectual virtue. Intellectual virtues, such as a proficiency in foreign languages, are partly the result of the talents with which a person is born, and owe a great deal to teaching, whereas the moral virtues are learned by living them. By making an effort to live a virtuous life, people develop the habits of virtue, and virtue then becomes part of the character rather than an effort – people today who are keen on healthy eating often use the same sort of argument, claiming that if you make the effort to eat sensibly, after a time you stop wanting large meals of rich food and healthy eating becomes habitual. Aristotle was convinced that virtue is something which we acquire, and not something which we have when we are born; different people are not inherently good or bad, but become good or bad according to the habits they develop in themselves. Virtue can only be acquired by doing it; Aristotle made the comparison with a craftsman, who learns his craft by constant practice and observation of others who have this skill. He also pointed out that it is not enough to have the know-how or even the habit of behaving as the virtuous person does; the actions are not as important as the character, and therefore the virtuous behaviour must be done with the right motivation, as the virtuous person would do them.

For Aristotle, the best way of learning about the virtues was to follow the example of the virtuous man. This could be an 'ideal type', following the example of how we imagine a virtuous person would behave; or it could be following a real example of an actual saint or hero, such as Socrates, Jesus, Gandhi, Mother Teresa or Nelson Mandela.

c) The revival of virtue ethics

Virtue ethics is often said to have begun to come back into popularity with the publication in 1958 of **Elizabeth Anscombe**'s article 'Modern Moral Philosophy'. In this article, she argued that the concept of moral rules and of moral obligation is flawed. She attacked the traditions of Utilitarianism and of Kant, which both set out principles for people to follow and which look at the morality of different actions, rather than at the character of the person. Anscombe argued that the idea that we have obligations to keep rules makes no sense unless people believe in God. Even if an ethical system is not, on the face of it, a particularly religious system, the only reason for keeping a moral law is if there is a judge, or law-enforcer, to reward or punish people according to their behaviour. Without any absolute law-giver, there is no sense in following laws in ethics. She saw that ethical systems which try to establish rules even after the idea of God has been abandoned are incoherent, not recognising that their basis depends on belief which many people no longer hold. For Anscombe, the way forward is to revive the concept of human 'flourishing', *eudaimonia*, which does not depend on any notion of God.

Philippa Foot's 'Virtues and Vices' of 1978 also had a profound influence on the renewal of interest in virtue ethics. Anscombe's article had concentrated largely on outlining the failings of other ethical theories, and the need for a new direction, without going into very much detail. Philippa Foot went further by setting out the reasons for her support of virtue ethics, arguing in particular that although virtue cannot guarantee happiness, it can often be an important part of achieving it. She also discusses some of the questions raised by virtue ethics, such as whether the person who is by nature virtuous is to be admired more, or less, than the person who has to struggle hard to be good and yet succeeds. In her article, she uses the example of Thomas Aquinas (a mediaeval Christian philosopher who was greatly influenced by Aristotle), and Kant (probably the most famous philosopher of the eighteenth century), to show how the concept of virtue was very much a part of their thinking – it is not a new way of approaching ethics, but part of a tradition with a long standing amongst respected thinkers.

Alisdair MacIntyre and **Richard Taylor** are two modern philosophers who have continued promoting virtue as a new direction in ethics, and who seek to combine the thinking of Aristotle with other ideas in an attempt to form a coherent system which can meet the objections of its critics.

The publication of Alisdair MacIntyre's book *After Virtue: A Study in Moral Theory* in 1981, has been the subject of a great deal of discussion by modern scholars, because of the scope of its arguments. In the book, he put forward a strong case for adopting an aretaic approach to ethics rather than considering the rules and principles by which people should live. However, he went much further than this, by suggesting that moral philosophy, and in fact the whole of philosophy of any kind, is too far removed from ordinary life. He claimed that it is not good enough for philosophers to spend their time debating the nature of ethical language, or forming logical, reasoned theories of morality, in a way which is far removed from real people and the lives they lead. Someone whose child has been murdered is not going to care at all about the precise ways in which the word 'bad' is to be defined; someone who has to make a decision about whether or not her elderly mother should be kept alive in an intensive care ward will not be interested in weighing the advantages and disadvantages of one ethical system over another. MacIntyre's book advocates a consideration of the virtues throughout history, to see how they work in the context of real life, in order to move towards a way of enabling people to cope with the moral problems they face, as individuals and as a community.

Richard Taylor's book, *Ethics, Faith and Reason* (1985), traces the ways in which, he believes, the ethics of Western civilization have been distorted and made unworkable by Christianity. He writes of *'the corruption of philosophical ethics by religion'*, arguing that the use of reason is essential for ethics but that religion has led people away from reason, by insisting instead on the need for faith and for blind obedience to an alleged 'divine command'. He supports a move back to the development of personal excellence, and away from concepts of absolute right and wrong. Taylor believes that religious ethics and the ethics of the ancient Greeks are not merely two different ways of approaching the same end, but that the goals themselves are different. He criticises Christianity which, in his view, encourages people to think of everyone as being equal; 'the poor, the weak, the ignorant and stupid' are promised the riches of heaven. Taylor believes that this discourages people from trying to become greater; there is no point in making an effort to be strong and noble if the weak and humble are the ones who gain the most. Pride in oneself, he argues, is a good example of something which should be developed as a virtue and yet which Christianity classifies as a sin. For Taylor, then, virtue ethics is a long overdue return to a system which has far more to offer the individual than Christianity.

Summary

- Virtue ethics concentrates on what a person is, rather than what a person does.
- The aim of virtue ethics is a good life of well-being, *eudaimonia*.
- It is a tradition which goes back to Aristotle; interest in it has recently been revived.
- Virtue ethics is a system which does not depend on any sense of obligation to a divine law-giver.

● The best ways to learn about virtue are to practise it, and to observe the examples of virtuous people.
● Individuals take their own responsibility for developing habits of virtuous conduct, and this improves their characters.

d) Advantages of virtue ethics

● Virtue ethics can fit well with a variety of philosophies. For example, a humanist view, which holds that there is no God but that humanity holds the key to its own success, could readily adopt a system of morality which had no need of a divine law-giver or sense of obligation to a creator. But virtue ethics can also harmonise well with, for example, a Christian view of living in the imitation of Christ as the prime example of virtue, and of developing faith, hope and love as 'cardinal virtues'; or with the Buddhist view of adopting the 'Middle Way' between extremes.
● The system can be readily understood and simply applied. Instead of adopting a complicated way of calculating the likely outcome of one's actions, for example, a person could aim to be good and do what a good person would do – something even a child could understand.
● Virtue ethics is based on the welfare of the whole community, and therefore is a good way for people to live together without anyone trying to impose on anyone else.
● Although the system is based on ideals, it is not unrealistic, because it looks to actual examples of virtuous people; it can therefore be seen to have attainable targets. Its aim is to achieve something which people genuinely want (*eudaimonia*), rather than being based on arguably incoherent ideas about the after-life.

e) Criticisms of virtue ethics

● One well-known criticism of Aristotle's concept of virtue as the 'Golden Mean', made for example by Alisdair MacIntyre, is that it does not work for every type of virtue; many virtues are not at a mid-way point between two evils, but are just inherently good. For example, promise-keeping, compassion or loyalty do not seem to lie between two extremes, where an excess of them would be a bad thing; they are virtues which do not appear to be striking a balance but are simply good in themselves. Also, Aristotle does not make it clear how we are supposed to know where the mean between the two extremes might be found – which point between foolhardiness and cowardice is the point at which courage lies?
● Some people, for example **Robert Louden** argue that virtue ethics is of little practical help for a person faced with a moral dilemma. He writes:

> We ought, of course, to do what the virtuous person would do, but it is not always easy to fathom what the hypothetical moral exemplar would do were he in our shoes...

If, for example, a woman discovers during the course of her pregnancy that the baby will be born with severe disabilities, virtue ethics would tell her to do what a good person would do – but how is she to know what that is? The problem is that virtues can sometimes conflict. How is she to choose between 'be brave', 'be compassionate' and 'be pragmatic'? This criticism is countered by **Rosalind Hursthouse**, amongst others: in her article 'Virtue Theory and Abortion', she takes the practical moral issue of abortion and shows how virtue theory might be applied in order to help someone come to a decision.

- **William Frankena** argues that virtue cannot realistically be separated from principles and rules, as a different system. We only know that, for example, generosity is a virtue, because we recognise the principle which says that we have a duty to those less fortunate than ourselves. Without rules and principles, we would not know how to judge whether a characteristic was to be admired as a virtue.

- Some people might object that virtue ethics is a very self-centred way of looking at morality. Rather than helping someone else out of genuine concern for the other person, virtue ethics encourages putting oneself first, and choosing a course of action that will be the most beneficial to one's own character, with the other person's needs coming second.

- It can be argued that 'being' and 'doing' in ethics cannot be separated in the way suggested by aretaic ethics, with one having priority over the other. A virtuous person cannot just 'be' virtuous, without doing anything; no-one can just 'be generous' in character unless this is accompanied by giving, and 'bravery' counts for nothing except when it is put into practice in times of danger. And a lot of people would think that good actions still count even if they are performed by someone who is far from virtuous, and someone who is generally believed to be virtuous will not always, invariably, do the right thing.

- Critics of Richard Taylor might argue that his understanding of Christianity is a distortion; Christianity does not teach that all people are equal in terms of their moral worth, but teaches that all have the same intrinsic value as created by God, which is not the same. Jesus criticised those who were, for example, hypocritical or greedy, and praised those who had faith and who gave all they had. Christians might argue that there is still the need for people to strive to become more like Christ as an example of virtue.

- Some argue that the concept of virtue is culture-dependent, and that it is therefore difficult to hold up virtue as the highest good when it can be seen in very different ways in different kinds of society. For example, in some parts of India it used to be the case that it was considered honourable and virtuous for a woman to throw herself onto her husband's funeral pyre and be burned to death with his body; but in some societies suicide is considered a crime as well as a sin, and not an indicator of virtue at all but the very opposite. This cultural dependency challenges the idea that we all recognise the virtuous person when we see him or her. It also challenges the idea that the virtuous character is an unshakeable fixture; and perhaps we need a more reliable way of judging moral worth.

● Some say that, because of its dependence on culture, virtue ethics has a built-in sexism which is oppressive for women. 'Virtue' itself comes from a Latin word for 'manliness'; the characteristics of the traditionally 'ideal man' are often very different from those of the 'ideal woman'. Aristotle's own views that women were inferior to men, morally as well as in other ways, has influenced centuries of thinkers, including some of the founders of Christian doctrine (such as Thomas Aquinas). A virtuous woman might be seen as one who successfully acts out her gender role as self-sacrificing, humble and non-assertive, and this concept of virtue is one which many modern women would not want to accept. Mary Wollstonecraft, a pioneering feminist and contemporary of Jeremy Bentham, complained in her *Vindication of the Rights of Women* that the concept of virtue excludes women as by definition it is involved with qualities of ideal manliness. Since virtue ethics has been revived, there has been considerable attention given to it by feminist writers.

● **Susan Wolf**, in her article 'Moral Saints', argues that it is difficult to be attracted by the concept of becoming a virtuous person. She opens her essay with the words: 'I don't know whether there are moral saints. But if there are, I am glad that neither I nor those about whom I care most are among them.' The main point of her argument is that people who resolutely cultivate the virtues are likely to become boring; people who devote themselves to helping the poor, being brave, patient, and in every way good-natured, are unlikely to find the time to read interesting books or develop a flair for cooking or a skill in playing a musical instrument. There would be no room in the world for the satirical wit so many of us enjoy, or for flamboyant personalities of any kind. Wolf argues that perhaps the virtues themselves should be practised only in moderation. In response to Wolf's article, **Louis Pojman** defends virtue, saying that dullness is a price worth paying for saintliness. He takes the example of Gauguin, a post-impressionist artist who abandoned his wife and five children in order to go to Tahiti and paint beautiful, vital pictures. Pojman asks whether Gauguin should have done his moral duty, stayed at home and 'gone through life as a quiet stockbroker and an undistinguished father and husband'; and concludes that he should have done just that, even if the rest of us would have missed experiencing Gauguin's art as a result. We cannot admire the results and ignore the immorality which was necessary for them to come about, any more than we can admire the results of medical research performed by the Nazis while ignoring the suffering of its victims.

f) Conclusion

Many of these criticisms lead towards the same point: a system which requires people to 'be truthful', 'be kind' and so on, relies on us all agreeing about what the virtues of truthfulness or kindness actually are. Before we can encourage each other to 'be good', we need to come to some agreement about what goodness is. Virtue theory, however, is not alone in facing this difficulty: other ethical theories, too, run into problems of definition, where the Utilitarian will be asked: 'How can the greatest happiness of the greatest number be identified?' and the Kantian: 'What is duty and how will we know it when we see it?'

Practice examination questions

1. **a)** Explain the theory of Virtue Ethics. (33 marks)
    b) 'The world would be a boring place if everyone in it were virtuous.' Discuss. (17 marks)

Guide

In part (a), an outline is required of the main principles of Virtue Ethics. It might be a good idea to refer to some of the leading thinkers, especially Aristotle, and to show that you are aware of more modern views, such as those of MacIntye. In part (b), you should make an assessment of whether virtue really is boring, perhaps by using some examples of real people – was Mother Teresa dull, for example? You could also consider whether dullness is a price worth paying for a moral society.

2. **a)** Explain what is meant by 'moral relativism'. (33 marks)
    b) 'There are some things which are always, absolutely wrong.' Discuss. (17 marks)

Guide

Part (a) is asking about a broad area, and you might need to plan your answer before you begin, in order to avoid wandering around aimlessly and running out of time. You could distinguish between relativism and absolutism, and you might be able to give some examples of each. You could also show understanding of other kinds of relativism, such as cultural relativism, although the main body of the answer should concentrate on the question itself. In part (b), you need to decide whether you are a relativist or an absolutist, and defend your view. Try to give examples to illustrate your answer. For higher marks, you should aim to give sound reasons, rather than just saying 'I feel' without much justification.

3. **a)** Describe some of the issues that are debated in meta-ethics. (33 marks)
b) How convincing is the view that when we are talking about morality, we are talking about facts? (17 marks)

Guide

In part (a), you should demonstrate your knowledge of meta-ethics by giving some examples of the questions it raises, and also perhaps indicating how different people have addressed them. You should show that you know the difference between meta-ethics and normative ethics, and show how meta-ethicists are concerned with questions of definition and use of moral terms, rather than with behaviour. In part (b), you should write about your own views of how moral language is used. Perhaps there is a particular scholar with whom you agree, such as Moore or Ayer, and you could use this in your answer.

Suggestions for further reading

Harry Gensler and Mary Grace Tokmenko, 'Moral Relativism', *Dialogue*, ed. John Waters
Joseph Fletcher, *Situation Ethics* (SCM Press, 1966)
Michael Palmer, *Moral Problems* (Lutterworth Press, 1991), Appendix
Mel Thompson, *Ethical Theory* (Hodder & Stoughton, 1999), chapters 4, 6 and 7
Peter Vardy, *The Puzzle of Ethics* (Fount, 1999), chapters 3, 4, 7 and 8
'Natural Law', an article by Peter Jackson printed in *Dialogue*, April 1999
Mel Thompson, *Teach Yourself Ethics* (Hodder & Stoughton, 2000), chapter 3
Richard Taylor, *Ethics, Faith and Reason* (Prentice Hall, 1985)
William Frankena, 'A Critique of Virtue-Based Ethical Systems', *Ethics* (Prentice Hall, 1973)
Louis Pojman, *Ethical Theory: Classical and Contemporary Readings* (Wadsworth, 1994) and Crisp and Slote, *Virtue Ethics* (Oxford University Press, 1997) are two anthologies of articles about ethics. The following articles in *Virtue Ethics* might be of particular interest:

G.E.M. Anscombe, 'Modern Moral Philosophy'
Philippa Foot, 'Virtues and Vices'
Robert Louden, 'Some Vices of Virtue Ethics'
Rosalind Hursthouse, 'Virtue Theory and Abortion'
Susan Wolf, 'Moral Saints'

3 Jewish scriptures (Old Testament)

KEYWORDS

Ancient Near East (ANE) – the name given to the geographical and historical context to which the Biblical texts relate

cuneiform – an adjective describing the wedge-shaped writing of ancient civilizations, such as the Babylonians

Diaspora – the dispersion of the Jews to live among Gentile populations in areas outside Israel

Form criticism – a type of Biblical study which considers the literary genre of a text in order to reach a better understanding of its meanings and purpose

Pentateuch – a word which comes from ecclesiastical Greek, and refers to the first five books of the Bible

Source criticism – a type of Biblical criticism which considers the different possible sources from which Biblical authors might have obtained their material

1 Dating the events of the Bible

The scriptures which make up the Jewish Bible were not all written at once, but over hundreds of years; and the events described in them cover a time from the creation of the universe until the beginnings of Christianity. Some of the writings come from periods when the people of Israel were settled and prosperous, and others were written during exiles and national crises, when the whole religion and way of life was under threat. Obviously these differences in context have a very great importance for the ways in which the texts are to be understood. It is also useful for the reader to know something of the social background of the texts, for example the usual customs surrounding inheritance, or the keeping of slaves, or the treatment of refugees, so that the behaviour of the principal characters can be judged within its context. Biblical scholars study the evidence within the scriptures themselves, and from other sources such as ancient documents and archaeological discoveries, in order to give the main events of the Bible this kind of context. They try to discover more about the times in which these people lived; what importance did they have as a nation among other nations? What were their everyday lives like; what animals did they keep, what did they eat, how did they trade? What were their social customs and family relationships? What was the nature of the other religions by which they were surrounded when Judaism was first beginning?

Of course, one of the issues which has caused the most controversy when trying to study the history of the Biblical narrative is that of whether the events described ever really happened. For many believers, this is not an issue at all: the Bible, as the Word of G-d, is more true than any other source of information, and therefore the events which it describes are necessarily true. If there is no external evidence to support this, or the discoveries of scholars suggest a different picture, then the Bible remains true, because the people who are doing the research are fallible whereas, for many believers, the Bible is not. However, there are also many people who are willing to accept that perhaps the Biblical accounts are true in a theological rather than an historical sense. The purpose of the text is to demonstrate the nature of the relationship between G-d and humanity, especially humanity's inclination towards sin and the ways in which G-d has intervened in the world to keep people away from evil. Sometimes, it is argued, the accuracy of the historical accounts might have been sacrificed in order to emphasise the theological point.

Many of the events described in the Jewish scriptures are very difficult indeed to date in an accurate way. There are many reasons for this, including:

● Most of the written records from these people and this period have not survived. Texts from elsewhere in the Ancient Near East (often abbreviated as ANE) have been discovered by archaeologists, sometimes because they were written on durable substances such as the terracotta used in Mesopotamia, and sometimes because the climate was dry enough to preserve writings made on flimsier materials such as parchment and papyrus. However, most Hebrew texts were written on insubstantial materials, and the climate was not particularly dry, and so only a few examples of texts have survived in exceptional circumstances, such as the Dead Sea Scrolls.

● The Jewish scriptures are believed by many to have originated as oral traditions rather than pieces of writing, which means that as they have been transmitted, they could have sometimes changed. Elements have been added or removed which make it very difficult for scholars to work out which parts of the text are historically reliable. Sometimes the texts refer to cultural features which may be of a later date than the story itself, and scholars have to speculate about which parts of a narrative are older than others.

● The Biblical writers did not have the same understanding of history as we do today. For them, history did not have to involve a completely accurate record of events that really happened and words which were actually spoken; it was quite accepted that a person's age or number of sons might be exaggerated to show that he was particularly blessed by

G-d, for example. If the writer wanted to demonstrate a special quality or characteristic that a person had, then an event might be introduced to illustrate the sort of way in which this person could be expected to behave, and it did not matter whether or not the event really took place. However, this different understanding of history should not be exaggerated. Modern historians and biographers, too, often have to make informed guesses where they do not know the facts, and although they have a much wider access to records and archives than the writers of the Bible, they still make mistakes in accuracy, and write according to their own biases.

● The writers of the Bible did not set out with the primary purpose of writing an accurate historical record. They were interested in the relation between G-d and humanity, and in particular the relation between G-d and his chosen people, Israel. What they chose to record is determined by this purpose, which makes it more difficult to date, because the people and events of the Bible were often of little concern to anyone else who did not share this particular religious interest. Important rulers and political events of international importance, which could give the Bible some firm dates if they were mentioned in the text, are ignored completely because they have no relevance for religious faith. Instead, the stories of the Bible are often about slave-girls, refugees, nomads, and others of whom nothing else is known.

In order to try to ascertain the dates at which the events described in the Bible might have happened, scholars use a variety of methods.

a) The evidence within the Bible itself

Some argue that a date can be found for any of the principal characters and events of the Bible, using the text itself; this depends on a belief that the Bible is historically accurate and reliable. If it is believed that the Bible is inspired by G-d and is never wrong, then Biblical dates which can be known with some certainty because of external evidence, can be used as reference points from which to calculate. The foundation of the Temple is described as being 'In the four hundred and eightieth year after the Children of Israel's exodus from the land of Egypt — in the fourth year of Solomon's reign over Israel' (1 Kings 6:1). If, as is usually agreed, this happened in year 967 (working on a system where year 1 is the first year after creation), the Exodus, then, can be calculated to have happened in 487. The Bible is often quite specific about the length of a man's life, or the number of years of a reign, and, as long as these are accepted to be true rather than poetic descriptions meaning simply 'a long time', then calculations can be made which place events at particular dates. Many scholars, however, are of the opinion that this is not a reliable method of dating events, because of the inconsistencies and difficulties that arise. Noah, for example, is said to have lived for 'nine hundred fifty years' (Genesis 9:28), and was born (according to a literal interpretation of Genesis 5) in the year 1056, well after the date ascribed by the same method to the Exodus.

b) Archaeological evidence

Until the end of the nineteenth century, it was assumed that it was impossible to give any kind of accurate dating to many of the events described in the Bible. Some judged that characters such as Abraham, Joseph or Moses had never really existed, but were mythical 'folk-heroes', personifying praiseworthy characteristics rather than having any basis in history. But since the First World War, archaeology has thrown considerable light on the societies which inhabited Israel and the surrounding countries. For example, excavations on the southern bank of the river Euphrates in modern-day Syria have revealed the existence of a city known as Mari. In the palace of Mari a collection of cuneiform tablets was found, dating from the nineteenth and eighteenth centuries BCE, and these have provided a wealth of information. They formed the city archives, and refer to legal, economic and other matters which help to build a picture of the ways in which people lived in the Middle Bronze Age. Haran, the city to which Abraham moved, is mentioned as an important political centre, and some of the people mentioned in the archives have names similar to those found in the Bible. There is no certain proof that Abraham and the other patriarchs lived at the time of the Mari archives, or even that they came from a similar type of society, but enough information is given to enable scholars to speculate. There is no evidence to prove that they existed, but there is also no evidence to prove that they did not; and the Bible says that they did.

The word 'Habiru' or 'Apiru' occurs in over 200 of the non-Biblical texts that have been discovered in the Ancient Near East. The term seems to refer to a class of people, rather than an ethnic group; they are seen as outsiders or strangers, a migrant group who sometimes work for the people whose writings describe them. Some scholars have noted the similarities between the word 'Habiru' and 'Hebrew'; perhaps the people mentioned in the ancient texts were the very same people who inhabited the world of the Jewish scriptures.

Other texts discovered by archaeologists include examples of early treaties, or 'covenants' made between different groups and sometimes between different countries. These are written agreements, where each party makes a promise as part of the bargain with the other. In what are called 'suzerainty' treaties, one party is much more powerful than the other. These treaties might have been drawn up after a battle, where the winning nation made a list of the rules which the losers would have to follow, the amounts they would have to pay, and so forth. In 'parity' treaties, both parties have equal power, and the agreement has the same conditions for each so that they can live peaceably side by side. The most useful ancient treaties, from the point of view of the historians, came from the Hittites of the Late Bronze Age. The treaties were set out in accordance with a pattern: first there would be a preamble, outlining the circumstances which led up to the treaty being formed, and then there would be the rules and conditions which were being agreed. This would be followed with a list of those who were witnesses to the making of the treaty, and then there would be blessings and cursings designed to encourage everyone to stick to what had been agreed. In the 1960s, scholars drew attention to the similarities between these treaties and the covenants in the Bible. The Biblical covenants, where G-d makes agreements at various times with humanity, follow the same kind of pattern as the Hittite treaties. In the Sinai covenant with Moses, for example, there is the preamble where it is remembered that G-d has brought the people out of the land of Egypt, and then the rules of the agreement are made; the Hebrews are to be a kingdom of priests and a holy nation, and in return they are to keep the laws they are given. The elders of the people witness the covenant, and the people are promised blessings and protection from their enemies if they keep to the agreement (Exodus 20–24). These similarities have led Biblical historians to the conclusion that perhaps the Biblical covenants date from the same time as those discovered from the Hittites, because of the ways in which they reflect such similar legal practices.

Names can provide other clues to the dating or geographical setting of a particular event. Forenames come in and out of fashion, and are typical of some regions but not others, and when scholars find evidence of other people with similar names to those of characters in the Bible, it could suggest a context for the Biblical writings.

As well as using documents from the Ancient Near East in an attempt to place the Bible in historical context, archaeologists have also searched for evidence of the existence of cities and buildings mentioned in Biblical stories. One of the biggest quests of archaeologists has been the attempt to discover the famous walls of Jericho, which by a miracle fell down at the seventh blast of the trumpet. During the 1930s, it appeared that archaeology had succeeded; remains of a Canaanite city were found, which seemed to have been destroyed dramatically by fire and earthquake. However, **Kathleen Kenyon**'s research in the 1950s disappointed many who had been pleased to think that archaeology supported the history of the Bible; it became apparent that the evidence did not agree with the Bible after all, because the destruction that had been discovered pre-dated the Joshua story by more than a thousand years.

Other Biblical sites, however, do have the support of archaeological evidence. The defeat of the city of Hazor, mentioned in Joshua 11, corresponds well with the excavations of a city which came to a sudden and violent end during the thirteenth century BCE. It does not provide solid proof, but in this case the findings of the archaeologists match the date of the story in the Bible.

Those who are trying to work out when the events described in the Bible might have taken place do not usually have firm evidence with which to work. Material from outside the Bible very seldom mentions Biblical characters at all; Moses, for example, is not referred to anywhere other than in the Biblical texts themselves. Scholars have to be content with making educated guesses. Details in the Biblical narratives sometimes give clues to the era in which the story is set; they might refer to weapons of iron, for example, so that scholars can match the story with a time when iron was a common material for weapon-making, or social customs might be mentioned which can be matched with the customs of people who lived in a particular period. But the task of dating Biblical stories is enormous and difficult, and there is a great deal of disagreement between scholars about the extent to which conclusions can safely be drawn from the available evidence.

c) Possible dates of the principal events of Jewish scriptures

Creation – The first chapters of Genesis are widely believed to deal in a mythological way with the creation of the world and an account of how sin and evil became part of everyday life. Some take these accounts to be literally true, and have tried to work out the date on which creation occurred; this is traditionally held to be in 4004 BCE. However, most scholars hold that the first eleven chapters of Genesis are myth rather than historical accounts, and that they should be interpreted for the concepts they are exploring, rather than for their literal historical accuracy. The myths themselves originated in pre-Israelite history, perhaps during or even before the Early Bronze Age.

Abraham and the Patriarchs – the early second millennium BCE – The story of Abraham (Genesis 12–25) begins a more historical account of G-d's relationship with humanity. The date of Abraham and Sarah and their immediate descendants is difficult to determine; they are widely held to have lived during the Middle Bronze Age, somewhere between 2000 and 1550 BCE, although there is no evidence of their existence apart from the Biblical record itself. The archaeologist **W. Albright** believed that Abraham was a nomad trading along the route from southern Sumeria to the Egyptian border, during the end of the second millennium BCE. Abraham's life-style, as depicted in the Bible, was typical of these people. He lived in a tent, rather than a permanent house, and was constantly moving from place to place, wherever he could find a well and somewhere safe to stay. According to the Bible, Abraham's grandson Jacob had twelve sons who are said to have founded the twelve tribes of Israel. They moved to Egypt in order to escape a famine, but as they grew in number they were enslaved by the Egyptians, until Moses led them out of Egypt in the Exodus towards the land they had been promised.

The Exodus – 1550–1280 BCE – No evidence for the Exodus itself has yet been discovered outside the Bible, and many Biblical scholars have been drawn towards the conclusion that the event described in Exodus was an idealisation, written many years after the event. The Bible tells how, after a series of miracles, the people were led out of slavery, and taken to Mount Sinai where they formed a covenant agreement with G-d, in which they were given commandments to follow and were promised G-d's special care as his chosen nation and 'kingdom of priests'. The Sinai covenant of Exodus 20 has significant parallels with official documents from the Ancient Near East. In particular, the Code of Hammurabai has noticeable similarities, and scholars have concluded that the Sinai covenant probably came from around the same time, when this sort of agreement or covenant was a common legal practice. The Hebrews used this literary genre, with which they were familiar, as a way of expressing their own ideas about their covenant relationship with G-d, dating it somewhere in the middle of the second century BCE.

The conquest and settlement in the Promised Land – 1280–1020 BCE – The date given for the Biblical battles and the eventual settlement is speculative, and some scholars, such as **Werner Schmidt**, are of the opinion that the Biblical accounts of miraculous victories are given for theological reasons rather than having any basis in history. Perhaps it is more likely that the Hebrew nomads gradually and peacefully began a new and more settled way of life. There is, however, definite evidence of the existence of the Philistines, who settled on the coastal plain of Canaan and moved eastward, presenting the Israelites with a challenge. Israel's need for central organisation under a king, rather than the previous haphazard system of organisation through elders and family groups, could date to around the time when the Philistines would have been considered a serious threat. Saul began to reign as the first king in around 1020 BCE; David succeeded him as king in about 1000 BCE, and Solomon reigned from 965–928 BCE.

The Unified Kingdom – 1020–922 BCE – The Israelites were prosperous under their first kings, Saul, David and Solomon. The tribes were united, and great building plans were made, including the great Temple of Jerusalem, the focus for worship, sacrifice, pilgrimage and festivals. But after the death of Solomon, the unity broke down, and the tribes of Israel divided themselves into two, some in the Northern Kingdom (Israel), and some in the South (Judah).

Israel and Judah – The Northern Kingdom only lasted until **721 BCE**, when it was conquered by the Assyrian empire, in accordance with the warnings given by the prophets Amos and Hosea. Judah was overthrown in **683 BCE**, but for reasons no longer fully clear, Jerusalem was not taken over but was allowed to continue as before, as long as tribute was paid to Assyria. Many of the Jews were scattered in different directions, some going to Assyria as slaves; some stayed where they were, married the foreigners who had settled in the land, and later became the Samaritans. The Babylonians overpowered the Assyrians during **614–612 BCE**; Nebuchadnezzar of Babylon captured Jerusalem in **597 BCE**, and put Zedekiah on the throne expecting his co-operation, but Zedekiah made an alliance with Egypt. Nebuchadnezzar returned in **587 BCE**, and crushed Jerusalem, including the Temple built by Solomon. Most of the surviving Jews were deported into exile in Babylon.

Babylonian Exile – 587–539 BCE – In the Bible, the Babylonian Exile is seen as a time of exceptional national crisis. Historians debate the exact date of this; some put it early, with the first deportation of the king and his family being placed in 597 BCE, but it is more widely held that 587/6 BCE is a more accurate date. Jeremiah has it that the exile lasted for seventy years (29:10) which would put the date for the return and rebuilding of the Temple at 517 BCE, but perhaps seventy years is a poetic number rather than an exact date.

Some of the most moving and important Biblical literature comes from this time: the beginnings of the hope for a Messiah, promises for the future, and psalms of lament:

> By the rivers of Babylon, there we sat and also wept when we remembered Zion. On the willows within it we hung our lyres. For there our captors requested words of song from us, with our lyres [playing] joyous music, "Sing for us from Zion's song!" How could we sing the song of HASHEM upon the alien's soil?

Psalm 137:1–4

Great prophets such as Isaiah and Jeremiah interpreted what had happened to the people in the context of the will of G-d, and looked towards the future of the nation.

Return and Restoration – 539–333 BCE – Historical records support the capturing of Babylon by the Persian ruler Cyrus the Great, who gave the Jews permission to return to Palestine. Historical records suggest that this return did not all happen at once, but that different groups of Jews returned gradually over time. Some had settled in Babylon and chose to remain where they were, beginning a phase when there were settled Jewish communities living and worshipping away from Jerusalem – the **Diaspora**.

For those who returned, the first priority was the rebuilding of the Temple as a focus for national and religious life. This was completed in 515 BCE, motivated by the prophets Haggai and Zechariah. Later, Ezra and Nehemiah presided over the reconstruction of the ruined city of Jerusalem; the book of Chronicles follows the story of the rebuilding of the city and the faith of the Jews. Nehemiah arrived in 444 BCE from Babylon and undertook the reconstruction of the city walls; he also began a series of religious reforms. Traditionally, Ezra comes before Nehemiah, but historical scholarship suggests that the correct order is the other way around.

333 BCE –70 CE – Old Testament history proper ends with the events described in the books of Ezra and Nehemiah. After the return and the restoration of the Temple, Judaea remained a Persian province, until the arrival of Alexander the Great. His victory at Issus in 333 BCE marked the beginning of the Hellenistic (Greek) period, when Greek culture, language, religion and government were promoted throughout the Greek empire. Although some Jews found a way of life which could co-exist with Hellenism, others deeply resented the ways in which their way of life was undermined, as is illustrated in the book of Daniel. The Maccabean uprising, led by Judas the Maccabee, was a reaction by zealous Jews, which succeeded for a short time in bringing back Jewish rule under the Hasmonean dynasty (142–63 BCE). Scholars have suggested that one of the Dead Sea Scrolls, entitled 'War of the Sons of Light against the Sons of Darkness' could relate to this period of Jewish struggle against Hellenising influence.

The Romans took control of Palestine in **63 BCE**, destroying the Hasmonean dynasty and imposing their own rules and ways of life. There was a great sense of uneasiness in the relationship between Jews and Romans; some wanted to live a peaceful lifestyle and were prepared to compromise, while others resisted Roman rule. Eventually the resentments escalated into a full confrontation between Jerusalem and Rome in the Great War of 66–70 CE, well-documented by, amongst others, the Jewish writer and historian **Josephus**. Jerusalem fell, and the second Temple, built during the restoration after the Babylonian exile, was destroyed.

Summary

- The events described in the Jewish scriptures are often very difficult to date with any degree of precision, although archaeologists and other historians use a variety of methods of research.
- For many believers, the evidence within the Bible is enough to convince them that these events genuinely happened as described.
- Some events, however, such as the destruction of the Temple in 70 CE, are well supported, and Biblical scholars can use these firm dates in order to make educated guesses about others.
- The dating of principal events in the Jewish scriptures is a difficult task, but important for the ways in which it gives greater understanding of the text.

2 Form criticism

Form criticism is the name given to one of the ways in which scholars have tried to add to our understanding of Biblical texts. It involves trying to recognise the form, or genre, to which a piece of text belongs, so that it can be appreciated more fully. All of our language, including our writing, can be classified as belonging to one genre or another: for example, we might read a holiday postcard, or an advertisement, we might tell someone a joke, or hear a song or a piece of poetry, write a business letter or a note to the milkman, or follow a recipe or listen to a news programme. We know, from the form the words take, how to interpret the language we read or hear, because we recognise the genre and we know the context in which it is used.

There are forms of words which are conventional to make the genre clear, so that other people know what we are trying to communicate, and we accept them and use them without thinking about it. As we grow up in society, we learn the forms of words normally used in different contexts, for example we use the same few phrases when greeting our friends, and we know that there are accepted styles to use when writing a letter of application for a job.

The context of our language has a great deal of importance for the way in which it is to be understood, and the language used prepares our minds to take a particular kind of approach to what we are about to read or hear. For example, if an article in a newspaper began 'A man walked into a bar' then we would expect the account which followed to be a fairly accurate representation of facts, and we would anticipate reading on to find out more about an incident that was significant in some way. However, if the words 'A man walked into a bar' were spoken by a comedian on stage, we would not have the same expectations, and to interpret what followed as being a true and significant story would be wrong and would miss the point. Identifying the genre can be crucially important in an understanding of language.

The form critic, then, looks at Biblical texts and tries to work out the genre of literature to which a text might belong, from the ways in which the words are used and particularly if they seem to fall into a predictable pattern or 'literary type'. This is not just so that the scholar can classify the passage, and put a label on it as 'parable' or 'myth' or 'saga' perhaps, but so that a greater insight can be gained into the intentions of the writer. Was this passage meant to be repeated during worship, as liturgy? Is it part of a story of the past, told and retold by members of the community as they gathered socially in the evenings? Is it a hymn, meant to be sung, perhaps for festivals? The form of a passage might give clues to the use it had when it originated, and the intentions of the writer; it can then be placed in context, and be better understood as the reader approaches it with appropriate expectations.

a) The origins of Form criticism of the Jewish scriptures

Heinrich Ewald was one of the first scholars to take an interest in the idea of the Jewish scriptures as a collection of stories which had begun by being passed down orally through the generations. He believed that these oral traditions had preserved memories which had some basis in fact, but which had also been idealised, so that the leading characters were presented as being more heroic, or more wicked, than they had probably been in real life.

Following Ewald's work, the first person to study the different literary genres of the Jewish scriptures was a German scholar named **Hermann Gunkel** (1862–1932). When Gunkel began his work, at the close of the nineteenth century, study of the Bible was very much dominated by **Source criticism**, which attempts to shed light on Biblical texts by looking at the date and authorship of the various different books. However, although Gunkel could see the value of being able to put a date and a geographical location on to the writing of a book, he was concerned that this did not give the whole picture, and he felt that a new approach was necessary in addition to Source criticism.

One of the ways in which source critics tried to work out the authorship of Biblical material was to look for differences in style, so that if the text came from more than one source and had been woven together at a later date, the separate strands could be recognised. Different sources in the Pentateuch were determined by noticing the ways in which different expressions are sometimes used for similar ideas – for example, Genesis 1 uses one word for 'G-d', while Genesis 2 uses another, and the source critics came to the conclusion that these passages must have had different authors. Gunkel, however, was interested not so much in the differences found in the writing, as he was in the similarities. He was struck by the ways in which passages with obviously different dates were nevertheless written in very similar styles – just as, for example, two business letters might appear similar even if they were written fifty years apart by different people.

Gunkel, like Ewald before him, was very much influenced by the work of the brothers Wilhelm and Jakob Grimm, who had collected together many folk stories and 'fairy tales' which had been told orally for generations, and had preserved them in writing. Gunkel recognised that there were similarities between the stories of the Brothers Grimm and those in the Old Testament; in both cases, the finished piece of text did not begin as the invention of the person who committed it to writing, but had originated as spoken word, and had circulated for many years in the context of having been heard and passed on by word of mouth. Gunkel was also fascinated by the new discoveries of archaeology, particularly in the religious writings of the Ancient Near East, which he thought showed remarkable similarities to parts of the Old Testament. The same literary genres were clearly apparent.

According to Gunkel, the folktale is the most primitive form of oral tradition. Stories are retold according to conventions, and similar themes or 'motifs' appear, not only in the Old Testament but also in folk literature from other cultures. There is, for example, the motif of the small boy who outwits the giant, such as David killing Goliath or Jack climbing the beanstalk to confront the ogre; or the story of the baby who narrowly escapes death and goes on to become a great leader, such as Moses or Hercules.

Gunkel did not address the question of whether or not the stories of the Old Testament were historically true, because he was far more interested in showing how they were used in practice, and in giving them a context in which to be understood. However, the ways in which he drew links between Biblical passages and other, non-Biblical folk-tales suggested to some that he was casting doubt on the authority of the Bible as the divinely inspired Word of G-d. Some people, therefore, reject form criticism entirely as a way of approaching an understanding of the Bible. It might seem as though these critics are saying that there is no more truth in the Bible than there is in the story of Rapunzel.

b) The literary genres of the Old Testament

The ways in which the forms of Old Testament literature have been classified varies from one scholar to another. There are also many possible subdivisions to be made within each genre. For example, under the heading 'song', the Dutch scholar **H. Brongers** has identified: work songs, sung during rhythmic occupations such as harvesting and winnowing; love songs, perhaps sung in courtship and at wedding parties; songs of victory, used in celebration after battle; songs of lament, which themselves are divided into personal laments for individual tragedies and political laments for loss in battle; songs of mocking, making fun of enemies; and so on. It is only possible, therefore, to consider a few of the types of literature found in the Jewish scriptures. These should be considered as examples, rather than as an exhaustive list.

Myth – myths, according to Gunkel in his book *Legends*, are 'stories of the Gods, in contradistinction to the legends in which the actors are men.' Not everyone, however, would agree with this understanding of the difference between myths and legends; and if Gunkel is right, then the Jewish Scriptures do not really contain much which could be described as myth, because Judaism is so strictly monotheistic that there is not the opportunity for interactions between gods in this way. Perhaps the conversation between G-d and Satan in the book of Job is all that could be considered a Biblical myth, in Gunkel's understanding. However, most scholars interpret the concept of myth rather more broadly, to refer to stories which may or may not contain literal truth, and which are produced in order to help societies to cope with difficult aspects of the world in which they live: how and why was the world created? What is the purpose of human life? Why do the innocent suffer?

Some of the myths are classified as 'aetiological myths' created to explain some feature of the world, in the same way as Rudyard Kipling's *Just So Stories* give fictional accounts of how the elephant got its trunk or how the leopard got its spots. The aetiological myths in the Bible, according to form critics, have a similar function. For example, the story of the creation of Eve from Adam's side could be classified in this way, because at the end there is an explanation: 'Therefore a man shall leave his father and his mother and cling to his wife and they shall become one flesh' (Genesis 2:24). The purpose of the story is to explain this feature of the world, and to answer the puzzle of why people marry.

Form critics have noticed strong similarities between Biblical myths, particularly those connected with creation, and the myths of other cultures in the Ancient Near East. Genesis 1–11 contains some material which also appears elsewhere, in non-Biblical sources such as the Babylonian creation myth 'Enuma Elish', and this suggests to some scholars that the Genesis stories are presentations of myths which were circulated widely in the Ancient Near East, using common motifs such as the flood, the attempt to gain immortality and become like divinity, the symbolic 'tree of life', and so on. Others reject this entirely, because of their belief that the creation story in the Bible is the inspired Word of G-d.

History – Although many of the writers of the Jewish scriptures did not set out to provide an accurate historical record of events, nevertheless there are books where the purpose is clearly historical. The books which are usually classified by form critics as 'history' are Joshua, Judges, Samuel, Kings, Chronicles, Ezra and Nehemiah. The first four are often known as the 'Former Prophets'. These set out to give a record of how the often-repeated promise that the people would be given a land of their own was fulfilled. The history covers the period from the entry into the land of Israel to the destruction of the Temple in 587/6 BCE, and then the first part of the exile which followed. Like all historical accounts, this is selective, including only those events which are seen to be relevant to the religious purpose, and ignoring those which were not seen to have anything significant to say about the relation between G-d and his people, or which might distract from the main theme. Important events are emphasised, and irrelevant ones omitted. The writer of Chronicles, for example, left out almost everything that took place outside Judah. He also brought together the important acts of King David into a condensed form in order to give the impression that David performed one great deed after another, thus emphasising his importance in Jewish history. The Biblical historians referred to earlier parts of the Bible, such as

Genesis, as source material, and also made use of other documents that were available at the time, such as those concerning battles and military installations. Although they did not have the facilities that we have today for reference, such as libraries and the Internet, they still recognised the importance of corroborating tales they had heard with supporting written evidence where possible. In their sources they included folk memories, and they sometimes made references to other books where the reader might learn more about some of the events described:

> The rest of the deeds of Jotham and all his wars and actions — behold, they are recorded in the Book of the Kings of Israel and Judah.
>
> *2 Chronicles 27:7*

This literary genre, then, served the same purpose that is served by historical writing today. It was written to preserve as accurate an account of events as could be achieved given the limitations of the time of writing, in order that the readers would have a true record of significant events of their past, to which they could refer. It was meant to be taken at face value.

Prophecy – Prophecy is a very noticeable literary genre in the Bible. People often think that a prophet is someone who tells the future, and this is sometimes the case, but not always; the main purpose of prophecy was for a messenger to transmit messages from G-d to the people. Sometimes the prophets were called 'seers', those who were given the gift of seeing visions explaining the purposes of G-d. The prophets told the people of the will of G-d, and the likely consequences if the people continued to practise their present way of life. They commented on the present, and gave warnings, threats, promises and hopes of future salvation.

These messages originated in the spoken word, rather than in writing, and because of this the books of the prophets in the Bible can be quite difficult to follow if read as a continuous narrative, because different sayings of the prophets from different speeches have been collected together and placed in an order which is not always coherent. Martin Luther (1483–1546) complained when he was writing lecture notes on the prophet Habakkuk that the prophets '… seem to observe no order but ramble along from one subject to another' (Luther's *Works*). The words of the prophets are often in poetic form, using striking and vivid imagery to capture the imagination of the audience.

Within the literary genre 'prophecy', various sub-divisions have been made by form critics. **Schmidt**, for example, classified 'stories about the prophets' where the books tell something of the life of the prophet, how he came to be called by G-d and his reaction to this call; 'visions', where the prophet receives the message he is to transmit by 'seeing' a vision which is of great significance for his message (eg Amos 7:1–8, Ezekiel 1–3); and the prophetic 'words' or speeches themselves. These are characterised by recurring phrases such as 'This is the word of HASHEM' and 'For HASHEM our G-d has spoken it', showing that the prophet is not only speaking his own opinions but is acting as a messenger on behalf of G-d.

Poetry – One of the outstanding features of the Jewish scriptures is the beauty of its poetry. Some of the poetry is contained within other genres too; for example, the words of the prophets are frequently expressed in poetic terms, especially in Isaiah and Jeremiah, and the book of Job, classified as 'wisdom literature' contains some of the most beautiful poetry ever written. But some books of the Bible are poetry first and foremost; these include the Book of Lamentations, and the Song of Songs (or Song of Solomon). The Book of Lamentations consists of five poems which express the grief of the Jews at the destruction of Jerusalem prior to the Babylonian exile. Some of them are acrostic poems, based on the Hebrew alphabet. Like all poetry, the texts try to find a way of expressing ideas, thoughts and emotions that are difficult to put into ordinary prose.

The Song of Songs is one of the most problematic of all texts in the Jewish scriptures. There is very little agreement on the date of the book or its authorship, and even its purpose is questioned, as it does not deal directly with themes of G-d (who is not mentioned at all), humanity and sin, but instead appears to be a collection of love songs and love poetry. In some ways, it is a genre all of its own in the Bible, although love poetry and erotic literature can be found in other Ancient Near Eastern texts.

The book of Psalms can be classified as poetry, as all of the Psalms are written in a poetic style. The relation between the Psalms and the worship of ancient Israel has been the subject of much debate over the last two centuries; were the Psalms invented for the purposes of worship, to be used at festivals and during ceremonies? Or did worshippers make use of this already existing literature, shaping their worship to fit it?

One of the distinctive features of Israelite poetry is the way in which it makes use of parallelism; this is where the second line of a poem mirrors or echoes the first. Sometimes the second line says the same as the first, using different words to emphasise the point:

Free me, HASHEM, from the wicked man; from the man of violence preserve me.

Psalm 140:2

At other times the second line puts the same idea the other way around, showing 'the other side of the coin':

The words of a wise man win favour, but a fool's lips devour him.

Ecclesiastes 10:12

Law – The laws of the Jewish Bible are considered by many to be the most important part of the text. They contain the essence of the covenant relationship, by setting out for the people the commandments which they have to follow in order to keep their part of the bargain made with G-d. For Jews, the law is essential because it gives the instructions for leading an *halakhic* life, 'walking with G-d'. The laws transcend time and culture, and provide a framework in which people can be confident that they are doing what G-d requires of them.

Written laws, as a literary form, predate the laws of the Jewish Bible by at least a thousand years. The existence of laws implies some kind of central organisation for a community, with a court and the facilities for making judgements and carrying out punishments, and this has led some scholars to the conclusion that the laws in the Bible were not formed until the eighth or ninth centuries BCE, and have been added into the narrative with hindsight.

Some of the laws of the Bible are casuistic, which means that they give rules which depend on particular circumstances:

> If you encounter an ox of your enemy or his donkey wandering, you shall return it to him repeatedly.
>
> *Exodus 23:4*

Others are categorical imperatives, commanding people to behave in a certain way at all times, regardless of the circumstances:

> You shall not steal.
>
> *Exodus 20:13*

Wisdom – Most scholars today classify 'wisdom literature' as a genre of its own, although up until the nineteenth century it was usually grouped together with poetry as part of the same genre. Archaeologists during the twentieth century found Egyptian and Babylonian texts which bear striking similarities to the material found in Job, Proverbs and Ecclesiastes; these Ancient Near Eastern texts suggest that the 'form' of wisdom literature was a common one throughout the ancient world, although the books from sources other than the Bible would probably not have been described in this way in the cultures from which they originated.

Wisdom literature could be said to contain the 'words of the wise', or sages, on all kinds of subjects pertaining to daily life. For the most part, wisdom literature is formed from collections of sayings, proverbs, pieces of advice and common sense, rather than providing a continuous narrative. The book of Job has a story theme running through it, but Proverbs and Ecclesiastes do not have anything which could be considered as a 'plot'. They cover, instead, a wide variety of topics as a collection. There is advice for the young man growing to adulthood, telling him what sort of company to seek and what to avoid, the importance of practising moderation and prudence, and the need to get his priorities right. There is teaching about the differences between the righteous and the wicked, explaining how they are characterised and what will happen to them in the end. There are also passages of reflection, where the writer shows awareness that life is not as simple as we might like; sometimes the wicked prosper, and the innocent suffer; sometimes there seems to be no reward for goodness and the bad escape unpunished. Wisdom literature expresses the fragile nature of human existence, the need to depend on G-d, and the need for acceptance of those elements of life which are beyond our understanding.

The book of Job is particularly important, and has generated vast amounts of discussion and literature. The 'wisdom' in it is contained within a narrative, introduced at the beginning and concluded in the closing chapters, but as well as telling a story it also contains some wonderful poetry considering the relationship between humanity and the creator, and the nature of good and evil. Some of the views expressed attack the position of the book of Proverbs; life is not so neat, and things do not always work out with the justice that we would like to see. The book of Ecclesiastes, too, shares this insight, and complains about the constraints of human life as well as celebrating its joys.

Liturgy – Liturgy is the name given to the language used in worship, where words are repeated according to a set formula. This gives the worshipper a sense of community with others saying the same words, and it gives structure to the worship and a sense of occasion. Many scholars have concluded that the Psalms, in particular, contain examples of liturgical writing, although they could have been intended for private meditation as well as for communal worship. There is little conclusive evidence about the ways in which the Psalms were used, although in some passages in the books of Chronicles it appears that songs made up from elements of different psalms were used in processions and at dedications (1 Chronicles 16:8–36, 2 Chronicles 6:41–1). Perhaps the Psalms were used in ceremonies for the rededication of the Temple after the Babylonian Exile.

Apart from the Psalms, there are other passages too which could have formed part of the liturgy of the Israelites. In Genesis 48, for example, where Jacob blesses Joseph's sons, the words used suggest a ritual form of language; and the prayer commonly known as the Shema, in Deuteronomy 6:4, has been at the centre of Jewish liturgy at home and in the Temple since ancient times.

Summary

- Form criticism is one of the methods used to aid an understanding of scripture, by looking at the literary genres found within the Bible. Some believe that this is an inappropriate approach to sacred writing, because

it could be seen to imply that some sections have less basis in fact than others; but others argue that it gives valuable insights.
● The Bible contains many different kinds of literature, and an understanding of the purposes of different kinds of writing can enable the reader to gain a deeper understanding of the message of the text.

Practice examination questions

I. a) Explain some of the methods that scholars use in trying to date the main events of the Jewish scriptures. (33 marks)
b) How important is it that the events described in the Bible should be supported by archaeological evidence? (17 marks)

Guide

In part (a), you need to give an outline of the main methods scholars use when they are trying to find an accurate date, or at least historical context, for Biblical events. You might find it easier to organise your material if you begin by making a list, and then use this as a framework for your answer. For part (b), you need to make some evaluation. You could explain the advantages of being able to place a date in its context, for example the light it might shed on the behaviour of characters in the stories, but you might also mention the views of those who believe that the Bible does not need any corroboration.

2. a) Explain the main aims and conclusions of Form criticism of the Jewish scriptures. (33 marks)
b) 'Form criticism implies that there are parts of the Bible that should not be taken seriously.' Discuss. (17 marks)

Guide

In part (a), you are asked to describe both the aims and the main conclusions of Form criticism. You should make it clear that you know what Form criticism is, but you do not need to go into a great deal of historical background here. Try to use technically correct terms, such as 'genre', and try to give some examples of the different literary genres you describe. For Part (b), you need to decide how fair you think the statement in the question is, as an evaluation of Form criticism. Some people might say that it implies that parts of the Bible are little more than folk tales, but there is also the view that Form criticism enables the reader to gain more from the text and that this is helpful; you might want to expand on opinions such as these, and also contribute your own view.

Suggestions for further reading

Kee, Meyers, Rogerson and Saldarini, *The Cambridge Companion to the Bible* (Cambridge University Press, 1997)
Encyclopaedia Britannica
Charpentier, *How to read the Old Testament* (SCM Press, 1982)
Drane, *Introducing the Old Testament* (Lion, 2000)
Richard Coggins, *Introducing the Old Testament* (Oxford University Press, 1989)

4 New Testament

KEYWORDS

Hellenistic – an adjective relating to Greek culture, language, history and concepts, of the period between the fourth and first centuries BCE

Pharisee – a Jew who was particularly concerned with maintaining standards of law-keeping amongst the whole Jewish community

Sadducee – a Jew characterised by a measure of power held within the community, by the refusal to accept 'oral law', and by association with the Temple

Zealot – a Jew whose attitude to Roman occupation was one of rebellion and refusal to compromise

1 First-century Palestine

Palestine once covered an area which is now divided between the state of Israel and Israeli-occupied territories; it was and still is a very important piece of land because of its situation as the natural link between three different continents. There has been fighting for control over this territory for almost the whole of its known history, and so the region has always been characterised by its political instability and by the many different cultural influences upon it. Not only does it share borders with different countries, but also it is an obvious centre for trade routes, with the result that the population has always been in close contact with a variety of different cultures and has struggled to maintain its own identity during many turbulent times.

King David, a thousand years before the birth of the New Testament, had successfully established a kingdom for the Jews, with a capital city in Jerusalem; and his son Solomon built a Temple there as a focus for Jewish worship and pilgrimage. But the reigns of David and Solomon were followed by many years of struggle, where the Temple was destroyed and the land was conquered by the Assyrians and the Babylonians, and then the Persians, under whom the Temple was rebuilt; they were followed by the Greeks whose leader was Alexander the Great. Palestine became dominated by Greek (often called Hellenistic) culture, and Greek was the language spoken and written by cultured people, including the writers of the New Testament, although it seems that Greek was a language which few Jews ever completely mastered.

While Palestine was under the influence of the Greeks, the most powerful group among the Jews in Jerusalem was the priests. They supervised the Temple, which was not only the focus of worship but was also the place where the Jewish wealth was kept and where individuals deposited their money for safe-keeping. The priests therefore had financial control as well as positions of authority in religion. Not everyone appreciated the extent of the priests' power; they were opposed by a group called the scribes, who taught and interpreted the Torah in accordance with an oral tradition going back at least to the time of the Babylonian exile. This oral tradition was word-of-mouth interpretation of the laws of the Torah, showing how it should be applied to contemporary life. Within the group of Jews known as the scribes was a section called the Hasidim, or 'Pious Ones', and these people are often (although not always) believed to have been the forerunners of the Pharisees as they appear in the New Testament.

a) The Romans in Palestine

The Roman general Pompey marched into Palestine in 63 BCE, capturing Jerusalem and reducing the Jewish territory significantly to Judaea and a few other small regions, such as Galilee. The Jews were now under Roman rule, and remained so for the time that provides the historical context for the New Testament. Herod I reigned from 37–4 BCE; he was a clever and politically ruthless man who had converted to Judaism for what many believed to be reasons of self-interest. The Romans were satisfied for Herod to rule this part of their empire on their behalf, as long as he kept the peace and prevented his subjects from stirring up trouble. Herod, with Roman support, managed to style himself 'king of the Jews', and extended the Jewish state again so that it covered nearly the whole of Palestine. His interest in keeping favour with the Romans meant that he promoted Hellenisation, building new modern-style cities and encouraging the people to adopt Graeco-Roman ways of doing things. He supported the Roman religion by building temples to Augustus in the non-Jewish cities, but he also sought the favour of the Jews with his determination to rebuild the Temple of Solomon, on an enormous scale and with no expense spared. Some Jews thoroughly approved of this; they could at last look forward to a time when they could worship together in the Temple again, and fulfil their obligations to the Torah laws by making their Temple offerings at the right times and performing the proper pilgrimages and sacrifices. Other Jews, however, were less convinced. They were not impressed by Herod's efforts to win Roman favour, and especially disapproved of his willingness to build the pagan temples. They suspected that his commitment to Judaism was entirely superficial; in their view, a Jewish Temple built by Herod was just as bad as having no Temple at all. Herod's Temple was begun in 20 BCE, and was finally completed in 64 CE, only to be destroyed in 70 CE when the fortunes of the Jews changed once again in their war against Rome.

When Herod died, the Jews asked the Romans not to allow any of Herod's family to take over from him; but the Romans ignored them, and divided up the Jewish territories amongst Herod's sons. Archelaus was given the largest and most important territory, which included Jerusalem. After his death in 6 CE, the area was placed under Roman administration, under a governor known as a 'procurator', for the purposes of tax and the law courts. The Jews were allowed to practise their religion, and were allowed to have charge of their own administration and law courts to some extent, but this was limited and supervised by Rome. The Sanhedrin was the Jewish court, permitted most of the time to conduct Jewish affairs, but only up to a point. The Jews could not, for example, recommend and carry out the death penalty without Roman sanction.

The ways in which Palestine was ruled during New Testament times are complicated to follow. Political leadership was given to people as a favour, when they pleased the emperor, and this favour was withdrawn abruptly from time to time if a perceived offence was committed, and the areas were reorganised with new people coming to power for varying lengths of time. Responsibility for the supervision of the Jews passed back and forth according to the whim of the monarch. Some of the Roman procurators were better at allowing the Jews their rights than others. Pontius Pilate, who was in charge from 26–36 CE, had a reputation for being cruel and ruthless, and for disregarding Jewish rights whenever it suited him. He tried to introduce busts of the Roman emperor for worship in Jerusalem, and was made very aware of the intensely anti-Roman emotions that this idol-worship provoked amongst the Jewish population. Eventually, Pilate was dismissed from his post because he caused so much bad feeling that it was adversely affecting the smooth running of the region.

Galilee, the area in which Jesus worked and taught, was run by one of Herod's other sons, Herod Antipas, a man referred to by Jesus as 'that fox'. The Jewish historian Josephus, writing at the end of the first century, explained how Herod Antipas had been responsible for the death of John the Baptist. Josephus believed that Herod thought John's message of repentance and the coming of the Messiah was dangerous as a possible source of resistance to his rule, and so had him executed. The Gospel writers thought that Herod's dislike of John was more personal, based on John's criticism of Herod's illegal second marriage. Whatever the motivation was, the evidence suggests that relations between the Jews and their Roman ruler were less than happy. Herod Antipas, after a while, fell out of favour with the Romans and was banished, and after a brief break Herod Agrippa I took over from him. The New Testament writers tend to refer to all the rulers as 'Herod', but they usually mean Herod Antipas.

The inhabitants of Galilee were thought by Judaeans to be very much inferior. Hellenisation had had its effects on Galilean life and culture, but a large proportion of the population lived in isolation, speaking Aramaic rather than Greek, and keeping up the old Jewish traditions without taking much notice of the changing fashions that other people thought of as progress. Galilee was known as an area where resistance to Roman influence was strong. There was a significant proportion of people who were prepared to defend to the death their right to follow the Torah and to live and work as Jews.

Relations between the Jews and the Romans were often strained. Some Jews, particularly those with money and influence, were anxious to keep the peace, to do as they were told by Rome as far as they were able, and to make compromises. Others were fiercely, sometimes violently, opposed to Roman rule. The New Testament only makes passing references to everyday life under Roman occupation, but questions about whether taxes should be paid to Caesar, and advice about what to do if a man makes you go with him one mile (to carry his belongings), give some insights into an existence where peace was precarious and rights to religious freedom only lasted for as long as the ruler's mood.

b) Groups within Judaism

We know about the different groups within the Judaism of the first century from three main sources:

1. the gospels and other early Christian writings
2. the writings of the rabbis, particularly in the Mishnah
3. the writings of the Jewish historian Josephus.

As with all historical sources, each of these three sources was written for very different purposes and for different audiences, and all were trying to persuade their readers to adopt a particular point of view, but not necessarily the same one; therefore there are times when it is difficult to know what the facts were.

The writings of **Josephus** have been particularly important for an understanding of Judaism at the time of the first century. He was a Jewish historian, politician and soldier who lived from about 37–100 CE; he came from a well-known priestly family, and spent some time at the court of Nero, after which he was given command of Galilee. He came into conflict with the Zealots, who rightly suspected him of having Roman sympathies; when the Roman forces invaded, he did not offer very much resistance but instead surrendered and then adopted the Roman name Flavius, which was the family name of Vespasian, leader of the invading forces. Josephus was an accepted member of the Roman court, particularly favoured because of his ability to speak with the Jews on their own terms and encourage them to co-operate with Rome. Although he was viewed by many as a traitor and a collaborator, Josephus wrote four works which were very much pro-Jewish, providing scholars with some of the major sources from which to gain knowledge of the Judaism of the first century and the groups within it. Sometimes he is believed to be unreliable, but much of the information in his writing has been confirmed by archaeological evidence.

Within the Judaism of the first century, there were many different groups, some of whom are mentioned in the New Testament text.

i) The Pharisees

The group of Jews known as the Pharisees are well-known, because of their frequent appearances in the gospels, where they are shown as having debates with Jesus or his followers about aspects of the Jewish law and how it should be kept. They were enthusiastic debaters, because of their deep commitment to *halakhah*. This term refers to the Jewish idea of 'walking with God'; the Pharisees took a great interest in the ways in which the laws of the Torah could be translated into practice, so that each Jew could know the right way to conduct his or her daily relationship with God. The application of the Torah to everyday circumstances gave rise to the Oral Law (*halakhoth*), which contained teachings that were not written down in the scriptures but which came from the traditions of the rabbis and were handed on from one generation to the next. The rabbis did not always agree; most famously within Pharisaism were the schools of the liberal rabbi Hillel and the more conservative Shammai, who frequently engaged in debates over practice.

In the gospels, the Pharisees are seen in debate with Jesus over issues of *halakhah*: in Mark's Gospel, for example, they ask questions about purity laws, in relation to fasting (2:18), hand-washing (7:1–5) and eating with tax-collectors and sinners (2:16–17). They also initiate debates about working on the Sabbath (2:23–28) and about divorce (10:2–11). Although they were lay people, Pharisees took very seriously the commandment in Leviticus 19:2 to be a kingdom of priests and a holy nation. They thought that this was their primary purpose as Jews. According to many New Testament scholars, such as **Jeremias**, Pharisees tried to encourage every Jew to follow the law to the same levels of purity as the priests, raising standards amongst ordinary people and 'building a fence around the law'. ('Building a fence around the law' refers to the practice of making extra rules which help to ensure that a law is not accidentally broken: for example, fasting for 25 hours rather than 24 so that no-one accidentally eats a few minutes after a fast day has begun or before it has ended.) Sometimes opponents of the Pharisees called them 'smooth interpreters', because they tried to find ways of interpreting the law that would make it possible for everyone to be law-abiding, and it was sometimes felt that they stretched this too far beyond the original intentions of the Law. However, the impact that the

Pharisees had on ordinary people was not huge, because for many, it was just impossible to follow Jewish laws (mitzvot), such as those about purity and tithing, when they were working in agriculture or in close proximity with Gentiles. More sympathetic views of the Pharisees stress their commitment to the 'priesthood of all believers', and their genuine interest in maintaining standards of law-keeping.

Originally, the Pharisaic movement may have come from the Hasidim, or Pious Ones, who were leaders of the Maccabean revolt. They began to emerge as a distinct group during the reign of the High Priest John Hyrcanus, the son of Simon Maccabeus. Their name may come from the word *perushim*, or separated ones, drawing attention to their characteristic separation from all things unclean and unholy; or it could be a corruption of the Hebrew for 'Persians', because they followed some of the new ideas which were brought into Judaism while Palestine was under Persian control. These new ideas added to beliefs found in the scriptures; for example, the Pharisees believed in life after death, particularly in bodily resurrection, and had a developed concept of angels and demons at work in the world as agents of God and of Satan. These were ideas which went beyond the concepts found in the written Torah. They believed that when all of Israel obeyed the Torah, the kingdom of God would be established. But the major characteristic of Pharisaic belief was commitment to the oral tradition, making explicit what the Torah had left unsaid so that every Jew could know exactly what was expected of him or her.

For a long time it was believed that the Pharisees were the origins of the traditional rabbinic literature, but in recent years this understanding has changed. It now seems likely that the rabbinic literature had several different component sources, of which Pharisaism was the most important, but not the only one; so it is not so easy to read back from the rabbinic literature and work out what the Pharisees must have believed. **Christopher Rowland** points out that rabbinic writing traces its origins back to the sages (*hakamim*), and keeps the word *perushim* for extremists. Possibly the word 'Pharisee' covered a wide range of different beliefs, considered extreme in different ways, and maybe when the Pharisees in the gospels are attacked, it is not always the same group of people holding the same ideas.

ii) The Sadducees

The origins of the Sadducees are rather more obscure than those of the Pharisees, and the accounts given of them by Josephus are sometimes contradictory. Their name, *tzedoq* in Hebrew (plural *tzedoqim*) has suggested to many that they may have been descendants or followers of Zadok, who was the High Priest of the Temple at the time of kings David and Solomon. However, they were also allied with the Hasmonean dynasty, otherwise known as the Maccabees. Some have suggested that the name Sadducee comes from the Hebrew word *tsedeq*, meaning 'righteous'. They were certainly wealthy people, of a higher social status than the Pharisees, and came from landowning aristocratic families, although **E. P. Sanders** is keen to point out that not all aristocrats were Sadducees. Unlike the Pharisees, whose claim to authority was based on their learning and their eagerness to obey the law, the Sadducees' claim to authority was based on their birth, wealth and social position. The New Testament links the High Priest Caiaphas with the Sadducees (Acts 5:17).

Because of the ways in which Rome ruled some of its territory from a distance, the leaders of the people were expected to keep order, acting as the representatives of Rome for the ordinary people, and sometimes too the representatives of the people to the Romans. The Sadducees seem to have occupied this kind of position. They still had a considerable amount of power in the time of Jesus, as long as they compromised with Rome, and they were allowed to keep their wealth, living a comfortable existence in comparison with many from more ordinary backgrounds. The Sadducees needed to ally themselves with the rulers at least to some extent, in order to keep their land. They had voting powers in the Sanhedrin, and were able to sentence people to death, although they did not have the power to carry this out without the agreement of the Roman rulers. They occupied rather an uneasy position; they were afraid of the Romans and of the power that they held, but they were also afraid of other Jews, especially those who were rebellious, because they did not want to excite a situation of conflict.

The Sadducees were more religiously conservative than the Pharisees. They were in constant disagreement with the Pharisees over details of the law, but most significantly, they disagreed over how far God was revealed in the Hebrew scriptures and in the oral traditions that surrounded them. The Sadducees believed that the only authoritative scripture revealed by God was the Pentateuch, the first five books of the Torah revealed directly to Moses by God. They rejected the idea that the other writings and books of the prophets were divinely inspired, and so, unlike other groups, they did not share a belief in the coming of the Messiah who would establish a new kingdom under the rule of God, because this is not in the first five books of the Bible. They were also anxious to avoid damaging their relationships with the Romans, which was another reason for rejecting belief in a spiritual 'king of the Jews'. They kept closely to the beliefs established in the Pentateuch; like other Jews, they believed in one God, who was to be worshipped at the Temple in the ways laid down. They believed that God had chosen the Jews as a special people, and that they had a purpose to be a holy nation and to represent God to the Gentile world. But they rejected beliefs which had developed after the writing of the Torah. They did not believe in angels, or in the immortality of the soul. They rejected the idea that there would be life after death, when the righteous would be raised and rewarded; but even though they did not look forward to the hope of future reward, they aimed to keep the laws of the Torah literally, and were, for example, ready to impose the death penalty where the Torah demanded it. They were not vicious, but could be seen by some to be inflexible in their unwillingness to accommodate more modern ideas. Most importantly, they rejected the belief held by the Pharisees that the oral traditions of Judaism were important. The Sadducees held that the Torah alone was authoritative, and not the traditions which had been built upon it by successive generations – even though, in fact, they had their own 'book of decisions' which was very similar to the oral traditions they claimed to reject.

Although the Sadducees had their inheritance of power and aristocracy, they did not have as much influence over the ordinary people as the Pharisees. They were generally disliked, even hated, because of their willingness to compromise with Rome. Some people must have felt that the Sadducees' strictly literal interpretation of the Torah was unrealistic for the ordinary agricultural workers who made up the majority of the population. For the Sadducees, Judaism centred on the Temple, but when struggles between Pharisees and Sadducees went in the Pharisees' favour, the Sadducees were excluded from the Temple. About ten years later, in 70 CE, the Temple was destroyed, and nothing more was heard of the Sadducees.

iii) The Zealots

The Zealots were a far more extreme and politically active group than the Pharisees or Sadducees. They despised the Sadducees' attempts to keep peace with the Romans, and thought little of the Pharisees' attempts at passive non-cooperation. The Zealots believed that God alone was their ruler, and they refused to pay tribute to Rome, looking forward instead to the arrival of a warrior Messiah who would lead them and re-establish Jewish rule. Many of them were actively involved in guerrilla tactics of opposition; one group, called the Sicarii or assassins, carried daggers under their cloaks and murdered those who were happy to live comfortably under Roman rule. They were particularly murderous during festivals, where they could stab someone quietly in a crowd and slip away undetected.

Judas the Galilean is named by Josephus as being the founder of the first century Zealot party, although it had links with other resistance movements dating from before the Maccabean revolt. In 6 CE, Judas led a revolt against an instruction for the population of Judaea to register. This took the form of a number of individual acts, which gradually gained momentum until they came to a head with the outbreak of the First Jewish Revolt in 66–70 CE. Because of Zealot activities, the Romans kept the land under strict control, and reinforced their command ruthlessly at the times of Jewish Pilgrim festivals when there was a stronger possibility of Zealot attack. It is possible that a Zealot revolt had been planned for Passover, when Jesus was arrested and crucified, and that this accounts for the way in which he was given a Roman form of execution usually reserved for rebels. Some scholars suggest that Jesus himself was a Zealot; his entry into Jerusalem, his passionate cleansing of the Temple and the fact that some of his followers were carrying knives at the time of his arrest have been seen by some to be evidence of Jesus' connection with the Zealot movement. However, others have pointed to Jesus' sympathy with tax-collectors – no Zealot would have had anything to do with someone who worked for Rome in this way – and to his insistence that the kingdom of God would be a rule of love given to all, even Samaritans.

The Zealots looked back to the leaders of the Maccabean revolt in 162 BCE as their heroes. The Maccabees had succeeded for a short time in gaining independent Jewish rule for Palestine, and the Zealots aimed to achieve this again. They believed that loyalty to God was inextricably linked with political action. They had faith in the imminent arrival of the Messiah, and thought that the Last Days, when God would finally establish his rule, were very close at hand. They were prepared to risk death in their efforts to keep Judaism pure, and many were brutally killed by the Romans, often by crucifixion.

iv) The 'amme ha-aretz'

The '*amme ha-aretz*' or 'people of the land' formed much of the Jewish community of the first century. They were not educated people, and did not observe the Law in all the ways prescribed by Pharisees or Sadducees. They were the masses, more concerned with working in agriculture than with keeping the Torah. There seems to have been a lot of resentment between them and the more scholarly groups of Jews, with the people of the land feeling that the Pharisees and Sadducees were making unreasonable demands of them, while they in turn were accused of letting down Judaism by neglecting their obligations.

2 The Acts of the Apostles

a) The author of Acts

Each of the four gospels is attributed to a named person: Matthew, Mark, Luke and John; but this does not mean that the books were actually written by people who had these names. The book of Acts is traditionally attributed to 'Luke', or whoever was the author of the third gospel. There are many reasons why people have assumed that the two books have the same author: they begin in the same way, they are written in the same style, which is distinctive and much more literary than other New Testament writing, and they have a similar message. Acts begins by referring back to the first part of the story which has already been written.

Most scholars agree that the two books were written by the same person, but there is disagreement about who this person was. Was the author the same person that is known elsewhere in the New Testament as Luke, a physician who was a friend of Paul? Paul, when writing to the Colossians, for example, mentions that he is with Luke, when he signs off at the end of his letter:

> Luke, the beloved physician, and Demas greet you.
>
> *Col.4:14*

There are several arguments in favour of the view that Acts was written by Paul's companion Luke:

● The early Church is unanimous in the view that Luke wrote Acts. Irenaeus, Bishop of Lyons, Clement of Alexandria and Eusebius, all of whom were leading figures in the first five centuries of the early church, are recorded as attributing Acts to the writer of Luke's Gospel. This tradition is uncontested; we do not have in existence any writings which attribute Acts to any other source.

● Acts contains passages which are known as the 'we-sections', because in these verses, the writer uses the first person plural to explain events, writing about what 'we' did on Paul's travels, implying that the writer was a travelling companion of Paul's:

> We set sail from Troas and took a straight course to Samothrace, the following day to Neapolis, and from there to Philippi, which is a leading city of the district of Macedonia and a Roman colony. We remained in this city for some days.
>
> *Acts 16:11–12*

Some people have suggested that these passages (Acts 16:10–17, 20:5–21:18, 27:1–28–28:16) come from a travel diary that one of Paul's companions kept, and that the author of Acts worked them into the text but was not himself the companion of Paul. But others argue that the literary style of the 'we' passages is so similar to the rest of the book that this theory is difficult to accept.

● Scholars sometimes consider that Luke's Gospel and Acts both use 'medical language'; they use terms which would have been familiar to a physician such as Luke.

However, there are also arguments put forward which suggest that Luke, the physician, could not have been the author of Acts. The writer **W. G. Kummel**, in his *Introduction to the New Testament* (1977) suggested several reasons why Luke might not have been the author:

- To some people, the book of Acts shows great similarities with the work of a Jewish historian called Josephus, who wrote in 93 or 94 CE. If the author of Acts knew the writings of Josephus, he could not have been a contemporary of Paul, unless he was a very young man when he was a contemporary of Paul and then lived to a very great age.
- Some scholars argue that the themes of Acts, showing universal salvation for Jews and Gentiles alike, are more appropriate for the second century than the first. It is argued that Acts was written with hindsight, to try and calm arguments between different groups within the church by showing that salvation for all was always a central message from the beginning.
- Some argue that there are important historical inaccuracies in Acts, which cannot have been written by a man who was there at the time but had to have been written later by someone who was using unreliable sources. The differences between Acts 15 and Galatians 2 are usually used in support of this argument, where there are noticeable differences in the versions of events.
- Scholars also point out the differences between the Paul whose personality comes across in his letters, and the Paul of Acts; for some, these differences are so striking that the writer of Acts could not have been someone who genuinely knew Paul well. Acts, far more than the letters, emphasises the view that Paul took his message first to the Jews, and then secondly to the Gentiles, whereas in the letters Paul describes himself as an apostle for the Gentiles (for example in Romans 9) and does not seem to have seen this part of his mission as secondary. Some see these differences as serious, while others believe that they show nothing more than that Luke was a travelling companion of Paul but not necessarily a very intimate friend.

b) The dating of Acts

The dating of Acts is closely linked with its authorship, because if the author is Luke, the companion of Paul, then clearly the book must have been written during the lifetime of someone who lived at the same time as Paul. However, as we have seen, some scholars are of the view that the book is later than this. There are no clear answers to this problem, because there are quite strong arguments on both sides of the debate but neither is conclusive.

In favour of an early date, it is pointed out that Acts does not mention Paul's later years or his death by execution, and the writer does not make reference to Paul's letters, which could suggest that the letters were not yet well-known. Nero's persecution of Christians must have had an impact on the early communities, and yet Acts says nothing about it, and nothing about the fall of Jerusalem and the destruction of the Temple; so perhaps it was written before 70 CE, or even before Luke's gospel, before any of these significant events happened.

Those who argue for a later date sometimes suggest that Acts might have been written for those who were disappointed that Jesus did not make an immediate return to establish his rule on earth (the *parousia*). The book could have been written with hindsight, as a later attempt to show that, in spite of this disappointment, God's promises were being fulfilled. It is also suggested that the writer of Acts tried to play down the differences in opinion between Peter and Paul in the early church. Someone looking back might want to pretend that everything had been more harmonious in the past. Another reason given for a late date is that nothing is said in Acts of an important collection for the poor in Jerusalem, made by Paul and mentioned in his letter to the Corinthian church (1 Cor.16:1); maybe, by the time Acts was written, this event was so long in the past that no-one was interested in it any more. Perhaps Acts was written in the 80s or 90s; some have even suggested the second century. Certainly, if Luke really was familiar with the writings of Josephus, Acts would have to be placed at a date later than 94 CE.

c) The purposes of Acts

Why was The Acts of the Apostles written? Certainly it was not to tell readers about the actions performed by the apostles; many of the apostles do not even get a mention, and some of the leading characters in the narrative, such as Stephen, Barnabas and Philip, were not apostles at all. For at least two hundred years, scholars have been suggesting that a better title for the work would be 'The Acts of the Holy Spirit', as a strong theme running through the narrative is the ways in which the power of the Holy Spirit enables preaching, courage in the face of persecution, miraculous events and conversions to Christianity. The title 'Acts of the Apostles' does not seem to come from the author, because the earliest texts have different wordings; perhaps one of the people who made a copy of the work used this as a title, and it stuck.

The writer then did not necessarily intend to record the actions of the apostles, but obviously must have had some purposes in mind when he began writing. Like the Gospel of Luke, Acts begins with an address to 'Theophilus':

> In the first book, Theophilus, I wrote about all that Jesus did and taught from the beginning until the day when he was taken up to heaven, after giving instructions through the Holy Spirit to the apostles whom he had chosen.
>
> *Acts 1:1–2*

This, then, is the author's stated objective: to write a sequel to the book he has already written, and to continue with the story from the point where he had left off. In Luke's Gospel, the stated aim is to give Theophilus a reliable and orderly account of these important events, so that he has the truth in writing:

Since many have undertaken to set down an orderly account of the events that have been fulfilled among us, just as they were handed on to us by those who from the beginning were eyewitnesses and servants of the word, I too decided, after investigating everything carefully from the very first, to write an orderly account for you, most excellent Theophilus, so that you may know the truth concerning the things about which you have been instructed.

Luke 1:1–4

The name Theophilus means literally, a lover of God. Perhaps the author was writing for someone who had this name, or perhaps it was a code name for a Christian who did not wish to be identified, for fear of persecution. It seems that Theophilus had been receiving instruction in the Christian faith, and that the author wanted to show him that the things he had learned were not just contrived myths or exaggerations but had their basis in historical fact.

The book of Acts is unique in New Testament literature. There are letters and gospels written by several other people, but this is the only attempt to write a history of the spreading of the gospel throughout the early church. It seems, from the literary style used, that the author was trying to write 'salvation history' in a way that would be comparable to the Greek translation of the Old Testament. The writer wanted to show that the history of the saving work of Jesus did not end when Jesus died; Jesus continued to work in the world through his Spirit, seen in action in the lives of the main characters of the book. **W. C. van Unnik** in 1960 put forward the view that the main purpose of Acts was to confirm the events described in the Gospel. The writer did not only want to show that Jesus fulfilled the promises of the Old Testament, but also to show that the spreading of the church, too, had been foretold by the prophets, and that everything that was happening was in accordance with God's plans.

Other purposes, too, have been ascribed to Acts:

- It seems to have been an attempt to encourage the early Christians to accept Gentiles as well as Jews into the church.
- It could have been written for political reasons, to show that the Christians were innocent of any charges that the Roman Empire might be thinking of bringing against them.
- It could have been written to try and heal rifts in the early church, by showing Peter to be more liberal than he really was, and showing Paul to be more sympathetic to Judaism than was true.

d) How does the book of Acts fit in with the writings of Paul?

The differences between the writings of Paul and the book of Acts have been the subject of many scholarly debates. For example, Galatians 1:13–24 in which Paul tells of his conversion is very different from the story given three times in Acts (9:1–30; 22:1–21; 26:4–18). But the most speculation has been concerned with Acts 15, in which there is a meeting in Jerusalem to discuss whether uncircumcised Gentiles could be allowed into the Christian community, or whether they had to be circumcised as Jews first before they would be acceptable. They also debated whether the food laws of Judaism still applied. The author of Acts obviously thought that this meeting was of great significance; his version of events is that the meeting went in favour of a full acceptance of Gentile Christians (although the question of circumcision is not entirely resolved), guidelines about food were given, and everyone was very happy about the outcome. Paul, however, does not refer to these discussions in his letters, even when he is writing about the same subjects. In Galatians 2, a very different account is given, where Barnabas let his friends down and everyone seemed to be careful about their speech and behaviour because they were afraid of the Jewish Christians.

Many questions are raised when the book of Acts is put alongside the letters of Paul. Maybe there were different visits to Jerusalem, and different discussions which led to different outcomes. Perhaps one author, or both, distorted what had happened because of a point they were trying to make. But the differences raise an important issue for the study of Acts: how far is the account historically reliable? Did the writer achieve his aim, to set out the facts for Theophilus so that he would have a true record, or were other factors involved?

Summary

- Acts raises a lot of difficult issues about date, purposes and authorship.
- Most scholars believe that the author of Acts is the same person as the author of the third gospel. There is less agreement about the identity of this person and the time of writing.

3 Source criticism of the Gospels

Source criticism is the name given to the type of scholarship which investigates and speculates on the sources that Biblical writers might have used when compiling their work. For some people, the question of the source of Biblical material does not arise; they believe that it all came directly from God, and that the writers were miraculously inspired to copy down, word by word, whatever God told them. But this way of looking at the Gospels raises some questions: why are there four gospels, rather than just one? Why do the gospels contain different versions of what seems to be the same event, if it all came four times directly from God? It seems that there is at least some element of human involvement in the writing of the gospel stories, with each author presenting his own understanding of what happened. Studying the sources of the Bible involves subjecting the Bible to literary criticism in just the same way as, for example, the works of Chaucer or Shakespeare. For some people, this is too disrespectful to be considered. The Bible is a sacred text, not an ordinary piece of literature, in the views of many. But others hope that a study of Biblical sources will lead to greater understanding, for believers and non-believers alike. Where did the Biblical writers get their information; how did they know what Jesus had said and done? Were they committing to writing the words of people who had known Jesus and heard him speak, or were they simply recording later ideas, based on things that people wished had been said?

Scholars investigate the possible sources of Biblical material in an attempt to discover the truth behind the narratives. If one piece of writing is shown to be much earlier in origin than others, then perhaps it might be close to the actual words of Jesus and his followers; although maybe the later writers had a more accurate picture, because they had the benefits of hindsight and were able to gather more material.

One way of looking at the question of gospel sources is to suggest that each of the four gospel writers independently gave his own account of events, from his own perspective, unaware that others were also writing their own versions of the life and teaching of Jesus. Perhaps details of the life and words of Jesus were being passed down, through an oral tradition, and each of the gospel writers had heard some of it and wanted to put it into writing. But this idea raises issues when the gospels are studied closely. Ever since the eighteenth century, Matthew, Mark and Luke have been known as the 'Synoptic' gospels, from the Greek 'synoptikos' or 'seen together', because they contain so much material in common. It is not just that they tell the same stories; they often structure them in the same way and they even use the same wording in many places, giving the strong suggestion that there is a literary connection, with some of the writers having a thorough knowledge of other gospels and copying some passages word for word. John's gospel is very different from the others in both style and content. Events occur in a different order, or are different events entirely, and the way in which Jesus is presented gives a very distinct and unique perspective. Matthew, Mark and Luke, however, all give an uncannily similar picture, suggesting not only that they knew the same oral traditions but that in some way, there was copying from one gospel to another:

> And when Jesus had been baptized, just as he came up from the water, suddenly the heavens were opened to him and he saw the Spirit of God descending like a dove and alighting on him. And a voice from heaven said, "This is my Son, the Beloved, with whom I am well pleased."
>
> *Matthew 3:16–17*

And just as he was coming up out of the water, he saw the heavens torn apart and the Spirit descending like a dove on him. And a voice came from heaven, "You are my Son, the Beloved; with you I am well pleased."

Mark 1:10–11

Now when all the people were baptized, and when Jesus also had been baptized and was praying, the heaven was opened, and the Holy Spirit descended upon him in bodily form like a dove. And a voice came from heaven, "You are my Son, the Beloved; with you I am well pleased."

Luke 3:21–22

The relationship between the three Synoptic Gospels has been the subject of debate for centuries. Which of the gospels was written first, and then copied by the others? **St Augustine**, who lived in the fourth and fifth centuries, thought that Matthew's gospel came first, and was copied by Mark, which was then copied by Luke. He thought that Mark wrote an abridged version of Matthew, which Luke then expanded because he had extra material of his own that he wanted to include. An eighteenth century scholar called **Griesbach** also believed that Matthew was written first, but his view differed from Augustine's because he thought that Luke came second, using Matthew, and that Mark had then used them both. For many years, most people accepted the theory that Matthew was the first gospel, and there are people today who still hold this view, particularly within the Roman Catholic church; B. C. Butler, OSB, for example, has recently presented a case defending the priority of Matthew. Matthew's gospel is particularly important to Roman Catholics because it contains verses in which Jesus appoints Peter to be the founder of the church.

But many scholars have not been convinced by the view that Matthew was written first, for several reasons:

- Mark is the shortest of the three Synoptic gospels. If Mark was written later than the others, he would have gone through his sources cutting things out, such as the Sermon on the Mount, which seems unlikely given the importance of the gospel story for Christian believers. It is perhaps more probable that Mark was the earliest, and that the others used his material but wanted to add things of their own because they knew of important teachings and incidents which Mark had not recorded.
- Mark's written Greek is the least polished and sophisticated of the three. It seems more probable that a later author would want to improve on the quality of language of his sources, rather than make it worse.
- Mark's gospel is written in a rushed, breathless kind of style. He uses words like 'immediately' a great deal, giving the impression of a story which was fresh in people's minds, where one incident happened straight after another. Matthew and Luke take things rather more

slowly, and stop to explain, which might suggest that they were written when people had had longer to reflect on the significance of what had happened.

● Mark's portrayal of the disciples is less flattering than the way in which they are presented in Matthew and Luke. In Mark, the disciples are often seen to be rather stupid, misunderstanding Jesus' sayings, and it seems likely that the other gospel writers would have wanted to tone this down because of the respect in which the disciples came to be held as time went on.

The theory that Mark was the first gospel to be written is widely accepted today by most scholars. There are many different ideas about how the gospels came to be compiled, and where each writer gained his information; the two most widely held are called the **two-document hypothesis** and the **four-document hypothesis**. These theories try to deal not only with the problem of which gospel has priority of authorship, but also, they try to explain why Matthew and Luke sometimes have material in common with each other but which is not in Mark.

The two-document hypothesis – this theory was developed in Germany in the nineteenth century. The idea is that Matthew and Luke both used Mark for a basic outline of the story of the life of Jesus, and often reproduced Mark's own words when they recounted events. They also both had access to a second source, which Mark had not known about. This source is known as 'Q' for the German word 'Quelle', meaning 'source'. It is suggested that Q was another gospel account which has since been lost.

The four-document hypothesis – this theory is a refinement of the two-document hypothesis, and it was developed by a Biblical scholar called **B. H. Streeter**. He produced evidence to illustrate his theory that Matthew and Luke each had their own special sources as well as Mark and Q. Matthew had his own source, known as M, which contained material that Luke did not know about, and Luke too had a source L of which Matthew was unaware. This would explain why the visit of the wise men to the infant Jesus in Matthew 2 does not appear in the other gospels, for example, and why Luke has passages such as the Magnificat (Luke 1:46f) which the other writers leave out. This theory was widely accepted for many years as providing the most reasonable and coherent explanation of the Synoptic Problem, and today, many scholars still believe that it provides the most plausible solution.

The debate about the sources of the gospels is far from over. Recently, several scholars have raised objections to the idea of the source 'Q'. The main objection is that there is no evidence for its existence at all. No Biblical writer or writer from the time ever makes any reference to this alleged work, and scholars who have tried to reconstruct what it must have been like have never been able to come up with a coherent and convincing picture. If Q did exist, it could provide a reasonable explanation for the similarities between the Synoptic Gospels, but there are other possible explanations too which do not involve the hypothesis of a 'lost' book, and many modern scholars are of the opinion that it is best to stick with the simplest explanation; Mark was written first, and then Matthew followed by Luke – or the other way around – with no need to suggest a mysterious lost source.

Some people think that this idea does not work, because there are parts of Matthew's text which do not appear in Luke, and parts of Luke which are not in Matthew. They argue that it is unlikely that a gospel writer would have deliberately left out stories which revealed something important about the life and work of Jesus. But possibly, there are these differences because each author had a particular audience in mind when writing. Matthew seems to have been writing for a Jewish audience. He assumes that his readers are familiar with Old Testament prophecy, and are looking forward to a Messiah, and he stops frequently in his narrative to explain how Jesus fulfilled the prophecies. Luke, in contrast, seems to have been writing for a wider audience, including Christians who had been Gentiles rather than Jews before their conversions. He is less interested in emphasising Jesus as the fulfilment of Jewish prophecy, and more interested than Matthew in showing that the 'good news' is for everyone, Jew or Gentile, male or female, prominent public figure or outcast; so he might well have ignored the parts of Matthew's gospel which were out of keeping with his aims.

Summary

- The gospels of Matthew, Mark and Luke have such striking similarities that most people believe they must have some literary connection. The nature of this connection is known as the Synoptic Problem.
- Some scholars have postulated the existence of a document known as 'Q', to account for these similarities, and this is an idea which still has a considerable following today.
- Other scholars believe that there are more straightforward possibilities, which are more likely solutions.

Practice examination questions

1. **a)** Describe the main characteristics of the Zealots. (33 marks)
    b) 'Most Jews in New Testament times were in sympathy with the Zealots.' Discuss. (17 marks)

Guide

Part (a) asks for a demonstration of your knowledge and understanding, You could contrast the Zealots with other groups, but the answer should not wander off too far into descriptions of people who are not mentioned in the question. In part (b), you need to give an evaluation; you should show that you understand that there were those with Zealot sympathies, but that other groups had different ideas about relationships with Rome.

2. a) Explain why many scholars believe that the author of Acts was also the author of Luke's Gospel. (33 marks)
  b) 'The writer of Acts cannot have been a companion of Paul.' Discuss. (17 marks)

Guide

In part (a) you need to explain as many different reasons as you can which support the idea that Luke wrote Acts. You could give examples from the texts to illustrate your answer, for example you might be able to quote the opening addresses from the Gospel and from Acts to Theophilus. For part (b), you need to show an awareness of the debate about whether the writer was actually present with Paul. You could explain something about the 'we-passages', and you might be able to make reference to some of the books you have considered when studying this topic.

3. a) Explain why source critics have taken particular interest in the gospels of Matthew, Mark and Luke. (33 marks)
  b) Discuss the view that Matthew and Luke must have based their writing on Mark's gospel. (17 marks)

Guide

Part (a) asks you to demonstrate an awareness of the importance of the Synoptic problem for issues of source criticism. You should show that you know what it is, and the reasons why these gospels are considered to be synoptic; you might be able to give some illustration by quoting passages which are similar. In part (b), you are asked to consider the view that Mark was written first, and to make an evaluation. You might be able to compare the thinking of different scholars, and you could evaluate the strength of the case for the priority of Matthew, for example.

Suggestions for further reading

E. P. Sanders, *Judaism* (SCM Press, 1992)

Jacob Neusner, *Judaism in the beginning of Christianity* (Augsburg Fortress Publishers, 1984)

Introductions to commentaries on the Acts of the Apostles

R. E. Brown, *An Introduction to the New Testament* (Doubleday, 1997)

E. Charpentier, *How to Read the New Testament* (SCM Press, 1982)

H. C. Kee & F. W. Young, *The Living World of the New Testament* (Dartington, Longman and Todd, 1972)

K. O'Donnell, *Introduction to the New Testament* (Hodder & Stoughton, 1999)

5 Developments in Christian Thought

KEYWORDS

Christology – a part of theology which investigates the nature of Christ as both human and divine

demythologising – the term used to describe taking the mythical elements out of Biblical texts in order to uncover the 'true' meaning

fundamentalism – the belief that a religion needs to return to its fundamental elements, including a literal interpretation of sacred texts. Within Christianity, it usually includes creationism and conservative views about family life

Redaction criticism – a type of Biblical criticism which looks at the ways in which the Biblical writers have selected and edited their

1 The inspiration and authority of the Bible

One of the issues which causes major divisions within Christianity is the question of the authority of the Bible. What does it mean to call the Bible 'the Word of God'? Was the Bible in some way written by God, and is everything it says absolutely true? Can the Bible be relied upon for accurate historical, scientific and moral information?

There are many different ways in which Christians have approached questions like these.

Almost all Christians would want to say that the Bible comes from God in some way; but there is considerable disagreement about how this should be understood. Some Christians are happy to consider that certain parts of the Bible, such as the creation stories of Genesis, are myth, rather than literal accounts of exactly what happened at the beginning of the world. Others insist that the Bible is the absolute authority and can be trusted to give accurate information.

Similarly, some argue that there are commandments which are inappropriate for modern society, such as those in Exodus 29 concerning animal sacrifice; it might be argued that these rules can be safely ignored in the modern world. However, other Christians believe that it is very dangerous to choose to disregard parts of the Bible in this way, and argue that if Christians allow the authority of the Bible to be called into question, then the whole message of Christianity is at risk.

a) Fundamentalist views of the interpretation of the Bible

The word 'fundamentalism' is commonly used to describe a very conservative and literalist approach to the Bible. The original Christian fundamentalists were part of a Protestant movement in the USA at the beginning of the nineteenth century, who set out to preserve the 'fundamentals' of the Christian faith. In their view, this included the inerrancy of the Bible. In this understanding, the Bible is the actual word of God to the extent that it was literally dictated by God, word for word, to the people who wrote it down. All the human authors had to do was to copy correctly the words that they were given.

According to a fundamentalist position, then, every word of the Bible is entirely the work of God and should never be changed, challenged or questioned. The Bible is 'inspired', or 'breathed in' to the people who wrote it down, in much the same way as the breath of life was breathed into Adam in Genesis 2:7; it comes directly from God. If society moves to a point where the Bible seems no longer appropriate for it, then for the fundamentalist it is the society which must change and not the book, which is infallible.

Henry Morris, an American writer, sums up this way of thinking in his commentary on the book of Genesis, which he believes to be the perfect word of God:

> It is always dangerous to alter God's Word, either by addition (as do modern cultists) or by deletion (as do modern liberals). God, being omniscient, can always be trusted to say exactly, and only, what He means (Deuteronomy 4:2; Proverbs 30:5; Revelation 22:18,19); and finite man is inexcusable when he seeks to change God's Word.

> *The Genesis Record, 1976*

Fundamentalists believe firmly that the Bible can be absolutely trusted as the truth, because it comes from God and God does not make mistakes. Their justification for their position is often taken from the Bible itself; because if the Bible is the source of the truth of God, then it can speak for itself with authority:

> All scripture is inspired by God and is useful for teaching, for reproof, for correction, and for training in righteousness, so that everyone who belongs to God may be proficient, equipped for every good work.

> *2 Timothy 3:16–17*

This verse is often used to support the view that the Bible is infallible – if the Bible itself says that it is infallible, then it must be.

> First of all you must understand this, that no prophecy of scripture is a matter of one's own interpretation, because no prophecy ever came by human will, but men and women moved by the Holy Spirit spoke from God.

> *2 Peter 1:20–21*

This way of thinking rejects the suggestion that God spoke through people who then used their own ideas and personalities to shape their writings in their own ways. It is argued that, if God had allowed his words to be shaped in this way, then human sin and wickedness would become involved. The Bible would have to be accepted as flawed in parts, and those verses of the Bible which claim that God's words are perfect would be false.

i) Advantages of a fundamentalist position

- The words of the Bible can be accepted as being infallible, and can be accepted unthinkingly. Every piece of historical information in the Bible, for example, need not be questioned but can be accepted as fact. A believer can know at once whether or not to accept the theories of scientists, geologists, historians and so on, by comparing their findings with the words of the Bible, which are already known to be true.

- People never have to rely on their own interpretation and judgement, and so there can be no danger that the Bible might be misunderstood. The Bible can be trusted entirely; whereas other views, which allow that the Bible might sometimes be mistaken, cast doubt on every verse.

- Moral decisions present fewer problems, because often the believer is able to use the Bible to find out how to behave, and then can be confident of doing the right thing.

- If the only people who are considered to be Christians are those who take a fundamentalist view, there are fewer disagreements and differences of belief, and when these occur they can often be resolved by reference to the Bible. For example, someone who wanted to know whether women should be allowed to preach in church could be shown the passage of the Bible which says: 'I permit no woman to teach or to have authority over a man; she is to keep silent' (I Timothy 2:12), and then he or she would know without doubt the answer to the question.

ii) Criticisms of a fundamentalist position

- A fundamentalist view of the Bible is difficult to reconcile with many of the theories of modern science, particularly those theories which deal with the origins of the universe and the origins of humanity.

- The Bible is not a single text, but a collection, with 39 books in the Old Testament and 27 in the New, written over a very long period of time. These different books give clear evidence that the human authors had at least some part to play in the writing. There are many moods and many styles, many different pictures of the nature of God, and different responses to life; there are many different kinds of literature, with poems, history, songs, stories and genealogies. It is difficult to accept a view which does not take into account the part played by the wide variety of authors. A reading of the Gospels, for example, gives strong evidence that Matthew was writing for a Jewish audience, taking trouble to show how Jesus was the Messiah for whom they had been waiting, while Luke seems to be writing for a largely Gentile audience, and bothers to explain some of the Jewish festivals and customs to his readers. Biblical scholars called Redaction critics study the text of the Bible in order to discover the particular themes and approaches of the human authors.

- Also, an attempt to interpret the Bible as a single inspired infallible creation raises more questions than it answers. Why, for example, if the Bible has been literally dictated by God, are there four Gospels instead of only one? It is far more logical to assume that four different authors each used their own source material to compile their own different understandings of the importance of Jesus, than to believe that God dictated each of the Gospels in turn, with some differences in detail in the stories. (For example, in Luke's account, at the crucifixion Jesus' last words were "Father, into your hands I commend my spirit", whereas in Matthew, Jesus says "My God, my God, why have you forsaken me?") Why are there two creation stories in Genesis, rather than just one, and why are things created in a different order in the two stories? It is difficult to reconcile the apparent contradictions in the Bible with the belief that every word was directly inspired by God.

- Many people argue also that it is circular to use the Bible as evidence for the truth of the Bible, and that other supporting evidence must be found beyond the text itself.

- Some writers, such as **James Barr** (*The Scope and Authority of the Bible, Fundamentalism*) argue that a fundamentalist approach to the Bible does harm, in that it often distorts the original intention and meaning of the Biblical writer. If the Biblical writer expressed his experience of God in poetry, then it is wrong to take the words at face value and not look for a poetic meaning.

- Barr also believes that Christians should try to work alongside one another and live amongst non-Christians, but that a fundamentalist approach makes this difficult; fundamentalists often suggest that the only true Christians are other fundamentalists, which can be divisive rather than welcoming. A fundamentalist perspective also involves an 'exclusivist' view of non-Christian religions: if the Bible is infallible, then non-Christian religions do not contain a way to God. In John's gospel, Jesus says: "I am the way, and the truth, and the life. No one comes to the Father except through me" (John 14:6). A fundamentalist would consider this to show that, without exception, only Christians have God's approval.

The view that the Bible was dictated without mistakes, where God completely overrode the personalities and minds of the writers, has never been widely accepted by Christian thinkers. One problem which did not escape the earliest Christians was that Jesus had given teachings which were, in some parts, a deliberate contrast to the teachings of the Old Testament: 'You have heard … But I say to you …' (Matthew 5:21f.). It is difficult to accept that the New Testament and the Old Testament were both written directly and infallibly by the word of God, if the New Testament contains explicit re-interpretations of the Old.

b) Liberal views

Some Christians believe that it is impossible for modern people to accept very many parts of the Bible as being either literally or infallibly true. Our understanding of science in particular can lead us into difficulties. Most people now believe that the earth is a small part of a very large universe; that humanity evolved from other creatures; that people suffer from mental illness rather than demonic possession, and so on.

Rudolf Bultmann caused great debate when he insisted on the need for what he called 'demythologising' the New Testament, as well as the Old. He argued that the language and imagery of the Gospel accounts were unacceptable to modern people, and that the mythical elements have to be taken out in order for the real significance of the Gospels to be found. He believed that many of the narratives of the Gospels (for example, the Virgin Birth), depended on us suspending disbelief to an impossible extent, and he wanted people to be able to take away the outdated world views in order to reach what he saw as the real point. In Bultmann's writing, even ideas such as the resurrection were called into question as historical, literal accounts.

Bultmann considered that the central message of the gospels was Jesus summoning his followers to the point of making a personal decision. The story of Peter at Caesarea Philippi was, to him, the most crucial part of the Gospels: Peter is put on the spot and asked whom he believes Jesus to be; Peter has to make a decision, and declares that Jesus is 'the Christ'.

The Myth of God Incarnate, a book edited by **John Hick** and published in 1977, caused the same kind of outrage as Bultmann had done. A collection of scholars, some of them ordained ministers of the church, contributed essays based around the idea that Jesus as the incarnate Son of God is a myth. The concept of Jesus being God in human form was meant to convey important truths, but is not literally true. The scholars who contributed to the book argued, in various different ways, that modern people could no longer accept this world-view, and that part of the reason why Christianity is in decline in the developed world is that people are unable to accept the understanding of the world which the Bible puts forward. Modern people are often happy with the ethics of the Bible, but the elements suggesting magic, or supernatural power, are generally unacceptable, and therefore people are rejecting the whole package because of its outdated wrapping. In this book, a variety of writers discussed Christology, looking at how the concept of Jesus as God incarnate could be understood if it is not taken as infallible, literal truth. In different ways, they discussed how it could be reinterpreted so that it had something meaningful to say to people in the second half of the twentieth century.

The former **Bishop of Durham**, **David Jenkins**, followed this way of thinking and became a popular target for attack by the press, when he suggested that elements in the Gospel stories, such as the Virgin Birth and the Resurrection, need not necessarily be taken absolutely literally. It could, he argued, get in the way of a person's faith, if that person could not believe that such things literally happened, however hard they tried. If other kinds of interpretation were allowed, then these same people might be able to discover the really important truths of the Bible without tripping over the outdated mythology.

Liberal views, then, accept that the Bible was not written directly by God but by people, who were encouraged by their own religious experiences to try to communicate their beliefs to others. They wrote using different literary styles, and according to their own cultures and traditions, using their own understanding of the world and the ways in which it worked. Some of these understandings were appropriate for the time of writing, but are inappropriate today. Although the Biblical writers were motivated by the power of their religious experience, they were capable of making mistakes. The Bible must be reinterpreted in order to be acceptable for modern minds.

i) Advantages of a liberal position
- Liberal views allow people to maintain their religious faith without having to try and force themselves to believe stories which, intellectually, they find impossible.
- Liberal views are much more readily accommodated into a modern scientific understanding of the world. They might be seen to make religion more respectable; religion is not set in opposition to scientific discovery, but can work alongside it, and people do not have to choose between science and religion.
- Liberal positions make people think for themselves about the real meaning of the Bible; they do not just accept stories as they are, but look for the deeper significance, which might be missed by someone who is more willing to believe that the story is describing a real historical event.

ii) Criticisms of a liberal position
- Many people argue that it is wrong to question and reject parts of the Bible in this way, because the Bible, by its very nature, is truer than anything which people claim to have discovered. Modern society and modern ideas should be judged against the Bible, not the other way around.
- It can be argued, and frequently is, that liberal interpretations destroy the whole point of the Bible. If concepts such as the Virgin Birth, the

Incarnation, the miracles and even the Resurrection are taken to be other than historically accurate, the whole essence of Christianity is removed. Christianity becomes diluted to the extent that it is indistinguishable from a general desire to be kind to other people.

● Some people might argue that religious belief requires effort, and people should pray for faith, not just reject anything they find difficult. Religious belief which fits in comfortably with other, secular, ideas, perhaps is not worth having.

c) Traditional views of the interpretation of the Bible

'Traditional' views of the right way to understand the Bible are more difficult to define. Many ordinary Christians believe that the Bible is full of truth, and that God is revealed in the Bible, but they also believe that some parts of the Bible are 'more true' than others, in a way which is difficult to pin down. Many 'traditional' Christians would admit that, in some cases, there could be mistakes in the Bible, reflecting the historical context in which it was written and the human fallibility of the author. The 'traditional' Christian might believe that, although the Bible is full of truth, some parts of it have to be reinterpreted, but there might be some disagreement about which parts these are.

However, many Christians would argue that some ideas are so important for the whole point of Christianity that they cannot be regarded as myth, as insignificant, or as outdated. These ideas might include: the importance of the Ten Commandments; the Virgin Birth; the Incarnation (the idea that God came to earth in human form as Jesus); and the Resurrection.

The earliest Christian writers, those who were responsible for shaping Christian doctrine, recognised the difficulties of treating the whole Bible as infallible. They saw that there were apparent inconsistencies, and that these needed to be explained for fellow Christians.

In the second century CE, **Marcion** came to the conclusion that the Old Testament should be rejected completely as not a Christian book at all; this view was considered to be heretical (not compatible with Christian doctrine), but had to be countered.

Irenaeus (c.130–c.202 CE) dealt with the problem by saying that certain parts of the Old Testament were symbolic, and other parts were temporary, given as a kind of interim understanding of the world and humanity's place in it, until the final revelation of Christ. This has become a traditional view of the Christian church: the idea that the Old Testament is full of truth, and that the prophets had spoken through the work of the Holy Spirit, but that some allowance has to be made for the fact that pre-Christians had a limited understanding of the nature of God before he revealed himself in Christ. In this view, the Old Testament cannot be properly understood without the New.

Irenaeus argued that, for example, the parts of the Old Testament which indicated the need for animal sacrifice were symbolic; they showed a need for people to sacrifice their lives to God, and they indicated the way in which Christ would come to be a perfect sacrifice for humanity. But he thought that it would be a mistake to consider these verses to be infallible when taken at face value.

Augustine (354–430CE), too, argued that Genesis was to be taken symbolically, and that the 'days' of creation were to be understood to mean the different stages in knowledge acquired by the angels. He argued that part of the purpose of the Church was to tell people how to interpret the Bible: 'We must show the way to find out whether a phrase is literal or figurative.' Augustine also pointed out that a human author might sometimes have written or said things without recognising the deeper meaning behind the words, and that in this way God might be seen to be at work.

In the twentieth century, probably the most influential thinker with a 'traditional' understanding of the way in which the Bible could be considered to be the word of God was **Karl Barth**. He was a strong critic of Bultmann and of other attempts to bring what he saw as the authoritative revelation of God into line with modern thinking. For Barth, God chose to reveal himself to humanity completely and finally in Christ, and humanity should be judged against this; it is not God's own revelation that should be measured and altered to fit. The Old Testament, therefore, can be tested to see how far it matches what we know to be the truth through Christ, and the New Testament is in some ways superior to the Old. Revelation, in Barth's view, is conveyed through the witness of the Bible; the Bible is not identical with the word of God, but it testifies to it – Scripture points to the word of God, rather than being literally the words spoken by God.

i) Advantages of a traditional approach
● Parts of the Bible which are very difficult for people today to accept as actually having happened can be understood to have a different kind of significance other than literal truth; but the important elements of the Christian faith are never doubted. Modern believers can accept the theories of science about the origins of the world, for example, without having to abandon the essence of their belief in Jesus as the Son of God.
● A traditional approach might help to resolve the problems raised by the sometimes very different ways in which the nature of God is portrayed in the Old Testament and in the New.

ii) Criticisms of a traditional approach
● This way of looking at the Bible, where some parts are regarded as essential truths and others as less significant, leaves many questions unanswered. If Christians are to interpret the Bible as fallible up to a point, but no further, how are they to know where that point is?

● This difficulty of knowing whether a certain passage is to be regarded as absolutely authoritative, or whether it can be conceded to be less relevant for today, causes considerable divisions amongst Christians. For example, the issues surrounding the ordination of women included discussion of whether St. Paul's teaching about the role of women in church was still appropriate for today, or whether it belonged to a different time and culture. Opinion was sharply divided, and many people felt that they could no longer take part in the Eucharist alongside people whose views differed from their own.

Summary

Views of God as the ultimate author of the Bible, then, are divided, from those who see God as the sole author, to those who see God contributing as co-author through human writers, perhaps supervising the writing to be done according to the cultural context of the writer. Others understand the Bible to be the words of human people who were inspired by their individual religious experience to write; in this view, the Bible is not the only source of God's revelation. God might be revealed through the writings of later people who claim to have had profound religious experiences (such as Julian of Norwich); and there is the possibility that God might be revealed in the cultural context of other world religions apart from Christianity.

2 An introduction to the teachings of the Bible

a) The treatment of the weak and the oppressed

The way in which people should behave towards those who are weak or oppressed within society is treated quite consistently in the Bible. There are some passages which suggest that those who are prosperous are being blessed or even rewarded by God; for example in the book of Job (42:10, 12), at the end of the story God gives Job many beautiful children, cattle, property and a long life. This might seem to imply that health and wealth are a reward from God, and that therefore poverty or weakness is some sort of punishment which has been deserved. However, the great majority of Biblical teaching on this subject shows that wealth or poverty is not an indicator of merit. This is something which some of the Psalmists found difficult to understand; it offended their sense of justice to see wicked people enjoying the good things of life.

Both the Old Testament and the New give a strong message that the righteousness of God will not allow people to mistreat one another. Those who are in a position of strength have a duty towards the weak, and they will be held accountable for the ways in which they respond to this. Psalm 82, for example, pictures God in the role of a judge, demanding justice for the weak, the orphans and the destitute. The covenant made by God with the Hebrews at the time of the Exodus involved many laws which detail the correct ways in which other people are to be treated. For example, Exodus 22:21–22 tells people to do no wrong to strangers, widows or orphans, and Exodus 22:25 forbids taking interest on loans made to the poor. The prophet Amos, in the eighth century BCE, warned his audience of the destruction which would meet them

> because they sell the righteous for silver,
>   and the needy for a pair of sandals—
> they who trample the head of the poor into the dust of the earth,
>   and push the afflicted out of the way;

> *Amos 2:6–7*

God, in the Old Testament, is frequently described as 'righteous', demanding that his people never take advantage of the weak, for example the writer of Deuteronomy explains that God 'executes justice for the orphan and the widow, and who loves the strangers, providing them food and clothing. You shall also love the stranger, for you were strangers in the land of Egypt' (Deut. 10:18–19).

The New Testament also makes clear that people have a duty towards the poor, who are God's particular concern. In Luke's gospel, Jesus begins his teaching by quoting from the prophet Isaiah:

> "he has anointed me
> to bring good news to the poor. He has sent me to proclaim release to the captives
>   and recovery of sight to the blind,
>   to let the oppressed go free"

> *Luke 4:18*

The first aim of Jesus' ministry seems to have been to provide rescue for the weak and oppressed. In Luke's version of the beatitudes, Jesus teaches:

> "Blessed are you who are poor,
>   for yours is the kingdom of God.
> Blessed are you who are hungry now,
>   for you will be filled."

> *Luke 6:20–21*

Luke is concerned throughout his gospel to show that the 'good news' includes the poor. Matthew, in the Parable of the Sheep and the Goats, shows Jesus pointing out that care for the poor, the weak and the oppressed is an obligation, not an option:

> "'Lord, when was it that we saw you hungry or thirsty or a stranger or naked or sick or in prison, and did not take care of you?' Then he will answer them, 'Truly I tell you, just as you did not do it to one of the least of these, you did not do it to me.'"
>
> *Matthew 25:44–45*

Although many Christians interpret these passages to mean that they should give to charity and be kind to their less fortunate neighbours, some have taken the ideas much further, believing them to show that Christians have a moral obligation to fight against injustice and oppression, to join civil rights movements or to take up arms against unjust regimes.

Summary

- Throughout the Bible, God demands that the weak and oppressed should be treated with justice.
- The most common complaint against the people by the Old Testament prophets is a lack of concern for the weak. Harsh punishment is promised for those who continue in their indifference.
- The New Testament, particularly the Gospel of Luke, emphasises the inclusion of the poor in the Kingdom of God.
- Concern for the weak is an obligation, not an option.

b) The use of violence

The teachings of the Bible about the use of violence are less consistent. Some passages, particularly in the Old Testament, depict a God who controls the armies, who defends the right and defeats the wrong, and who sends his people into battle in order to fulfil his plans.

One of the oldest pieces of writing in the Old Testament is believed to be the Song of Moses in Exodus 15, which praises God for having destroyed the enemy Egyptians and enabled the Hebrews to escape from slavery. This illustrates an understanding of God as a warrior king. Similarly, in the book of Joshua, the Israelites fight the battle of Jericho with God firmly on their side; at the end of the battle, the Israelites did as they were instructed and 'they devoted to destruction by the edge of the sword all in the city, both men and women, young and old, oxen, sheep, and donkeys' (Joshua 6:21).

It appears that all the inhabitants of the city, even the children and the cattle, were killed in the belief that this was what God wanted. Joel the prophet encourages his listeners to prepare for war:

> Beat your ploughshares into swords,
>   and your pruning hooks into spears
>
> *Joel 3:10*

Psalm 137, believed to have been written at a time when the Israelites were in exile in Babylon, looks forward to a future in which the prisoners of war will get their revenge on their captors by murdering their children:

> Happy shall they be who take your little ones
>   and dash them against the rock!

Psalm 137:9

Violence, then, is often seen as an acceptable way of ensuring that the right side is the winner; it is seen to have the sanction of God, and sometimes violence is commanded by God. Those who are on the wrong side frequently meet horrible fates, which seem to be presented as only right and proper (see, for example, Exodus 12:29 in which the firstborn of the Egyptians lose their lives, or Daniel 6:24 in which Daniel's accusers are punished). According to some passages of the Bible, violence is an acceptable way of dealing with wrong, and this includes not only violence in war time but violence on a more individual scale as a means of exacting a proper revenge.

However, both the Old Testament and the New also contain many passages which condemn the use of violence and which have an explicit message of peace. Peace is seen as a blessing which God gives to the people in Psalm 29:11. In particular, the passages in the Old Testament that look forward to the coming of the Messiah emphasise the peace which the Messiah will bring. Micah, in a passage echoed in Isaiah, reverses the message found in Joel:

> they shall beat their swords into plowshares,
>   and their spears into pruning hooks;
> nation shall not lift up sword against nation,

Micah 4:3

The Messiah to come is described as a 'Prince of peace' (Isaiah 9:6). The New Testament also views the kingdom of God as a rule of peace, for example in the beatitudes Jesus teaches: "Blessed are the peacemakers, for they will be called children of God" (Matthew 5:9). People are taught to be peaceful in their personal relationships: "Love your enemies and pray for those who persecute you" (Matthew 5:44) and to avoid even feeling angry with other people (see Matthew 5:21, 38–42). Paul, in his letter to the Romans, advises the early Christians not to seek revenge by using physical violence, but to respond to aggression with Christian love:

> Do not repay anyone evil for evil, but take thought for what is noble in the sight of all. If it is possible, so far as it depends on you, live peaceably with all. Beloved, never avenge yourselves, but leave room for the wrath of God; for it is written, "Vengeance is mine, I will repay, says the Lord." No, "if your enemies are hungry, feed them; if they are thirsty, give them

something to drink; for by doing this you will heap burning coals on their heads." Do not be overcome by evil, but overcome evil with good.

Romans 12: 17–21

But the New Testament message is also not completely on the side of pacifism; Jesus says to his disciples; 'Do not think that I have come to bring peace to the earth; I have not come to bring peace, but a sword' (Matthew 10:34). In context, the passage suggests that Jesus knew that his message would divide people, and that violence was an inevitable consequence.

Summary

- Biblical teaching about the use of violence is inconsistent; there are passages which support its use, and others which condemn it.
- Christians can find Biblical support for all different opinions about the ethics of war and of using violent means to overcome injustice. Some will argue that Christians should be pacifists, and others argue that the Bible teaches of a need to fight against evil using violence when appropriate, in order to protect the weak.

c) The role of women

The Judaism of the Old Testament and of the beginnings of Christianity was a patriarchal society; men had the dominant roles, and women were seen as the property of their fathers until they married.

The creation stories of Genesis 1–3 are often given particular attention for an understanding of the place of women in the Bible. In the first creation story (Genesis 1), man and woman are made at the same time and in the image of God, suggesting equality:

So God created humankind in his image,
   in the image of God he created them;
male and female he created them.

Genesis 1:27

However, in the second story, Adam the man is created first, out of the dust of the ground, and it is only later that the woman Eve is made when God decides 'I will make him a helper as his partner'(Genesis 2:18). Eve is made from Adam's side, rather than from more dust, and it is Eve who is the first to be tempted by Satan. The way in which Genesis depicts Eve in the role of Adam's helper, and as the morally weaker partner, has been very influential in the history of Christian thought. This is noticeable in the first letter of Paul to Timothy; Paul gives explicit instructions that women should remain silent in places of worship, and he cites Genesis as his reason:

'I permit no woman to teach or to have authority over a man; she is to keep silent. For Adam was formed first, then Eve; and Adam was not deceived, but the woman was deceived and became a transgressor' (1 Timothy 2:12–14). Paul, then, clearly believed that Eve defined femininity, as existing for the purpose of helping men, and as the weaker sex.

The letter to Titus also expresses an understanding of women in a subordinate role, as helpers and supporters of their husbands, but not as leaders:

> Likewise, tell the older women to be reverent in behaviour, not to be slanderers or slaves to drink; they are to teach what is good, so that they may encourage the young women to love their husbands, to love their children, to be self-controlled, chaste, good managers of the household, kind, being submissive to their husbands, so that the word of God may not be discredited.
>
> *Titus 2:3–5*

Old Testament laws about compensation and property rights often include women in the list of a man's goods, suggesting that a daughter or a wife were considered to be part of a man's property. For example, in Deuteronomy 22:28–29, the punishment for rape involved compensation payable to the father of the raped woman, and the rapist also has to marry the woman. Her possible feelings about being made to marry a rapist are not discussed.

The book of Proverbs ends with some beautiful poetry praising the qualities of 'a capable wife'. Her role is clearly very different from that of a man; she works in the home, cooking, sewing, taking care of the children, selling some of the goods she produces and bringing credit to her husband. In spite of this somewhat limited (by today's standards) expectation, the reader is left with feelings of admiration for a woman of energy and strength, and perhaps some envy for a woman who is judged primarily for her character rather than her looks (Proverbs 31:10f).

In spite of frequent references to women as subordinate 'chattels' of men, there are also many women in the Old Testament who are powerful and colourful characters. Deborah, in the book of Judges, was a prophet who clearly had considerable influence and authority in the local community. Esther was a brave and diplomatic queen who saved the Jews from their enemies in the book which bears her name. Ruth, although in some ways dependent on men and on marriage for her survival, is nevertheless an example of courage and loyalty. There are also women who exerted a powerful influence over men in encouraging them to do wrong, for example Jezebel (1 Kings 16–21) thoroughly manipulated the weak king Ahab, and the legendary strength of Samson was not able to stand up to the wiles of Delilah (Judges 16).

In the New Testament, too, women certainly have a lower status than men in society, but this does not prevent some strong female characters from making their mark. Luke's gospel, in particular, is often referred to as 'the gospel for women', because of the ways in which he shows how the Kingdom of God is to include women as well as men. Although the disciples of Jesus were all men, Luke makes it clear that Jesus had friends and followers who were women, such as Martha and Mary (Luke 10:38–42). Mary the mother of Jesus is given a special status in the Gospel of Luke; and female followers were the first to see Jesus after his resurrection. Although Eve might have begun the story by being the first to fall away from God, it was also women who were the first to believe in the risen Christ. Luke continues his story in the Acts of the Apostles, where, again, women (such as Lydia and Priscilla) have a not insignificant part to play, even though it is in the background.

Galatians 3:28 is often quoted by Christians to show that in Christianity, women are not meant to be subordinate to men but equal: 'There is no longer Jew or Greek, there is no longer slave or free, there is no longer male and female; for all of you are one in Christ Jesus' (Gal 3:28).

Summary

- Society at the time during which the Bible was written was male-dominated, but this did not prevent some exceptional women from contributing to events.
- Women in the Bible are usually, but not always, seen as subordinate.
- Although Luke in the New Testament makes a point of showing that the kingdom of God was inclusive, there are also passages, particularly in the writings of Paul, which explicitly give women a secondary role.
- There is not just one consistent attitude towards women in the Bible, but many different attitudes, and also many different women.

d) Attitudes towards other religions

The ways in which the Biblical writers viewed religions other than Judaism and Christianity is not always explicit, or consistent. The writers would not have known of the existence of the great Eastern traditions of Hinduism and Buddhism; religions such as Sikhism and Islam began after the Bible was completed. However, they would probably have come into contact with the beliefs and practices of neighbouring tribes. The Israelites, in their journey to occupy the Promised Land, had to contend with Canaanite religion in particular, which, with its fertility rites and lack of emphasis on morality, must have seemed very attractive to some.

The first of the Ten Commandments in Exodus 20 makes it plain that the Jews are to worship no other gods. This could be interpreted to mean that all other religions are wrong; but it could mean that Jews are to follow Judaism, while members of other faiths can follow their own traditions.

In the Old Testament, the God of Israel is often intent on destroying the religions of other nations. For example, in Deuteronomy the people are told that when they arrive in their new land:

> You must demolish completely all the places where the nations whom you are about to dispossess served their gods, on the mountain heights, on the hills, and under every leafy tree. Break down their altars, smash their pillars, burn their sacred poles with fire, and hew down the idols of their gods, and thus blot out their name from their places.

> *Deut 12:3–4*

When the prophet Elijah is confronted with the Baal religion in 1 Kings 22, he stages a competition between the God of Israel and Baal, setting up an altar to be consumed by fire, and then sitting back and waiting to see which will answer the prayers. There is no suggestion that Elijah's God is true, and that the followers of Baal are also right in their own way; God wins, Baal is defeated and shown not to have any reality at all, and Elijah kills all of the four hundred and fifty prophets of Baal in the finale.

The New Testament often seems to be quite certain that salvation can only be found through Christ. A verse which is often quoted comes from John's Gospel, where Jesus is speaking to his disciples about the future: Jesus said, "I am the way, and the truth, and the life. No one comes to the Father except through me" (John 14:6). Many Christians have interpreted this to mean that religions which do not accept Jesus as the Son of God are wrong, false religions, and that believers from these other religious traditions are not going to reach God, however hard they try and however devoutly they might believe in their own traditions. Acts 4:12 gives a very similar message: 'There is salvation in no one else, for there is no other name under heaven given among mortals by which we must be saved.'

However, there are other passages which suggest that the message of Christianity may not be completely exclusive. Jesus certainly did not distance himself from Judaism, but was recognised as a rabbi, a teacher of the Torah, from which he often chose to quote. The Gospel stories of Jesus' Transfiguration show him standing alongside Moses and Elijah, representatives of the Law and the Prophets, a tradition continuing in Jesus; and there is no suggestion that Judaism is to be rejected in favour of Christianity. However, the Acts of the Apostles deals with the question of whether Gentiles who wanted to become Christians had to be circumcised first, as a symbol of having converted to Judaism. Both Peter and Paul came into conflict with 'Judaisers' on this point, as well as in relation to the Jewish food laws.

Peter and Paul did not insist that Gentiles followed the Jewish traditions, which could be argued to show a Christian belief that Judaism is mistaken in continuing to follow all the laws of the Torah.

In Matthew's gospel, Jesus tells the crowds 'For whoever does the will of my Father in heaven is my brother and sister and mother' (Matthew 12:50).

This could be interpreted to include all people who sincerely try to follow what they understand to be the will of God, regardless of the way in which they do it; perhaps anyone who genuinely tries to worship God is right, regardless of the name of their religion. Also in Matthew's gospel is an occasion where Jesus explains how to tell true prophets from false, by comparing them with trees: 'In the same way, every good tree bears good fruit, but the bad tree bears bad fruit. A good tree cannot bear bad fruit, nor can a bad tree bear good fruit' (Matthew 7:17–18). It could be argued therefore, that Jesus was saying that the test of 'true' religion is the way in which its members behave, regardless of their words. Perhaps it could be considered a Biblical view that whoever leads a truly spiritual life is not going far wrong. Paul in Galatians lists the 'fruits of the Spirit', as a way of demonstrating whether a person is genuinely 'walking with God'. Possibly the Bible could be understood to be saying that anyone, of any religious tradition, can be regarded as following the right path if their lives show that 'the fruit of the Spirit is love, joy, peace, patience, kindness, generosity, faithfulness, gentleness, and self-control' (Galations 5:22–23).

Summary

- Many passages of the Old Testament strongly suggest that only the Biblical God is to be worshipped, and that other religions are false and wicked.
- There are several passages in the New Testament which state that salvation is found only through Christ, and that the eternal destiny of everyone depends on whether or not they confess Jesus as Christ.
- Some people interpret other passages of the Bible as suggesting that the real test of 'true' religion is in the behaviour of the believer. Those who look after the sick, clothe the naked and visit prisoners are working for Christ all the time – perhaps even if they belong to a different religious tradition.

e) Attitudes towards racism and equality

The Bible is almost universally disapproving of any kind of racism. However, there is one short passage in Genesis 9:18–27, which some people have used as a justification for treating black people as inferior. In the Genesis story, Noah is sleeping in a tent and the robe which was covering him falls to the floor. Ham, one of the sons of

Noah, sees his father's nakedness and goes to tell his brothers. The brothers go into the tent and avert their eyes while helping to cover their father. Noah wakes and is angry with Ham for his response; he curses him, and tells him that his descendants will be servants, or slaves. Some people have used this passage to support the slave trade, or to support apartheid, arguing that Ham's descendants were black people who clearly deserved their fate. However, there is no other supporting evidence for this view in the Bible, and many would regard the racist interpretation as spurious.

Elsewhere, the Bible is clear that all people are made 'in the image of God' (Genesis 1:27). The people of the Old Testament are told that they must treat people of other races and from other countries in an acceptable way, remembering how they felt when they were the strangers: 'When an alien resides with you in your land, you shall not oppress the alien. The alien who resides with you shall be to you as the citizen among you; you shall love the alien as yourself, for you were aliens in the land of Egypt' (Leviticus 19:33–34). This passage is unequivocal in its message that members of other races are not only to be treated well but also to be given equal rights as citizens.

The Parable of the Good Samaritan in Luke 10:25–37 is often given as an example of Biblical teaching which challenges racist attitudes. The Samaritans were descendants of Jews whose territory had been captured by Assyrians; the Assyrians had expelled or deported many of the Jews who lived there, but some had stayed and intermarried with the Assyrians. The Samaritans of the time of Jesus were therefore regarded as mixed-race and as traitors; Jesus' parable deliberately places the Samaritan as the hero. The story could have been told so that the principle of neighbourliness was illustrated by a kind Jew who helps a poor Samaritan; however the Samaritan here is not the victim but the one who shows up the Jewish characters who pass by and do nothing. Members of other races, therefore, are not just to be treated with a patronising kindness and tolerance, but are to be respected for the content of their characters – an ideal that was still far in the future when Martin Luther King made his famous speech in Washington, in 1963.

Paul's letters, too, make it clear that ancestry is not important, and that Christians are to be united and to recognise each other as part of the same 'body of Christ' (see 1 Corinthians 12). Galatians 3:27–29 emphasises that people are not to discriminate against one other, and Colossians 3:11 gives the same message:

> In that renewal there is no longer Greek and Jew, circumcised and uncircumcised, barbarian, Scythian, slave and free; but Christ is all and in all!

Summary

● Apart from the passage in Genesis, where racist meanings have sometimes been read into the text, the Bible absolutely condemns racism.

● Christians and Jews are told to treat members of other races as their neighbour, to love them as they love themselves, and to recognise that they too are made in the image of God.

Practice examination questions

1. **a)** Describe what is meant by a 'liberal' approach to the Bible. (33 marks)
   b) To what extent is a liberal approach helpful for the modern Christian? (17 marks)

Guide

In part (a), you need to be able to distinguish a liberal approach to the Bible from other kinds of approach, such as a fundamentalist or a traditional view. You might be able to give specific examples of scholars, such as Bultmann or the writers of 'The Myth of God Incarnate', in order to illustrate the points you make. Remember that here, you are being asked to describe, rather than evaluate, so you only need to explain this position. In part (b), you are asked for your evaluation, and you need to be able to point out the strengths and weaknesses of holding this kind of view.

2. **a)** Describe the ways in which women are regarded by the writers of the New Testament. (33 marks)
   b) How fair is the claim that in the New Testament, women are seen as the 'weaker sex'? (17 marks)

Guide

In your answer to part (a), you should aim to give specific examples from Biblical texts, rather than just writing generally about the patriarchal society of the New Testament. Remember that the New Testament presents different attitudes; Luke, for example, does not seem to hold the same views as Paul about the proper place of women in Christian life. In part (b), you should evaluate the idea that women are the weaker sex in the New Testament, by considering how fair the term 'weaker' really is as a summary of New Testament attitudes. Probably some writers did think that women were weaker, and used this as a reason for suggesting that they kept quiet in church, but other examples might be used to show an understanding of women as having their own strengths.

3. **a)** Describe the attitudes of Biblical writers towards the use of violence in times of war. (33 marks)
b) 'Pacifism does not feature in Old Testament teaching.' Discuss. (17 marks)

Guide

Part (a) asks for a display of understanding of different attitudes, so you should make sure that you show you realise that there are different views expressed. You should aim to give specific examples. You do not need to have memorised and be able to repeat large chunks of text, but you should know the material well enough to be able to refer to it with confidence. If you cannot remember the exact chapter and verse, just say 'in Exodus' rather than leaving out the example altogether. In part (b), you need to think about whether pacifism is an entirely New Testament concept, or whether there are elements of it in the Old Testament as well. Again, you need to show a thorough understanding of the texts you have considered, and be able to use them in support of your argument.

Suggestions for further reading

Use any Bible commentaries available, to add more detail to your knowledge of these examples.

Re-visiting GCSE textbooks on Christian attitudes to moral and social issues could provide an extra source of appropriate Biblical material.

Books which take a literal interpretation of the Bible include:
Henry Morris, *The Genesis Record* (Baker Book House, 1976)
James Barr, *The Scope and Authority of the Bible* (Xpress Reprints, 1993)
Wilfred Cantwell Smith, *What is Scripture?* (SCM Press, 1993)

6 Eastern Religions

Hinduism

KEYWORDS

dharma – this is often translated as 'religious duty' or 'natural law', but it is a word without a direct English translation

monism – the belief that essentially, all things are One, and that all the different things that can be seen in the world are aspects of the same reality

monotheism – the belief that there is only one God

pantheism – the belief that there is no real distinction between God and the universe

polytheism – the belief that there are many different gods, or deities

rta – an early version of dharma, found in the Vedas; the eternal, natural laws of the universe

sanatanadharma – eternal, imperishable religion, everlasting truth. Hindus often prefer this term to 'Hinduism'

smriti – literally, 'that which is heard'

sruti – literally, 'that which is remembered'

1 The origins of Hinduism

Most religions can easily trace their origins back to a particular founder or to an event at a specific time in history, but Hinduism cannot pinpoint its origins in the same way. Hinduism is probably the very oldest living religion, and has gradually evolved and developed into the shape that it has today over many hundreds of years, not from a single leader but from a very ancient and remarkable culture: the Indus valley civilisation.

a) Archaeologists in the Indus Valley

Evidence of this vast and complex civilisation was first brought to the attention of the public in 1924, when Sir John Marshall wrote about his new archaeological project in the 'Illustrated London News'. While exploring the remains of some Buddhist sites of pilgrimage, Marshall, together with R. D. Bannerjee, found to their astonishment that they had uncovered the remains of an entire urban culture, built on the flood plains of the Indus river in what is now Pakistan.

Archaeologists have a tradition of naming their discoveries after the site at which they were first found, so when the first discoveries of this culture were made, it was called the Indus Valley civilisation, although it did not exist only in the area surrounding the great River Indus (from which the name 'Hindu' derives) but extended far beyond it. Evidence of the civilisation has been found on the alluvial plains of other rivers, covering an area estimated to be larger than Western Europe – some scholars therefore refer to it is the Harappan civilisation, using the name of one of the great cities (Harappa). So far more than twelve hundred Indus villages, towns and cities have been discovered, in India, Pakistan and Afghanistan. Many of these have not yet been excavated, and much remains to be learned about the people who lived there.

The archaeological work in the Indus Valley has been interrupted many times; Marshall's original excavations came to a halt when Marshall himself was no longer able to carry on. He was the sort of man who was a very inspiring leader, filling others with enthusiasm for the project. However, he found delegating tasks to other people more difficult; and when he was no longer able to work as an archaeologist, the project had no leadership, lost momentum and finally ground to a halt. The Second World War subsequently meant that there were no men to do the work and there was no money for it. After the Second World War, excavations began again, this time under the leadership of Sir Mortimer Wheeler. He was a well-known figure in British archaeology, renowned for his success with women and his splendid moustaches. He succeeded in bringing far more meticulous methods to the archaeologists at work on the site than they had ever used before, and also made the work of archaeologists more popular with the public, as he frequently appeared on television in its early days and was even voted 'Television Personality of the Year'. However, although he was such a popular figure, and is still much admired for his methods, some aspects of his work are now treated with considerable caution. Modern scholars are less keen to draw the confident conclusions that Wheeler drew, making links and parallels between Indus valley religion and the religion of Hindus today; although Wheeler readily recognised the dangers of reading too much into discoveries, he nevertheless enthusiastically found elements of primitive Hinduism in many of the items uncovered, whereas modern researchers are more cautious.

The work of uncovering the culture of the Indus Valley continues; major archaeological projects led by renowned scholars such as Jonathan Mark Kenoyer are piecing together the evidence as it is unearthed, and gradually coming to a greater understanding of the lives and beliefs of the people who once prospered in an area which is now barren desert.

b) Indus Valley society

The Indus valley civilisation flourished for about fifteen hundred years, sometime between 3000 and 1500 BCE. Three major sites of interest have so far been found, at Mohenjodaro in Sind, Harappa in the Punjab, and Ganweriwala in Bahawalpur. Ganweriwala is a relatively new discovery and is largely unexcavated, but Mohenjodaro and Harappa have been studied since the first discoveries in the 1920s, and many interesting theories have been produced about the ways in which the Indus people lived, and the religious beliefs which they might have held.

The society of the Indus valley, as far as we can tell, was highly organised and had its basis in agriculture; the people grew wheat, barley, dates, sesame, melons, and the earliest known examples of cotton. The large towns of Mohenjodaro and Harappa are built on a grid system, with straight roads running north to south and east to west, suggesting that, unlike the towns of Ancient Egypt and Mesopotamia with their winding streets, they were planned before being built as a whole, instead of growing gradually: the earliest known examples of town planning. The roads and the lanes were made to precise measurements, and the buildings, some of which were multi-storey, were made of kiln-fired bricks of a uniform size and shape. There were staircases to the upper floors and the roof, and a bathroom in each house. Alleys, onto which many of the houses opened, separated the streets. On street corners were single-room buildings, possibly housing watchmen who patrolled the streets at night. There was an organised drainage system, with inspection holes, linked with even the humblest of the houses, and there were plenty of public wells. All of these features suggest that this was a highly sophisticated culture, with central organisation and specialist workers.

At the western end of each of the cities of Mohenjodaro and Harappa were huge citadels, artificially raised from the rest of the town on platforms of bricks. These citadels housed the public buildings, and had massive walls, bastions and towers, implying that there were soldiers to defend them. There is evidence of substantial structures which were once thought by scholars such as Mortimer Wheeler and Jacquetta Hawkes to be granaries, the early equivalent of the state treasury; more recently, doubt has been cast on this because no trace of grain can be found between the bricks of the walls. Whatever the buildings were used for, they clearly had great significance, as they occupy a prominent place in the town and were given special defences. Some buildings have been found which may have been used as temples, but this is not obvious, and they do not form a predominant feature of the cities. At Mohenjodaro there is a structure which is likely to have been an artificial pool of some kind, waterproofed and with broad flights of steps leading down at either end, and next to it, a very long building with a courtyard, verandas and a row of cell-like rooms. Possibly this had some kind of religious function, and could have been used for purification, as there are many examples today in India of sacred bathing places. Perhaps the long building was a monastery or a religious college of some kind; maybe the little cells were used for meditation. Scholars have suggested that the Great Bath might have formed a focal point for the religion of the Indus Valley people – whatever it was used for, it is a wonderful example of early engineering skills. The long life-span of the Indus Valley towns and cities shows that there must have been an availability of resources, and a well-structured system of trade with neighbouring peoples.

c) Indus Valley seals and figurines

Some of the most important findings in the Indus Valley have not been large impressive buildings, but much smaller objects and artefacts. In particular, a large number of decorated seals have been found, as well as small figurines, and these have attracted a lot of attention from scholars. Indus metal-workers were not very skilled, but the potters were far more competent, even experimenting with glazes; many of the seals and figurines were made from terracotta.

The designs on the seals include a wide range of animals, which give archaeologists some idea of the kinds which lived in the Indus Valley at the time, or which the inhabitants knew about through trade associations. The animals are almost always accompanied by some writing. Most popular of all is an ox-like animal with a single horn, or perhaps it is a way of drawing a two-horned animal in strict profile. In front of the animal is a strange object which continues to puzzle scholars; it looks like a bowl or table-top on top of a pole. Perhaps it was a feeding manger for the animal; or possibly it could have been an incense holder or a torch of some kind; or perhaps it was some kind of filter used for the preparation of the intoxicating drink soma. One seal found in Mohenjodaro portrays this 'unicorn' being carried in procession, which suggests ritual and a religious element. The short-horned bull is another popular representation on the seals, but many other animals have also been depicted, including tigers, elephants, crocodiles, scorpions and antelopes. Some of the animals are composite, which gives strength to the idea that there was a religious or mythical significance to them; for example, a man's face with the trunk and tusks of an elephant, a bull's horns, the front of a ram and the hindquarters of a tiger. It is possible that these creatures were early representations of Hindu ideas: for example, a seal showing an eagle or vulture in conjunction with a snake could anticipate Garuda, an eagle who is a vehicle of Vishnu and who flies with a snake in his beak. The bull could be an early example of Nandi, the vehicle and emblem of Siva, and the tiger could be associated with an early form of the goddess Durga, but these associations are not certain.

A few seals are carved with a three-faced figure, probably a god, with a huge horned headdress, seated on a low stool with the soles of his feet together in a yoga-like posture, his hands resting lightly on his knees. He is surrounded by animals: a tiger, an elephant, a rhinoceros, a buffalo and two deer or goats, all animals which appear on other seals and perhaps were objects of worship. This image has been suggested by many scholars to be an early version of the god Siva, in his aspect as Lord of the Beasts (Pasupati); Wheeler suggested that there may have been larger representations used in Indus temples.

The seals found in the Indus Valley may contain clues to the beliefs of the earliest Hindus.

Many terracotta figurines have been discovered of an almost nude female with a necklace and an elaborately plaited hairstyle, made of rolled 'sausages' of clay. Some are pregnant, and some carrying a child. These have often been assumed to reflect some kind of mother goddess belief, but the seals and buildings do not have any obvious mother goddess elements, and the figurines themselves do not have all the typical elements of a fertility symbol. These figurines exist in large quantities, and are crudely made, which suggests mass production and perhaps that most households had them as part of some kind of domestic cult; maybe they stood in little household shrines and were believed to bring prosperity, fertility and protection. Some have suggested the possibility of a link with the goddess Lakshmi.

d) Interpreting Indus Valley religion

The religious beliefs of the people of the Indus Valley are still something of a mystery. Objects have been discovered which seem likely to have had a religious significance, and the Great Bath might well have been used for religious reasons; but it is always very difficult to look at objects and use them to work out what was believed by the people who owned them and used them. Objects alone will not be able to give an accurate picture of the true content of belief – perhaps there was more than one religion prevalent in Indus Valley society. Our knowledge of other ancient civilisations, apart from that of the Indus Valley, suggests that the religious and secular elements of life were not as sharply divided as they are for most of us today; ordinary objects used in everyday life could have had a religious significance as well as a practical use. There is the danger of assuming too much, and imagining that similar objects must once have been used in the ways that they are used today. We have our own ideas about religion, and there is sometimes the danger of interpreting evidence to fit our own preconceptions.

Added to this is the problem that many of the researchers have Western understandings of Hinduism, so not only are they interpreting the Indus Valley religion in the light of modern Hinduism, but also their understanding of modern Hinduism is coloured by Western ideas. It is, of course, impossible to approach any kind of study with a blank mind, and deal with it entirely objectively, but people are not always aware that they have preconceived notions which they then try to make the evidence fit. Archaeologists have to remember that they could be entirely wrong in their theories, and that they rely partly on the evidence and partly on intelligent guesswork.

However, it is difficult to look at the discoveries in the Indus Valley without drawing comparisons with Hinduism today. Animals and composite animals seem to have had religious significance; the 'standard' depicted on the seals suggests some kind of fire offering, and at a site called Kalibangan several 'fire altars' have been discovered; the Great Bath and the female figurines also are reminiscent of Hindu bathing rituals and mother-goddess worship.

e) The Indus Valley script

One of the major problems for archaeologists investigating the Indus Valley civilisation is that although writings have been discovered, they have not been deciphered and it seems unlikely that they ever will be, although more than a hundred theories have been put forward and the most sophisticated computers have been employed. Three and a half thousand specimens of the script have been found so far, with roughly 450 different signs used on them. Many examples of the writing are on seals carved out of stone; other examples are in moulded terracotta and on faience amulets (faience is a kind of porcelain-like material, made out of quartz crushed together with ashes and then fired – it seems to have been an important material for the Indus people). However, although there are many examples of the script, they are all very short, with an average of five signs each, and so far, no relationship has been established between the Indus script and any other; this makes the problem of understanding what the writing is trying to communicate almost impossible to solve. There are two main views among scholars about the kind of language represented by the script: some are of the view that it is part of a group of languages called Dravidian, and others believe that it is an early example of a group known as Indo-European.

There have been many enthusiastic attempts to decipher the signs, but none have been widely accepted. One of the most far-fetched ideas tried to show similarities between the Indus Valley script and symbols found on tablets in Easter Island, but it is highly improbable that there would be genuine links between cultures so far away from each other; and the Easter Island tablets have themselves not been deciphered; so even if there were a link, it would not be of much help to people trying to read the Indus Valley writings.

The fact that written records remain inaccessible to us means that many mysteries still surround the objects discovered. No large-scale statues have been found, nor any frescoes painted on the walls that might provide clues about the people who lived in the Indus Valley so long ago. The original findings of the archaeologists of the 1920s were not documented according to the meticulous methods used today, which also causes problems, when people can no longer be sure exactly where something was found. There are, then, many questions which remain unanswered: who used the seals, and for what? What do the carved and sculptured animals symbolise, and what beliefs and customs are indicated here? When and by whom were the great baths used, and did they have religious significance? How far can the Hinduism which thrives today be seen in the lives of these long-dead communities? Without written evidence, it is always possible that archaeologists may have completely misinterpreted the clues; perhaps, if the script is ever deciphered, it will completely refute everything which has been suggested. One scholar, **Gunther Urban**, writes: 'Far from finishing the Indus puzzle, we have hardly started to assemble the pieces.'

The Indus Valley civilisation was one of the most important and most interesting in the ancient world, and yet it is one of the least well-known. Most children of primary school age know at least something about the Ancient Egyptians, and there are many colourful books easily available about it; but relatively few people have ever heard of the Indus Valley civilisation. Perhaps one of the reasons for this is that a large part of the excavation of archaeological sites has yet to be carried out. Towns, cities and villages have been discovered but have not yet been explored; more than 80% of the area known to have been inhabited is still under the earth and shrouded in mystery.

Another reason which is sometimes suggested for the relative obscurity of this culture is that Hinduism has a different view of time from that of the Western world. In the West, people understand time as a line, and have a strong sense of past, present and future, whereas in Hinduism time is seen as a circle. Seasons follow each other, round and round, and so do the years; people are born, die and are reborn, and so time repeats itself. Possibly this is part of the reason why the history of Hinduism is not as well documented as that of other religions, because the sense of the past is not as strong for Hindus as it is for those with a more linear view of time.

However, this view is something of an over-simplification. There have been many Hindus who are very keen to show the rest of the world that theirs is a faith with a history. Particularly during the nineteenth century, when there was a lot of Hindu contact with Western missionaries who tried to persuade Hindus to abandon their religion and become converted to Christianity or Islam, Hindu reformers were keen to show that Hinduism is just as respectable as the religions of the West. Hinduism has its own enduring system of beliefs, 'sanatanadharma' or eternal truths, which have stood the test of time and which can be traced back through the centuries. There is much support from Hindus in India and Pakistan for the work of the archaeologists in the Indus Valley, because as they gradually uncover more of the mysteries of this great ancient culture, they show that the Hindu religion has a pedigree which is probably older than that of any other world religion.

f) The decline of the Indus Valley civilisation

The Indus Valley civilisation seems to have gone into a rapid decline somewhere between 1800 and 1700 BCE; the towns and cities seem to have decayed, slums developed, and eventually people abandoned first the cities and then the smaller towns and villages. Different theories have been suggested to explain this decline, and there is strong disagreement amongst scholars about what really happened.

● Some argue that groups of people known as **Aryans** invaded the Indus Valley in around 1700–1500 BCE, when the civilisation had already gone into a decline. The Aryans came from central Asia, and while some moved into Iran, others moved into the Indus Valley through the mountain passes of Afghanistan. They had superior skills in war and dominated the Dravidian-speaking Indus Valley people. The Aryans worshipped a fire-god called Agni, a warrior-god called Indra, and a plant with hallucinogenic juices, called Soma. The name 'Aryan' means 'noble'. They were lighter-skinned than the Indus Valley people, and when they moved into the area, the Aryans formed the higher social classes and the original Indus Valley people the lower. The combination of Aryan beliefs and the beliefs of the people of the Indus Valley became interwoven, and formed the basis of early Hinduism; evidence for the existence of these Aryans can be found in the Rig Veda Samhita, which is the earliest piece of Hindu literature. This point of view has been the one traditionally accepted by scholars for many years: **Kanitkar** and **Owen Cole**, for example, write: 'The Aryans were a people of European origin ... they entered India in about 1700 BC, and replaced the dominance of the Indus Valley culture with their own' (*Teach Yourself Hinduism*, p.155).

- Others, such as **Poliakov**, **Shaffer** and **David Frawley** are more sceptical about the idea of an Aryan invasion. Their view is that modern archaeological evidence does not support it, and that too much has been made of a comparison between languages; they argue that the Indus Valley people spoke an Indo-European language, not Dravidian, and that Aryan culture developed within the Indus Valley itself. These scholars point out that it is very unlikely that invaders would adopt some of the beliefs they found in the country they had invaded, and would instead have replaced them.

Whether or not there was an Aryan invasion of the kind traditionally assumed, it seems probable that this was not the cause of the decline of the Indus Valley civilisation; it had already crumbled, probably because of environmental factors such as flood or drought.

Summary

- The archaeological discoveries in the Indus Valley suggest the existence of a sophisticated civilisation and perhaps an early form of Hinduism.
- The buildings, seals and figurines give many clues about the beliefs of these people.
- It is difficult to know how much can be concluded from the evidence available. Many sites are not yet excavated, and the script has not been deciphered.

2 Vedic religion

Hinduism does not have a single holy book in the way that many other religions do. There are very many different sacred writings, mostly in Sanskrit, and some in Tamil, which have important religious significance for Hindus; but most Hindus will be unfamiliar with the vast majority of them, as Hinduism is not a 'religion of the book' in the way that Christianity, Judaism and Islam are.

The writings with the most authority for Hindus are also the most ancient, and are called the Vedas, which means 'knowledge'. They are 'sruti' texts, which means 'that which is heard'; this is in contrast to other Hindu texts, called 'smriti', 'that which is remembered'. 'Sruti' is believed to be an eternal sound, which does not come from any human source – it is eternal. This 'sound', or 'word', was first heard by wise men (rishis) from the Aryan culture, and then passed down from teachers (known as gurus) to their students, as the Vedas, in the holy language of Sanskrit. Sanskrit has patterns in its syllables which make it particularly memorable, and the words of the Vedas have remained virtually unchanged over many hundreds of years. 'Smriti' writings are recognised to have had some human authorship, and so they have a lower status although they are very much loved and respected.

In fact, although the Vedas are the most authoritative literature for Hindus, they are not the most popular or well-known. Many ordinary Hindus in India will be far more familiar with some of the smriti texts such as the Mahabharata, which contains the Bhagavad Gita, and the Ramayana. These are epic stories containing many exciting episodes which can be told as tales and dramatised to illustrate different Hindu teachings. The Vedas, in contrast, are usually studied only by Hindu Brahmins and people with an education, although parts of them will be more widely known because of their use as chants (mantras) in rituals such as private prayers, weddings and funerals, and at festivals. Hindus, then, are much more likely to know parts of the Vedas through hearing them and remembering them than through reading them.

a) The Vedas as sacred texts

One of the first things that should be realised about the Vedas is that the concept of 'sacred writings' is really a Western concept, suitable for understanding the Torah, the Bible and the Qur'an. The Vedas, in contrast, were not written down for perhaps the first thousand years of their existence; they were passed down by word of mouth, through a tradition of reciting, from teacher to student. The Rig Veda was not produced as a 'book' until the nineteenth century, and not by a Hindu but by a European scholar called Max Müller. The idea that sacred words should be written down and made into books is not Hindu (and therefore Hinduism does not have the rituals connected with showing respect to a book, which can be found in many other world religions). Many Hindus can neither read nor write, and the Vedas continue to be passed down by being spoken, repeated and remembered from one generation to the next. They should be considered, therefore, in the context of their use as spoken words, rather than as some kind of parallel to the Christian Bible, for example.

There are four Vedas: the Rig Veda, which is the most ancient and the most important; the Yaju or Yajur Veda; the Sama Veda; and the Atharva Veda. The Rig Veda is a collection of hymns in praise of the gods, divided into ten 'mandalas'; the Sama Veda gives instruction about melodies and chanting; the Yajur Veda contains the words to be used in sacrificial rites and the Atharva Veda has magical spells and charms. These four are divided into layers: the Samhitas, the Brahmanas, the Aranyakas and the Upanishads.

The Samhitas are the oldest parts of the Vedas, and when people talk about the Vedas they are often referring to the Samhita sections. These Samhitas consist of hymns to different gods, and words to be repeated in worship. The Brahmanas explain the hymns and deal with the ways in which they should be used in rituals and sacrifices, and the Aranyakas and Upanishads take the teachings of the other sections further. The Upanishads are particularly important in Hinduism; the name means 'sitting near', which suggests that the teachings are more secret, given to the student privately by the guru only when he is ready for them. The Upanishads deal with some of the most important areas of Hindu philosophy, including the nature of reality, the achievement of wisdom, and death and immortality.

People disagree about exactly when the Vedas were formed. Hindus traditionally believe that the Vedas are eternal; some Hindu mystics look at the astronomical evidence in the texts and place them at around 4000 BCE; modern scholars usually place their origins at around the time of the decline of the Indus Valley civilisation, perhaps somewhere near 1500 BCE.

In the Rig Veda, the universe is divided into three: the earth, the atmosphere, and the sky. Each of these three layers is inhabited by deities (gods), and most of the gods are related to nature: to fire, to the sky, to the sun and the moon, to the forest and the rain. There was believed to be a constant movement between the inhabitants of these three levels, with the deities coming into the world to help humanity, people making visits to the gods in order to receive wisdom, and so on. The hymns of the Vedas contain some wonderful pieces of poetry, and show that the early Hindus had a great sensitivity to the beauties of nature and also to its power. The deities required sacrifices to be made, or at least, the people believed that sacrifice was the appropriate response to deity, and these sacrifices formed a prominent part of early Hindu worship.

In the Vedas, the most important deities have different names from the ones most commonly worshipped today. The main deities of the Vedas include Agni, the god of fire, Indra, the warrior god of rain and thunder, Varuna the universal monarch, and Soma, the god of a plant which produced an hallucinogenic juice used in worship.

- **Indra** is the most prominent deity of the Rig Veda; almost a quarter of the whole collection is devoted to him, and there are many myths associated with him. He is described as driving a golden chariot, and being the force of thunder and lightning. Indra kills Vrita, who is a deity who holds back the waters and stops the rain from falling; because of Indra, water is released for people to use. Indra's face is the sun; he lights all three regions of the universe, and he is described as the 'lord of force', moving swiftly with his fiery golden horses. He is seen as a friend and protector.

- **Agni** is the deity connected with both fire and sacrifice; when the sacrifice is made, Agni consumes it and presents it, bridging the gap between humanity and the gods in an almost priestly role. Sometimes Agni is the god of fire, and sometimes fire itself; he is both great and humble, the sustainer of life and capable of great destruction but also a servant of people, being used in domestic tasks such as cooking and heating. He is present everywhere, in heaven as the sun, in water as lightning from the storm clouds, and on earth hidden in kindling.

- **Soma** is the deity derived from the intoxicating plant used in India and Persia for sacrifice; it heightens experience and is believed to give strength and immortality. The hallucinogenic effects of the juice give the worshipper a greater sense of religious experience. In the Vedas, the process of filtering the juice from the plant becomes associated with spiritual processes of separating the pure from the impure, the soul from the body, etc., and in some places Soma becomes lord of streams. The juice of the soma plant was often consumed mixed with milk and water, and the god Soma became associated with the bull and with fertility, giving strength over enemies.

- **Varuna** is only celebrated in ten hymns, but he is still considered to be one of the greatest deities in the Rig Veda. Varuna is all-seeing and all-knowing; he knows the paths of the birds, the courses of the ships, and the activities of all people and animals. He moves in the world and has an army of spies to observe everyone's deeds. He is described as the universal king, ruling over the gods as well as the world; he has a palace with a thousand gates, and a golden throne. He is lord of the sky; but perhaps most importantly, he is the controller of rta, concerned with moral behaviour, with weapons to destroy sinners but also with a merciful character. Varuna is the deity who gives commands not to kill, not to be deceitful, and not to gamble.

In the nineteenth century, scholars of Hinduism often portrayed the deities of the Vedas as nature-gods, and Hinduism itself as polytheistic, with different deities representing different aspects of the natural world. However, Vedic religion is not as simple as this.

There are certainly many different divine forms, and different aspects of deity and of human consciousness are symbolised in them; but in the Vedas, monotheism, polytheism, pantheism and monism are all woven together. Vedic religion does not fit into any one of these categories, but has elements of all of them. When the ancient writers praised one of the deities, they often addressed him or her as the greatest of them all, and attributed characteristics borrowed from an entirely different deity; and sometimes, the deities were explicitly identified with each other. In a hymn in the Rig Veda known as 'The Riddle of the Sacrifice', for example, the writer explains:

The wise speak of what is One in many ways: they call it Agni, Yama, Matarisvan.

In some ways, then, all of the characteristics of the different deities are representations of the Ultimate, or the Absolute. They are all different ways of looking at the same reality. However, at other times the Vedas give each of the different deities, distinctive characteristics and attributes. The question of the relation between the One ultimate truth, and all the different phenomena in the world (the Many), is one to which Hindu spirituality has returned time and again throughout the centuries.

Vedic religion, then, is not a simple, ordered whole which can be easily understood. Just like human life, it is all-encompassing, containing varied and often seemingly contradictory elements, and it is frequently expressed in riddles and unanswerable questions. It often seems as though the intention of the hymns is to perplex and to disturb the mind.

These ancient Hindu writings do not set out to answer questions, but rather to raise them. Mysteries such as the creation of the world, death and immortality, and the nature of wisdom, are considered from different angles and aspects, and are portrayed in myths, poetry and magic, to be wondered at, and understood at different levels, or perhaps not at all.

b) The concept of rta in the Vedas

From the hymns in the Rig Veda addressed to Varuna, it seems that ever since the Vedas began, Hinduism has had a sense of universal order, called rta. Rta is a word which is impossible to translate into English; it refers to a cosmic pattern, or natural law which is universal. Rta can include the physical laws of nature, such as gravity and the orbits of the planets, and also moral law, an absolute standard of right and wrong. Everything, including the gods, is subject to this law.

In the Rig Veda, Varuna makes regulations about moral behaviour and about natural laws such as the courses of the sun, moon and stars. However, this is not a deity choosing rules for the universe to follow, giving his own commandments; Varuna tells the different components of the universe that they are to behave in accordance with rta, and Varuna himself is subject to it. Rta, then, is an eternal order, not dependent on the will of the gods but governing their behaviour along with the behaviour of everything else. The role of the ancient rishis (wise, learned men) was to enable people to play their part in sustaining and re-enacting this eternal law.

c) Rta and dharma

Many scholars believe that the concept of rta is an early version of dharma, which is such an important part of Hinduism today. Dharma is an impossible word to translate into English: it includes elements of duty, of law, of righteousness, of right religion, and of eternal order. It is also 'that which sustains existence'; it is the very structure and framework of the universe. According to Hinduism, the world operates according to eternal, unchanging laws; and everything within the world has its own dharma, its own rules which apply and which should be obeyed. For people, these rules include moral behaviour and religious behaviour; there are rules which apply to everyone, such as not lying or cheating, and rules which are specific to particular roles, such as the right behaviour for a wife, or a student, or a trader. Dharma also includes following customs and traditions, and performing religious duties such as pilgrimage and rites of passage.

People who follow their dharma will gain merit, and this will affect their future rebirths. This is not the same as the Western concept of reward and punishment; behaviour is not judged at the end of a person's life, but is seen to carry within it its own consequences. Hindus see the world as an endless chain of cause and effect; people have some control over their own destinies, because they can choose which effects they want to bring about, and act in a way which will bring them merit, keep them away from sin and lead them to a better future. By following dharma, people know that they are gaining themselves merit.

Dharma can be learned in several ways. Most usually, within the family, through custom and example, a child will be taught the elements of dharmic practice which are appropriate for his or her social status and gender. Traditional stories and myths, such as those from the Ramayana and Mahabharata, also help to communicate the principles of dharma; these stories are repeated from generation to generation, and are remembered and often re-enacted at festival times. Dharma is also learned from a study of the Vedas, either from reading them or, more often, from hearing them read and explained.

d) The Purusha Sukta

The Purusha Sukta, as an example of Vedic literature, is a very interesting and important piece of literature for an understanding of the sacrificial beliefs of Vedic religion and for its influence on the development of Hinduism. It is quite a late hymn in comparison with many of the others, and perhaps does not completely reflect earlier society, but it contains many important ideas which have pervaded Hinduism from earliest times.

The Purusha Sukta is a hymn referring to the creation of the world, and showing that all of the universe comes into existence through one supreme power and the sacrifice of a great 'cosmic giant', called Purusha. Everything in the universe has a basic unity, because it all originates from this same source. The theme of momentous sacrifice is a common one in ancient mythology. The hymn begins:

> A thousand heads had [primal] Man,
> A thousand eyes, a thousand feet:
> Encompassing the earth on every side,
> He exceeded it by ten fingers' [breadth].
> [That] Man is this whole universe, —
> What was and what is yet to be,
> The Lord of immortality
> Which he outgrows by [eating] food.
>
> *verses 1 and 2*

In these verses, the all-encompassing nature of reality is shown, stretching beyond the bounds of both time and space. The Primal Man grows beyond the world, transcending that which needs food to grow or is the food (such as Soma) and that which eats (such as Agni); he grows beyond the world of immortality.

> This is the measure of his greatness,
> But greater yet is [primal] Man:
> All beings form a quarter of him,
> Three-quarters are the immortal in heaven.
> With three-quarters Man rose up on high,
> A quarter of him came to be again [down] here:
> From this he spread in all directions,
> Into all that eats and does not eat.
>
> *verses 3 and 4*

The hymn explains that there are different levels of existence, and that the worldly level is only a quarter of it; the rest is eternally existent, but linked with the human world as coming from the same source. There is no suggestion that the physical world is more real, or less real, than the world of immortality.

From him was Viraj born,
From Viraj Man again:
Once born, — behind, before,
He reached beyond the earth.
When with Man as their oblation
The gods performed the sacrifice,
Spring was the melted butter,
Summer the fuel, and autumn the oblation.
Him they besprinkled on the sacrificial strew, —
[Primeval] Man, born in the beginning:
With him [their victim], gods, Sādhyas, seers
Performed the sacrifice.

verses 5, 6 and 7

Here, the powers of existence, called the Gods, sacrifice the Cosmic Person (Purusha), and make his life-force the origin of existence in other forms. The world becomes ordered through this sacrifice, into seasons, which themselves are seen as parts of a sacrifice; the whole created order participates in an ongoing cycle where sacrifice continues to create and sustain the existence of the universe. It is not just a response by humans to creation, but is part of the whole creative process, and the gods take part in it as well as the people. (Viraj is the name of the female creative principle, which in later Hindu thought became known as Prakriti, an untranslatable term for material, energy and change. Sadhyas is a word referring to demi-gods.)

From this sacrifice completely offered
The clotted ghee was gathered up:
From this he fashioned beasts and birds,
Creatures of the woods and creatures of the village.
From this sacrifice completely offered
Were born the Rig- and Sāma-Vedas;
From this were born the metres,
From this was the Yajur-Veda born.
From this were horses born, all creatures
That have teeth in either jaw:
From this were cattle born,
From this sprang goats and sheep.

verses 8, 9 and 10

In these verses, the animals and birds are formed from the energy of the sacrifice, symbolised as the melted fat or mixture of sour milk and butter used for sacrifices. Also created were the chants, songs, rhythms and sacred words which have been passed down and used in worship ever since creation.

When they divided [primal] Man,
Into how many parts did they divide him?
What was his mouth? What his arms?
What are his thighs called? What his feet?
The Brahman was his mouth,
The arms were made the Prince,
His thighs the common people,
And from his feet the serf was born.
From his mind the moon was born,
And from his eye the sun,
From his mouth Indra and the fire,
From his breath the wind was born.
From his navel arose the atmosphere,
From his head the sky evolved,
From his feet the earth, and from his ear
The cardinal points of the compass:
So did they fashion forth these worlds.

verses 11 to 14

These verses have attracted particular attention because they show how Hindu social structure is seen to have originated in creation, as part of the natural, eternal order of existence. Purusha is divided into parts, and the different parts of the body have a higher or lower status; these form the different social groups, or varnas, present in Hinduism, from the priestly class at the top to the servant class at the bottom. Not only are the different groups of people formed from Purusha, but also the moon, the sun, and the deities; showing again that they all share an essential nature, as coming from the same source. The principle of rta can be seen here; the place of individuals in society is dictated by the eternal law of the universe.

Seven were his enclosing sticks,
Thrice seven were made his fuel-sticks,
When the gods, performing sacrifice,
Bound Man, [their sacrificial] beast.

verse 15

This verse is quite difficult to understand; Koller suggests that perhaps it relates to the music used at sacrifice, or to the practical elements of ritual. O'Flaherty explains that the enclosing-sticks were meant to prevent the fire from spreading, while the fuel-sticks were used as kindling.

With sacrifice the gods
Made sacrifice to sacrifice:
These were the first religious rites (dharma),
To the firmament these powers went up
Where dwell the ancient Sādhya gods.

verse 16

In the closing verse, the hymn shows the cyclic nature of sacrifice; creative existence is offered to itself, because it is ultimate, there is nothing which precedes it. The rituals which are part of daily life are seen to go back to the beginnings of time, maintaining the heavens, the world, and the natural order and social structures within it.

The Purusha Sukta, therefore, deals with one of the primary issues of Hindu thought: the relation between the One and the many. How can our experience of the world, full of many different people, different objects, senses, times and spaces, be related to the Ultimate, which by definition has to be singular? The mythology of the Purusha Sukta provides one approach to this question: all the many different phenomena of the world are brought into life by an eternal, cosmic sacrifice, and sustained by ritual.

Summary

- The Vedas are best understood in the context of their use as spoken words, rather than as sacred texts.
- There are many different understandings of the nature of the gods, or God, in the Vedas. Some of the Vedic deities are no longer worshipped; others seem to have evolved into other deities which are more often chosen today as a focus for worship.
- The Purusha Sukta, as an example of Vedic literature, shows one way in which Hindus have addressed the mystery of the origins of the world.

Practice examination questions

1. **a)** Describe the archaeological discoveries in the Indus Valley which are believed to be of religious significance. (33 marks)
   b) How far is it possible for archaeologists to be certain that the Indus Valley people held Hindu beliefs? (17 marks)

Guide

Part (a) is a test of knowledge and understanding. Aim to give as detailed an answer as you can, referring to specific examples of discoveries where possible. Notice that the question asks about the discoveries which are of religious significance, so you should concentrate on the seals, the figurines and so on rather than the town planning. In part (b), you need to show your evaluative skills, and demonstrate an awareness of the limitations of learning about belief from physical objects.

2. **a)** Describe how the Purusha Sukta portrays the creation of the world. (33 marks)
   b) 'The mythology of the Purusha Sukta is of little value for societies which do not practise sacrifice.' Discuss. (17 marks)

Guide

In part (a), you need to be able to summarise the main points made in the Purusha Sukta about the world's creation. If you can, give quotations from the text; you do not have to be able to remember long passages, but phrases are a good way of showing that you have read the text for yourself rather than just relying on your teacher having read it. In part (b), you need to evaluate whether the mythology of the Purusha Sukta is only of value for people who perform sacrifices, or whether it might have something to teach people today.

3. a) Explain the nature and role of the Vedas in Hindu religion. (33 marks)
b) How fair is the claim that the deities of the Vedas are nature-gods? (17 marks)

Guide

For part (a), you should demonstrate knowledge of the Vedas as sacred words. You should show that you understand their use, mainly in speech rather than as written text, and you should say something about the different Vedas and the kinds of writings they contain. For part (b), you might consider whether the deities you have looked at are just a 'god of fire' and so on, or whether they are more complex than this. You might want to look at the view that the Vedic deities are sometimes all seen as aspects of the same reality, rather than belonging to distinct elements of nature.

Suggestions for further reading

K. M. Sen, *Hinduism* (Penguin, 1984), chapters 8 and 9
Kanitkar and Owen Cole, *Teach Yourself Hinduism* (Hodder & Stoughton, 1995), chapter 8
R. C. Zaehner, *Hinduism* (Oxford Paperbacks, 1966), chapter 1
Gavin Flood, *An Introduction to Hinduism* (Cambridge University Press, 1996), chapter 2
Koller, *The Indian Way* (Macmillan, 1982), p. 42 f.
'The Purusha Sukta, or Hymn of Man', in *The Rig Veda* (Penguin Classics)

Buddhism

bhikku – a fully ordained Buddhist monk. A nun is called a **bhikkuni**

Buddha – Awakened or Enlightened One

dhamma (dharma) – Universal Law, or Ultimate truth; the teachings of the Buddha

kamma (karma) – Action. Intentional actions that 'bear fruit' and affect one's circumstances in this and future lives

nibbana (nirvana) – 'blowing out the fires' of greed, desire and hatred; a state of bliss, the goal of Buddhism

samsara – Everyday life. The continual round of birth, sickness, old age and death which can be transcended by following the Eightfold Path and Buddhist teaching

Sangha – the community or assembly of monks and nuns. In some countries, lay people can also be included in the Sangha

1 The life and work of Gautama the Buddha

The name 'Buddha' means Enlightened or Awakened One, and Buddhism traces back its origins to the life of a man who is known as 'the Buddha'; a man whose name was Siddharta (which means 'he who has accomplished his aim') and who came from a clan called Gautama in the Shakya kingdom of India. He is also sometimes called the Buddha Shakyamuni, which refers to his tribal origins, the 'sage of the Shakyas'; and sometimes as Tathagata, often translated as 'he who has reached the truth'. But although there are very many stories in existence about the birth, life and death of Siddharta Gautama, nevertheless there is little that can be known about him with any degree of certainty. The ideas attributed to him have had such a profound influence on the shaping of Buddhism that it is difficult to tell which of the stories are historically accurate, which are myths with an element of truth embroidered over time, and which are fiction. Scholars disagree about the time when the Buddha was born, and even whether he ever existed at all as an historical character. Many of the stories show the effect of the Buddha figure on the imaginations of his followers, rather than giving historically accurate and reliable information.

Most scholars in the UK, the US and India, however, believe that the Buddha lived in around 560–480 BCE, although the Japanese place him about a hundred years later. The first attempt at a coherent biography of the Buddha's life was not written until about 700 years after his death, by Asvaghosa, and was called the **Buddhacarita**; but of course it was written so much later than the events it describes that it has to be considered as a collection of stories and legends, rather than as an accurate historical source. Apart from this, other details and legends of the Buddha's life can be found scattered around in various different parts of the Buddhist scriptures.

One source which is popular amongst Buddhists for details of the Buddha himself is a collection of writings known as the Jataka tales. The **Jataka** tales contain stories of the various different lives that were experienced by the Buddha before he lived in the sixth century, and before he was enlightened. Although they contain little material that might be considered useful for an accurate historical understanding of the origins of Buddhism, they do contain a lot of important teachings and concepts typical of Buddhist thought, and they show how the figure of Siddharta himself came to be understood as a representative of Ultimate Truth.

Stories of the Buddha, then, have to be recognised as stylised accounts. The people who formed the stories and passed them down through the generations were not particularly interested in historical accuracy; it was the significance of the events that mattered, not how or whether they had actually happened. Teachings ascribed to the Buddha point out the necessity for each person to take responsibility for his or her own path of discipline. The Buddha demonstrated the way, but does not achieve enlightenment on behalf of the followers; they have to do that for themselves. To some extent, then, it could be argued that it would not matter if Siddharta Gautama had ever really existed, as the truth of his teaching matters far more than his historicity.

a) Stories of the Buddha's early life

The Buddha's father was called Suddhodana, and is often described as a king or a ruler of his region, which was in north-eastern India, near the Nepalese border. Because he was a ruler, Suddhodana would have belonged to the Kshatriya class of Hinduism, a person who had responsibilities for maintaining social order and, if necessary, fighting in battle. His wife, the Buddha's mother, was called Mahamaya, or the Great Maya, and she is said to have conceived her son in a way that was spiritually significant. Some sources say that he was conceived without any human intervention, and others say that although he was naturally conceived, his mother remained pure, and went through pregnancy and birth without any of the usual discomforts and pain. When the time came for the Buddha to be born, Maya decided that she wanted to withdraw from the palace into the forest where she could practise meditation, and so she and the king went to a forest grove called Lumbini for the birth. When the stars were arranged in the most propitious way, the child was born, miraculously out of his mother's side and without causing her any pain. He had already lived for many lives in the round of rebirth, and so by the time of this birth he arrived in the world already filled with wisdom and awareness.

His mother died seven days after his birth, and so he was brought up by Suddhodana's second wife, Mahayapati. He lived a lifestyle appropriate for the heir to the throne, with everything he needed, and was protected from the harsh realities of the outside world. It is said that he grew from a perfect child into a perfect adult, and married his cousin Yasodhara; they had a son, named Rahula, who was later to become one of the Buddha's leading disciples.

b) Encounter with suffering

Although Siddharta lived in luxury as a prince, he was aware of his privileges, and at the age of twenty-nine, he decided that he wanted to venture into the world outside the palace. Some stories say that his father the king immediately arranged for anything unpleasant to be removed from the route Siddharta was planning to take, and that the events which followed happened despite the king's efforts; different stories give different ideas of the extent to which Siddharta had been protected as he grew up. There are also different accounts of whether Siddharta's encounters in the outside world happened on the same outing, or whether he went out several times in separate attempts to understand more about the nature of life.

As Siddharta left the palace, he caught sight of an old man who could no longer walk upright, and he asked his charioteer what was the matter with this man; he was told that it was only old age, which happened to everyone eventually. He also met a sick man with a terrible fever, and then a funeral procession, with a corpse being carried and followed by weeping mourners. These famous encounters with old age, sickness and death led Siddharta to the realisation that suffering is inescapable, even for those with wealth and privilege. Fitness, health, youthfulness and even life itself are all only temporary. Finally Siddharta saw a monk, begging for simple food to enable him to carry on with his religious devotions, and was very impressed by this. He understood that there was an alternative to the life into which a person had been born; it could all be renounced, in favour of an individual search for truth and understanding.

The profundity of the effect of encounters with suffering on Siddharta is emphasised by stories of how he had been protected during his childhood. He was seriously shaken by his recognition of the universal nature of suffering, and the ways that it is inescapable, and he became resolved to discover the truth, just as the monk was trying to do. In the middle of the night, he left the palace and his sleeping wife and child.

c) The search for enlightenment

Siddharta began to experiment with different ways of realising the truth, by following the example of others. Wandering hermits were a common sight in his time, and he conformed with this custom, renouncing all his possessions and adopting a yellow robe to show that he was a monk. Along with five friends, he tried extremely ascetic practices, similar to those of Mahavira, the founder of the Jain religion. Siddharta went naked in every kind of weather and he went without food and sleep, in the hope that denying the needs of the body would bring him a greater philosophical understanding. This kind of behaviour is known as **tapas** in Hinduism; it is believed by some that peace will result from harsh treatment of the body. Even in Hinduism, however, this is usually recognised as being an inferior way of finding enlightenment, and Siddharta came to the same conclusion but in a more final way: it did not work. After six years of austerity, he realised that he was faint from lack of sleep, and close to starvation, but no nearer to the truth than he had ever been. Siddharta concluded that a life of luxury did not help in discovering reality, but neither did severe asceticism; the best practice was moderation, or 'the Middle Way', in which the body is given neither too much nor too little care. Sufficient food should be eaten, not too much and not too little; a person should wear enough clothes for the weather not to be a distraction, but should not become obsessed with fashion and finery. This realisation was a radical departure from the beliefs of most religious people of his time, for whom tapas was one of the recognised ways of gaining enlightenment.

When Siddharta had rejected tapas, he was still no nearer to finding the truth. He had become aware of the nature of **samsara**, the endless cycle of birth, death and rebirth, with countless lives which are transient and which inevitably involve old age, sickness and death, and he wanted to find a way out of it. Determined to discover the nature of ultimate reality and the goal of all existence, he decided to adopt the path of meditation, and sat down in the lotus position to meditate under a Bo tree in a small village called Bodh Gaya, facing the east. He was determined never to move from that spot until he had attained absolute wisdom. His followers later named the place 'Bodhinanda', or 'seat of blessedness'.

According to some Buddhist traditions, Mara, the enemy of truth and wisdom, set out to try to prevent Siddharta from reaching enlightenment. Mara is depicted in Buddhist literature as a kind of deity, a hater of spiritual and mental freedom, one who rules over the world of the passions and who encourages people to allow physical desires and attachments to keep them in the endless cycle of birth and death. He had three sons, whose names can be translated as Gaiety, Flurry, and Sullen Pride; and also three daughters, called Thirst, Delight and Discontent. Mara's sons and daughters noticed that he was concerned, and asked him why; he pointed out the figure of Siddharta seated under the Bo tree, and told them that here was a great threat because Siddharta was about to break away from Mara's influence, and lead others with him. Mara threw himself and his armies into an attack on Siddharta, trying to lead him away from his goal and back to a world of pleasures, but Siddharta resisted him, pointing out to the Evil One his contempt for wealth and privilege, not only in this life but in many lives before. Mara was forced to retreat.

In the month of May, when it was the full moon, Siddharta used his great meditative skills and put himself into a trance. In the first watch of the night, he remembered the whole series of his former lives, thousands of past existences. In Hinduism as well as Buddhism, memories of past lives are considered to be a sign of a person of great spiritual wisdom and maturity, and no-one can reach enlightenment without going through many different lives, as an animal, as a man and as a god. As he recalled these births and deaths, he felt moved with compassion for all living things and the ways in which they always have to leave everything they love and move on, never stopping, from one life to the next and the next. The first stage of his enlightenment, then, was a recognition that the world of samsara is totally insubstantial, and nothing in it can be held on to as truly real.

In the second watch of the night, Siddharta received a pure 'heavenly eye' of wisdom, enabling him to see with great clarity the whole world. He saw the ways in which all creatures are driven by the workings of karma, and how all deeds have their 'fruits', either as rewards for goodness or punishments for wrongdoing. He understood the ever-present threat of death, and realised that the endless chain of becoming and rebecoming is, like the world, totally insubstantial.

In the third watch of the night the Buddha meditated on the real essence of the world, and the twelve links of the chain of cause and effect, understanding how ignorance leads inevitably to old age, sickness and death. He saw the means to break this chain, through the practice of the Noble Eightfold Path (see pages 163–4).

Finally, in the fourth watch of the night, a great light spread into his mind, and he achieved Enlightenment; from then on, he was known as the Buddha, or the Awakened One. He understood the ultimate truth about the world and about the nature of reality; but although this meant he had reached **nibbana** (nirvana), he chose not to leave the physical world but to remain on earth in order to teach others. The Buddha in his capacity of an Enlightened One who chooses to share his knowledge with others, rather than moving immediately to individual bliss, is known as the **Bodhisattva**. The term is used for anyone who, having reached enlightenment for himself or herself, is compassionate and remains in the world to teach and to set an example. For seven days the Buddha stayed where he was, looking deeply into his own mind. Afterwards, he continued to move about in the world, looking like other people, but, as the scholar **Conze** wrote in 1951:

> this ordinary human body of the Buddha was nothing but a kind of outer layer which both enveloped and hid his true personality ... The paintings and statues of the Buddha which we find in Buddhist art, never depicted the human body visible to all, but they always try to represent the 'glorious body' of the Buddha.

Edward Conze, Buddhism

Statues of the Buddha often try to depict his 'glorious body', showing through symbolism his great height, golden colour and 'third eye' of wisdom.

The Buddha decided to teach others through the giving of sermons. He chose five ascetic friends, known as **bhikkhus**, for his first teaching, which is known as 'Setting in motion the Wheel of the Law', or 'Dharmacakrapravatarna', and it was here in the sermon given in the Deer Park at Varanasi (Benares) that he set out his explanation of the secret of the meaning of life: the Four Noble Truths.

For an account of the Buddha's earliest teaching, we have to rely on the Pitakas, or 'Baskets of the Law', which contain the nearest writings we have to the Buddha's actual words. According to tradition, these were written after the Buddha's death to settle matters of doctrine that were causing disputes among the early Buddhists.

d) The sermon at the Deer Park

The Buddha began his sermon by pointing out that there are two extremes that people might choose to follow. There is the life of pleasure, given over entirely to greed and lust and the satisfaction of the appetites; and there is also the life of self-mortification, or extreme asceticism, which is painful and leads nowhere. The bhikkhus were taught to avoid both of these extremes and to adopt the Middle Way, which would lead to nibbana.

i) The First Noble Truth – dukkha

The Noble Truth of suffering is this: birth is suffering; ageing is suffering; sickness is suffering; death is suffering; sorrow and lamentation, pain grief and despair are suffering; association with the unpleasant is suffering; dissociation from the pleasant is suffering; not to get what one wants is suffering.

Dukkha is a word which is difficult to translate. It is normally translated as 'suffering' but this is inadequate to express the concept completely. It does refer to pain and suffering in the ordinary sense, and so is the opposite of the word 'sukha' which means 'happiness'. But dukkha also refers to all things which are lacking in perfection because of their contingent nature and because they are impermanent. Change and transience are inevitable characteristics of the universe; there is nothing in the world which lasts for ever, unchanging. Objects are corruptible, and decay. Relationships always come to an end, however happy they are, because people do not last for ever. At any moment, however happy a person might feel, there is not perfect happiness, because the moment will pass and cannot be retrieved. So dukkha includes the ordinary idea of pain and misery, when people are aware of being unhappy, the kind of suffering that the Buddha witnessed when he saw old age, sickness and death, which is sometimes known as **dukkha-dukkha**, suffering which is obvious at first sight.

But as well as this, there are wider implications. There is also the dukkha which arises when people are aware of the difference between what they wish for, and what they actually have, the suffering that comes from the knowledge that happiness cannot be captured but will pass away. This is the kind of dukkha which gives old family photographs their poignancy, when sunny weather shown in the picture has gone and winter has come, or the children in the photograph have grown up and left home, or the friends shown laughing together have lost touch since the picture was taken. It is called **viparinama-dukkha**, the pain which always arises because of change. In recognising that nothing lasts for ever, a person recognises this aspect of dukkha.

There is still another kind of dukkha, which comes about because of human nature. According to Buddhism, people are made up of five **khandhas** (often spelt **skandhas** from the Sanskrit): matter, sensations, perceptions, will and direction, and consciousness. These five, in combination, make up each individual; but there is nothing else beyond this, there is not any special extra element apart from these. People are not indestructible; they do not have any kind of eternal, everlasting aspect which is apart from the body, which might be described as a 'soul' or 'self'. When people realise that there is no more to anyone than the combination of these five elements, they have come to understand **anatta**, the Buddhist doctrine which teaches that there is no essential, eternal and independent Self. The Buddha taught that it was the ultimate in foolishness to believe that there is anything substantial or enduring which could be disentangled from the body and which might live on after death. There are only the five khandhas, and each person is no more than the sum of the ways in which these different elements happen to have combined, for a while. When we think of ourselves as 'I', and imagine that we merely inhabit our bodies but in some way exist in an extra way which goes beyond our physical and mental characteristics, we are fooling ourselves.

Samkhara-dukkha, then, refers to the kind of suffering that is inherent in human nature. People eventually come to realise that not only are they witnessing impermanence, change and loss in everything they experience around them, they are also part of it; they too are part of the sequence of change, and they too are impermanent and will be lost.

The First Noble Truth, then, could be simply summarised: suffering exists as an inevitable part of the human condition.

ii) The Second Noble Truth – the causes of dukkha – Samudaya

The Noble Truth of the origin of suffering is this: it is this thirst (craving) which produces re-existence and rebecoming, bound up with passionate greed. It finds fresh delight now here and now there, namely, thirst for sense-pleasures; thirst for existence and becoming; and thirst for non-existence (self-annihilation).

The causes of dukkha, according to the Buddha's teaching, are craving or greed. People do not recognise that nothing in the world has an absolute reality. In fact, we observe processes, not real objects, and we imagine that they have a permanent core but this is not the case. Everything is impermanent and changing, everything which has had a beginning will also come to an end: the recognition of this impermanence is known as the doctrine of **anicca**. Because of the false belief in the substance of the world, people give worldly objects far more importance and significance than they really have, and they become attached to them. Suffering inevitably arises; the material things turn out to be impermanent after all.

The things of the world that we desire, such as wealth, health, love and pleasure, carry with them dukkha, because either we want them but do not have them, or else we have them but are afraid of losing them. Attachment inevitably brings about dukkha for these reasons.

The unending sequence of birth, death and rebecoming, with all of its associated suffering, is explained in one of the most important Buddhist ideas, the idea of 'conditioned genesis', sometimes called 'dependent origination', **paticca-samupadda**. Human life, and all other kinds of existence, is bound by a chain of cause and effect, where each link in the chain is caused by the one preceding it, and causes the next one, in a circle. According to the Buddha's teaching, it has twelve links known as the **Twelve Nirdanas**, some of which are difficult to translate directly into English:

1. ignorance (**avidya**) leads to volition (or 'will', or 'intention') – it is deliberate actions which give rise to karma, they bring about 'fruits'
2. volition leads to consciousness
3. consciousness gives rise to mental and physical phenomena (the body and mentality)
4. mental and physical phenomena bring about the 'six faculties' (the five senses, plus the mind)
5. the six faculties cause engagement with the world, through experience
6. experience gives rise to feeling
7. feeling causes craving
8. craving causes clinging
9. clinging causes the process of becoming
10. becoming causes re-becoming
11. becoming and re-becoming, as a continuing process, cause growth, change, old age, decay, sickness and death
12. the effects of growth, change and so on bring about dukkha.

iii) The Third Noble Truth – the cessation of suffering – Nirodha

The third Noble Truth is quite simple to understand. Once a person has realised the nature of dukkha, and has understood the chain of cause and effect that brings it about, then the cure becomes obvious. A person must stop craving for the insubstantial things of the world, and must detach from clinging to them, instead recognising them for what they really are. Once someone has succeeded in this, he or she will no longer be part of the chain of rebecoming. The way in which this can be done is not through extremes, but through the Middle Way, by following the Noble Eightfold Path, which is the fourth Noble Truth.

iv) The Fourth Noble Truth – the Noble Eightfold Path – Marga

The Noble Eightfold Path is sometimes known as the Buddhist self-help guide to Enlightenment; it teaches Buddhists how to put into practice the concepts of the philosophy. Buddhists stress that the eight parts of the Noble Eightfold Path are not steps to be taken in sequence, like the rungs of a ladder, but are to be followed together, and are all equally important, like the spokes of a wheel (which is a frequently-used symbol in Buddhist art). Again, there are terms used to define each part of the Noble Eightfold Path which are difficult to translate directly, and different English terms will be found in books on the subject.

1. **Right Understanding, or Right Ideas** – this refers to the intellectual grasp of the central teachings of Buddhism, including the **Four Noble Truths**. Unless a Buddhist has a firm and clear understanding of these teachings, enlightenment will be impossible. The understanding is not just an intellectual assent, but an ingrained commitment, which results only after careful meditation.
2. **Right Resolution, or Right Motive** – this means that a person should make following the Noble Eightfold Path the centre of his or her life. Everything else should be seen in the light of it. The Buddhist ideal gives a clear direction, and the Buddhist should focus the whole mind on achieving this aim.
3. **Right Speech** – this relates to behaviour as well as mentality. The Buddhist should aim to ensure that every word spoken is true, courteous, wise and kind. The key to Right Speech is self-control.
4. **Right Action, or Right Behaviour** – this encompasses all of Buddhist ethical behaviour, characterised by the Five Precepts (**Pancha Sila**) which are five rules telling Buddhists what to avoid. The first is the rule not to kill, which is extended into the general principle of **ahimsa** or harmlessness; in practice this means life must not be taken through anger, for sport, for personal adornment or for food. The second rule forbids taking what is not given, or in other words, stealing, and covers every form of theft in personal life and business. The third rule is against adultery, and also includes purity and sexual self-control. The fourth

demands abstention from all forms of dishonesty, whether deliberate lying or withholding of the truth or intentionally misleading through inaccuracy, gossip or exaggeration. The fifth precept forbids the use of alcohol and other drugs, or anything which weakens a Buddhist's mental control.

5. **Right Livelihood, or Right Vocation** – this involves a Buddhist in following an occupation which is compatible with the Five Precepts. This rules out livelihoods which depend on war, gambling, prostitution, cruelty to animals, exploitation, and so on. In practice, some Buddhists find that the only lifestyle which enables them to follow this part of the Noble Eightfold Path adequately is the life of a monk.

6. **Right Effort** – this part stresses the need for the Buddhist not to be satisfied with the progress made so far, and not to be lazy, but to keep working towards the cultivation of unselfishness, charity and goodwill. The Buddhist should be zealous, determined and persevering; Right Effort involves the best use of a person's energies.

7. **Right Mindfulness** – with the understanding of the Four Noble Truths, and self-control of the body, the Buddhist will begin to achieve control of the mind. It involves the art of concentration, in order to avoid looking at the superficial appearance of things and to see them as they really are. Through practice, the Buddhist learns to put aside distractions and control his or her own mind, rather than being controlled by it.

8. **Right Meditation** – this is the most difficult term to translate (**dhyana**). It involves the development of inward concentration so that the individual is in a state of rapture, still able to observe and reflect upon life, but detached from it.

A follower of the Noble Eightfold Path would aim to be rid of all desires and cravings, and to live a morally pure life, in thought as well as in actions. In this way, nothing would be done that gave rise to karmic fruits, the chain of cause and effect would be broken, and the individual's involvement in the cycle of birth, death and rebirth would be brought to an end.

e) Buddhism as pessimistic

If the Buddha had taught only the fact of the existence of suffering as a universal condition, then Buddhism would have been a profoundly pessimistic philosophy; and indeed, some people think that it is. It might be seen as a way of thinking that over-emphasises the dark side of life. It might be true that happiness and pleasure are only transient and pass quickly away, but pain and misery also pass. Many of us manage to enjoy life in spite of the difficulties that we need to overcome and the losses that we face, and would want to agree with Tennyson:

'Tis better to have loved and lost, than never to have loved at all.

'In Memoriam'

In the end, perhaps, the good outweighs the bad, and a view of life which concentrates on the belief that for every silver lining, there is a cloud, might appear unnecessarily gloomy. The Indian scholar **Radhakrishnan** writes:

> In the whole history of thought no-one has painted the misery of human existence in blacker colours and with more feeling than the Buddha.

Sri Radhakrishnan, *Indian Philosophy*

But Buddhists frequently describe themselves as 'neither optimistic nor pessimistic, but realistic'. Rather than basing their hopes on false ideas of eternal souls, they recognise the world for what it is. Other people delude themselves and try to protect themselves from facing the facts by pretending that the world is not so bad after all. Confronting the fact of suffering is difficult, but necessary. The Buddha did not just draw attention to dukkha, but offered a way out of it, by looking at the causes of dukkha, and the methods by which it can be ended. Sometimes the analogy is made between the Buddha and a doctor; the diagnosis of dukkha is made, but then a treatment is proposed. Pessimism stifles the opportunity for hope, but the Buddha preached a positive message.

f) The end of the Buddha's life

The first **bhikkus**, who were the pupils of the Buddha, accepted his teachings enthusiastically and were ordained as members of the **Sangha**, the Buddhist monastic order. They became **arhats**, or 'perfected ones', taught others, and the number of disciples grew. The most famous, whom the Buddha personally admitted into the monastic order, were Sariputta and Mogallana; and amongst others, a favourite was Ananda, Buddha's cousin.

At his father's request, Buddha went back to visit the palace in which he had grown up. He had left it twelve years before as a prince, and now he returned as a beggar. The Buddha welcomed his father and stepmother and all of their household into the Buddhist community; but his wife, Yasodhara, would not come out to see him. She said that if Siddharta found anything of virtue in her, he would come in to meet her, and then she would worship him. With his two chief disciples, the Buddha went into her apartment, where she fell at his feet in adoration. Women were accepted from the first, although with some hesitation, and formed themselves into a community of nuns called **bhikkunis**.

Large numbers of the Buddha's clansmen became his followers, and monasteries were built for him and his followers in many of the important cities of the Ganges.

After having lived as a missionary for nearly forty years, the Buddha realised that it was time for him to die and enter **parinibbana**. **Nibbana** is attainable by the living, in the world, but **parinibbana** is realised only at death. There are many tales and traditions associated with the death of the Buddha, and a version of the story is recorded in detail in the **Maha-Parinibbana-Sutta**, or the 'Sutta of the Great Decease'.

The Buddha travelled to the village of Beluva, where he became seriously ill; but he was determined not to die without preparing and training his disciples. With an effort of will, he recovered, and decided to live for another three months. He asked Ananda to assemble all of the local monks in the hall of Vesali, where he announced to them his intention to leave them, taught them the essential truths of his doctrine, and advised them to teach it to others, out of compassion for their fellow beings.

Tradition has it that just before he died, the Buddha had a meal at the house of one of his followers, Cunda the blacksmith. The Buddha became ill in the evening after eating this meal; some say that he was poisoned by it. In ancient commentaries on the story, the food is said to be pork, although this seems unlikely given the Buddha's doctrine of harmlessness to all living things. The Buddha told Ananda that he was to make it clear to everyone that Cunda was in no way to blame for his death.

The Buddha and his close followers travelled on to the Sala Grove and asked Ananda to spread his couch for him. He lay down on his right side, under the full moon, in the month of May (Vesakha). Ananda moved away from the others because he was weeping, but the Buddha called him back, telling everyone present of Ananda's devotion, and pointing out that death is an inevitable occurrence. Local people came to pay homage, and then Buddha spoke his last words:

> All conditioned things are transient. Work out your own salvation with diligence.

After a week, the remains of the Buddha were cremated by the Mallas people, in Kusinara. Arguments soon broke out about the relics, and it was decided that they should be divided into eight portions. A **stupa** (chamber for relics) was built at each of eight sites, and these have been places of pilgrimage for Buddhists for many years, although today some of them are difficult to locate. It is difficult to imagine that the Buddha would have approved of the cult status of these relics. However, the Deer Park at Varanasi (Benares), where the Buddha was enlightened, is one of the spiritual centres of modern India and enormously popular as a site of pilgrimage and tourism.

2 Buddhism in its historical and religious context

No new religious movement or system of thought comes into existence in a vacuum. There are always other beliefs around, and the new ideas are in many ways affected by them, either adopting the old ideas and giving them a new angle, or rejecting them and proposing something else in their place. When Buddhism began, the area of north-eastern India where it originated already had Hindu beliefs and traditions of its own, and these helped to shape Buddhism. Some beliefs were incorporated into Buddhist thinking, while other aspects were rejected, and the reaction against them also gave Buddhism some of its distinctiveness.

The time around the sixth and fifth centuries BCE was one of social change in India. There was not one large empire, but several different tribes and clans, with their own territories, and there were several languages spoken; Sanskrit was the language used in the holy scriptures, the Vedas (see pages 143–52), and was also the language used for worship. There is evidence to suggest that the rural, tribal society was declining, and that people were moving to the towns and cities to take on a more settled and ordered way of life. This led to all kinds of change, including attempts to discover new ways of understanding ultimate questions about the world, about the nature of human life, and about death and immortality. Many different sects came into being, including the Jains whose religion still flourishes today. It was a time of experimentation and clashing theories. Some, including the Jains, tried to find the truth through ascetic practice, denying themselves food and clothing in the attempt to find spiritual purity. Some became involved in complicated philosophical discussions. Some turned to atheism, and cast doubt on everything supernatural, while others tried to make sense of ultimate questions through ritual observance and sacrifice.

Within Hinduism, which was the prevailing religion at the time of Siddharta Gautama, the most powerful group was the Kshatriyas, who had the duty of forming governments and defending their tribesmen in times of war. The Brahmins, or priestly class, were also highly influential, as the people who were in charge of performing the religious rites and sacrifices that were so important for Vedic religion. Religious observance for the tribal societies tended to take the form of sacrifices to the deities by the Brahmins, in order to keep the gods happy and to encourage them to look kindly on people.

Not all Hindus followed a belief system that was focused around rituals; the teachings of the Upanishads were also gaining in popularity, and these included many ideas which were incorporated into Buddhist doctrine. The Upanishads are Hindu scriptures which follow on from the Vedas. Rather than dealing primarily with different deities and the sacrifices which should be made to them, they concentrate on more philosophical themes, such as the nature of the 'soul' or 'self', death and immortality, and the concept of wisdom. Some of the key ideas of the Upanishads, which were either rejected or adopted and used by the Buddha, include:

Karma and rebirth – the Upanishads taught that each deliberate action had an effect, or a 'fruit'. Good actions cause good 'fruits', and bad actions cause bad 'fruits'; if people behave well, then their good deeds will bring them rewards, and if they behave badly then they will suffer later. This is an eternal law of nature. The endless chain of cause and effect keeps people trapped in the cycle of birth, death and rebirth. Buddhism adopted this idea, teaching that desires and attachments to the objects of the world trap people into performing actions which bear fruits, and so they are committed to the cycle of the physical world.

Escape from the endless cycle of birth and death – according to the Upanishads, a person who gains wisdom can escape from the cycle of birth and death, by practising detachment from the things of the world. If a person performs a good action without caring about the fruits it might bring, then the endless chain of rebecoming can be broken. The Buddha adopted this idea in his teaching about nibbana or perfect bliss, although the idea of **nibbana** is not the same as the Hindu concept of moksha (release).

Dharma – belief in dharma is belief in following the right way to live. It includes morality, the way someone earns a living, the status a person should have and the duties that they are supposed to fulfil. Buddhism adopted the idea of dharma, but changed it; for the Buddhist, dharma is the same for everyone, and it refers to the teaching of the Buddha.

Atman, or soul – Hindus believe that each person has an essential soul or self, known as Atman. It is this which is carried over from one person to the next, when one dies and another is reborn. Atman is eternal. Buddhism completely rejected this idea. The Buddha taught that it was foolish and ignorant to believe in the existence of a soul; people will only become wise when they have come to terms with the limits of their own existence. The Buddhist teaching that there is no soul is known as the doctrine of **anatta**.

Summary

- The focus of Buddhism is that everything is dukkha.
- The way to escape from dukkha is by following the Noble Eightfold Path.
- Buddhism differs from Hinduism because it has no belief in an eternal 'Self' or 'soul'.

Practice examination questions

1. a) Describe how, according to tradition, the Buddha became enlightened. (33 marks)
b) To what extent was the teaching of the Buddha a reaction against the religion of his time? (17 marks)

Guide

In part (a), you need to be able to give a straightforward description of the enlightenment of the Buddha. You will need to include some of the factors which led up to this event, but should not spend too much time giving information surplus to what is required by the question. You need to make it clear that you understand what 'enlightenment' means, and that you are aware of some of the traditional stories. For part (b), you need to evaluate by making some comparisons between the religion at the time of the Buddha, and the Buddha's own teaching. Aim to show some differences, and also some similarities.

2. a) Describe Buddhist teaching about dukkha. (33 marks)
b) How far can Buddhist ideas about dukkha be considered to be pessimistic? (17 marks)

Guide

For part (a), you need to be able to explain clearly what is meant by dukkha in Buddhist thought. You could do this in the context of the Four Noble Truths, and you might want to give some examples from the Buddha's own life to illustrate your explanation. In part (b), you need to demonstrate evaluative skill, and consider whether Buddhism is pessimistic in its outlook, or whether it is just facing facts.

Suggestions for further reading

Walpola Rahula, *What the Buddha Taught* (Oneworld, 1997)
Ian S. Markham (ed), *A World Religions Reader* (Blackwell, 1999) chapter 4 – a collection of translations of Buddhist texts with some useful commentary.

7 Islam

KEYWORDS

animism – the belief that spirits inhabit natural objects, such as trees, rivers, the sun and animals

Hijrah – Muhammad ﷺ and about 70 of his Makkan followers emigrate to Yithrab to escape persecution

Makkah – city where the Prophet Muhammad ﷺ was born, and where the Ka'bah is situated

Makkan – an inhabitant of Makkah

Night of Power and Excellence – the first revelation to Muhammad ﷺ in 610, when he was meditating in a cave on Mt Hira

polytheism – the belief that many different gods or deities exist

Qur'an – 'recitation', the sacred text revealed to the Prophet Muhammad ﷺ

ummah – the community or 'brotherhood' of Muslim believers, those who accept the oneness of Allah and the true prophethood of Muhammad ﷺ

1 Pre-Islamic Arabia

The religion of Islam dates back to the life of Muhammad ﷺ , who lived from around 570 to 632 CE. He was born in the city of Makkah, in what is now Saudi Arabia.

a) Society

The Arabian Peninsula, before the beginning of Islam, was inhabited by tribes of Bedouin nomads, who moved with their goats, sheep and camels from one area of desert to another in the search for grazing and water. It was a dry, unwelcoming kind of country, with only a few cities situated on oases in what was otherwise largely a barren desert stretching for a million square miles. South of the Arabs was Abyssinia, an affluent and thriving society, while to the north were the Sassanian Persian (modern Iran) and Byzantine Greek cultures. Arabia was situated at an important crossroads for trade routes; there was traffic from north to south, between the different empires, and also east to west, between the Indian Ocean and the Mediterranean Sea.

The nomads made their living by trading from one another and from the people who lived in the oasis cities, such as Makkah and Yathrib (later known as al-Madinah). They also supported themselves with agriculture, and from a system of raiding the camel caravans which carried goods from the sea to market. This raiding was so much an accepted part of nomadic life that it had its own code of honourable conduct, where it was agreed that caravans would not be attacked if, for example, they came from an area where the nomads had relatives.

The society of the Arabs, whether they were nomads or whether they lived in the cities, was centred around membership of extended families. Several related families together formed a clan, and a group of related clans made up a tribe. Each of the clans within a tribe had its own leader or *shayk*, a family elder, and the clan leaders together formed a kind of council for the tribe, which was the nearest the people got to any form of government. More powerful families no doubt had a greater influence over the tribal council than weaker ones, but group solidarity and family loyalty was a very cohesive force. Tribal customs and an unwritten oral law kept the clans together and protected them against each other, so that rivalries did not escalate into full-scale vendettas. The most important and most highly prized quality for a tribe member was manliness; he should be brave in battle, honourable in his dealings with other people and loyal to the group. It was a male-dominated society, where the leaders were men and the line of inheritance was male. Men could marry and divorce whenever they wanted to, and women were treated as little more than possessions of their fathers, brothers and husbands. However, there is evidence that in some tribes, women were allowed a greater role, and could even hold their own property. Muhammad's ﷺ first wife, Khadijah, seems to have been such a woman, as she is said to have been wealthy and a tradeswoman in her own right.

At the time when Muhammad ﷺ was born, society in the Arabian peninsula was undergoing a period of change. The cities, although quite few, were prospering because they were in such important geographical locations for trade, and this meant that many nomadic tribes were attracted by the idea of city life and began to give up their wandering agriculture in favour of a more settled and affluent existence. Places like Makkah and Yathrib were growing in population as well as in importance, and this gave rise to the usual tensions that are associated with urban growth: a struggle for power, a widening gap between rich and poor, and a questioning of previously held beliefs.

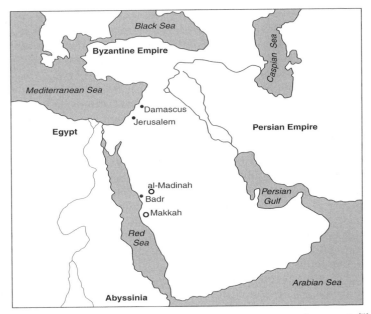

Arabia and the surrounding nations at the time of Muhammad ﷺ.

b) Religion

Most of the population of Arabia did not belong to any kind of formal religion, but the people did have contact with Christians, Jews and Zoroastrians, because of the large numbers of people passing through the desert, stopping in the cities and trading with the local people. Arabian nomads had polytheistic, animistic beliefs in a variety of supernatural forces. They believed that spirits inhabited natural objects; and there were also tribal deities, each of which offered protection to the tribe and was associated with sacred objects such as water sources and trees, the sun and the moon. These gods were treated with fear, and had to be appeased with rituals of sacrifice and pilgrimage so that they would continue to look after the fortunes of the tribe. There were local shrines for the gods, and also a central shrine in Makkah: the Ka'bah. This was, and still is, a building in the shape of a cube. In pre-Islamic Arabia, it was the place where idols of the deities were kept. Every year, there was a major pilgrimage to the Ka'bah, and as a sign of respect for this pilgrimage, raiding caravans was forbidden during the pilgrimage months. Many Arabs believed that there was one supreme god, which was the ruler of the others, the god of travelling and of the moon; this god was known as 'Allah'. He was believed to have three daughters, goddesses called Al-Lat, Manat, and al-Uzza. Arabian religion did not associate morality with religion; religion was about keeping the gods happy, so that they did not do anything which might adversely affect the fortunes of the tribe. Morality was an entirely human matter, and was practised for the peace of the tribe. There was no belief in life after death. The nearest that an Arab might come to being immortalised was to have his character and deeds captured in poetry, so that he would live on in tribal memory. Because poets had this power, they were feared and respected members of the community, but sometimes also viewed with suspicion, as also were the soothsayers, individuals who promoted themselves as tellers of the future and who were believed to have supernatural powers.

The empires surrounding Arabia at the time of Muhammad's ﷺ birth were not only more settled cultures, but they also had more formal religious beliefs than the Bedouin. The Byzantine Greek and Abyssinian empires were both officially **Christian**, and so they had a monotheistic culture, with a detailed, structured ethical code, corporate worship and belief in life after death and the judgement of God. They believed that Jesus was the incarnate Son of God, and that he had been raised back to life after his crucifixion. This was the accepted religion of these areas, supported and promoted by the rulers. Some Christians also lived in Arabia itself, having been attracted to cities such as Makkah by the trade, and settling there; but the Christians in Arabia seem to have been individual believers rather than whole communities, and there do not appear to have been any established churches in the cities. Where there were communities of Christians, they were settled on the edges of the Arabian territory, along the caravan trade routes where they made their living.

The Sassanian Persians to the north also had quite a sizeable Christian population, but the major religion there was **Zoroastrianism**. Zoroastrianism began in ancient Persia, and was founded by the prophet Zarathustra, roughly translated by the Greeks into Zoroaster. The sacred writings of Zoroastrianism are called the Avesta. The basic beliefs of Zoroastrianism include monotheism, believing in one God or Wise Lord called Ahura Mazda, who fathered twin spirits, one good and one evil. The evil spirit, Angra Mainyu, chose Lie, while the good Spenta Mainyu chose Truth, and humans too must choose between Lie and Truth, because at their deaths they will be judged and will go to heaven or hell as a result of their choices. There are also some similarities between Zoroastrianism and Hinduism; the ancestors of the Persians seem to have belonged to the same Aryan racial group as the people who lived in the Indus Valley at the time when the Vedas were compiled.

Although Zoroastrianism was a thriving religion at the time of Muhammad ﷺ, once Persia was conquered by the Arabs in the seventh century it converted to Islam, and today only a relatively small population of Zoroastrians survive; they are known as Parsees, or Persians, and live mainly in Iran and Bombay.

The other major formal religion with which the Arabs had contact was **Judaism**. All the areas surrounding Arabia had Jewish populations, and there were also Jews in Arabia itself. Some of the nomadic tribes associated themselves with Judaism entirely, as descendants of Jews who had moved out of Palestine into Arabia after the destruction of the Jerusalem Temple in 70 CE. There appear to have been many tribesmen who valued their ancestry in Israel as descendants of Abraham and his son Ismail, and who were familiar with the stories of the Hebrew scriptures. These were known as *hanifs*. The Jews, like the Christians, held monotheistic beliefs, and had a strict code of moral and religious behaviour to follow; although their beliefs about life after death were not as certain as those of Christians and Zoroastrians, they were certain that the judgement of God depended on obedience to his laws. There were thriving Jewish communities in several of the cities, including Yathrib.

When Muhammad ﷺ was born, then, it was into a society of religious diversity. Monotheism was well established, as were beliefs in sacred writings, angels, life after death, and judgement according to moral behaviour. Worship of idols was prevalent among the Arabians, as was pilgrimage and ritual. Islam did not begin in a vacuum, but against a background of different beliefs, some of which were to be condemned and others which were to be shaped and adopted into the Muslim religion.

2 Muhammad ﷺ

a) Muhammad's ﷺ early life

Muhammad ﷺ is the most respected human figure in all of Islam, both as the person to whom God revealed his messages, and as a role model. However, although a considerable amount is known about his life and actions after he was called to be a prophet, relatively little is known about him before this happened.

His family was part of the Quraysh tribe; this was quite an influential tribe within Makkah, although Muhammad's ﷺ own clan, the Hashim, was not particularly strong within the tribe. The Quraysh tribe had control of the Ka'bah and were in charge of the pilgrimages to it each year, and so they had considerable respect as well as a secure income from the pilgrim trade.

Muhammad ﷺ was born, according to tradition, in 570 CE, the son of Abdallah and Amina. Abdallah died before Muhammad ﷺ was born, and so his grandfather Abd al-Muttalib took over the care of him. When he was six years old, his mother died too, leaving him an orphan. It is difficult to know very much about his youth, because many legends have grown around his early years, just as they have about the childhood of other religious leaders such as Jesus and

Siddharta Gautama. One story, for example, tells how the child Muhammad ﷺ was visited by two angels, and his heart was washed with snow before being replaced in his chest, showing that he was not tainted by worldly concerns in the way that usually happens to growing children. Perhaps these stories are true, or perhaps the people who wrote them wanted to demonstrate their beliefs that such people, even from a very early age, were set apart from the ordinary.

Muhammad ﷺ is believed to have been fostered by a nomadic tribe as a child, living in the desert to grow up among the shepherds and learn a simpler, more wholesome way of life than might have been possible in the city of Makkah. Later, he was returned to his family, to live with his uncle Abu Talib, who was a merchant. Muhammad ﷺ learned his trade, travelling with him and meeting many different kinds of people from different countries. As he became an adult, he became a merchant himself, and was a business manager for a wealthy widow named Khadijah. She noticed the reputation he had made for himself, earning the nickname 'al-Amin' or 'trustworthy one', and was impressed; she made a proposal of marriage to him, and he accepted. He was twenty-five, and she was forty, according to tradition. They were married for fifteen years, and they had three sons and four daughters. None of the sons lived past infancy.

Although Muhammad ﷺ worked hard at his trade and was successful, he also took opportunities when he could to retreat into the mountainside for quiet contemplation. He was worried about the changes in his society and the tensions that it produced, and about the polytheism and worship of idols which was prevalent. He often went to a cave on Mount Hira, just outside Makkah, where he could be alone.

b) The revelation of the Qur'an

One night, when Muhammad ﷺ was forty, he received a call, described in Surah 96:1–5 of the Qur'an:

> Proclaim! (or Read!) in the name of thy Lord and Cherisher, Who created — Created man, out of a (mere) clot of congealed blood: Proclaim! And thy Lord is Most Bountiful — He Who taught (the use of) the Pen — taught man that which he knew not.

The angel called him 'rasul Allah', the Messenger of God. This was the first of a series of revelations made to Muhammad ﷺ, on a night which has become known in Muslim tradition as 'The Night of Power and Excellence', believed to be the 26th of Ramadan; the story of what happened is found within the Qur'an.

When Muhammad ﷺ returned home to his wife, he was very troubled, and confided in her that he thought perhaps he was going mad. He was afraid that he had been possessed by spirits, or *jinns*. However, Khadijah's cousin Waraqa, who was a Christian, recognised that this message was the same in origin as that which had been received by Musa (Moses) and Isa (Jesus). Muhammad ﷺ was not entirely convinced, and went through a time of doubt which lasted perhaps three years; but then he was overcome by a strange sensation. He wrapped himself in his cloak, but heard a voice which said: 'O thou wrapped up (in a mantle)! Arise and deliver thy warning!' (Surah 74:1-2). After this, Muhammad ﷺ recognised that he had been called by God and that he had an important task to perform, although he was very reluctant, and with good reason. Muhammad ﷺ continued to receive messages from God, over the next twenty-two years, and as he recited the messages, they were collected and written down to form the holy scripture of Islam, the Qur'an.

All Muslims believe that the Qur'an has its origin in Allah. The Qur'an was revealed to Muhammad ﷺ , not all in one go but in portions, as God chose, and the medium of communication was the angel Gabriel, or Jibra'il in Arabic. This began with the call of Muhammad ﷺ in around 610 CE and continued until the Prophet's death in 632 CE. In total, the Qur'an contains 114 chapters, known as surahs, which are of varying lengths; some have only three verses and the longest (the second) has 286. Although the word 'qur'an' appears in the text, it is not used as a title for the whole work; the word 'qur'an' means 'recitation', because it was originally recited to Muhammad ﷺ , who then recited it in prophecy, and it continues to be recited by Muslims in their daily worship. Muslims do not refer to their holy scripture simply as 'the Qur'an'; it is always given some other adjective, to indicate its incomparability and miraculous nature. It is 'qur'an sharif' – the illustrious Qur'an, – or 'qur'an majid' – the noble Qur'an, and, when translated into English, the holy Qur'an.

The exact nature of Muhammad's ﷺ role in the receiving of the Qur'an has been the subject of some debate. The Muslim historian **Ibn Khaldun** (1332–1406) was convinced that Muhammad ﷺ had not played any part at all in the shaping of the Qur'an: 'The Qur'an is alone among the divine books, in that our Prophet received it directly in the words and phrases in which it appears.' Khaldun draws a distinction between the Qur'an and other holy texts such as the Torah and the Gospels, which, he said, were inspired in the form of ideas in the prophets' minds during the process of revelation. The Qur'an, in contrast, is not Muhammad's ﷺ ideas based on his experience of Allah. Muhammad's ﷺ own personality and interpretations had nothing to do with the text: every word is directly the word of God, and Muhammad ﷺ was simply the channel by which it was given. Because of this, the Qur'an must be in Arabic, its original language. Translations of it into English and other languages are paraphrases, and many of the meanings and nuances are lost.

Some Muslims, however, have considered that Muhammad ﷺ had a more active role in the process of revelation. The twentieth-century writer **Fazlur Rahman** drew attention to the superior qualities of Muhammad's ﷺ character, and tried to explain how, through the grace of Allah, Muhammad's ﷺ consciousness was raised to the extent that, at times of revelation, it became identical with the Divine Word itself.

Some modern Muslims, therefore, consider that there is a human element in the Qur'an, but the great majority believe that it is wrong even to question the origins of this sacred text.

Although the Qur'an was recited to Muhammad ﷺ, according to most Muslims he was illiterate, and therefore he could not copy down what he had been told into writing but had to preserve it in his memory as it was revealed. Usually, the explanation is that some of Muhammad's ﷺ followers acted as scribes, writing down the different revelations on a variety of different materials; these writings were checked once a year by the angel Gabriel, but were not collected and assembled into order until after the Prophet's death.

c) Muhammad ﷺ as preacher

After Muhammad ﷺ was convinced that the revelations were real and that he should accept his role as the messenger of God, he began to preach. Like the prophets of the Jewish scriptures, Muhammad ﷺ taught of the need for people to turn away from evil and to recognise the existence of one all-powerful God, who would judge them according to their treatment of one another. He spoke out against the practices common in urban Makkah: the poor were being ill-treated and neglected, the rich were being greedy, and were lending money in ways which exploited the poor. Early converts to Islam included Abu-Bakr, a wealthy merchant, and Uthman ben Affan who later became a caliph. Some people reacted to the message with curiosity, and some were converted and became his followers, particularly slaves, the poor and women, who readily responded to the call for equality. However, there were also very many who saw Muhammad ﷺ as a threat. He was preaching monotheism, and this contrasted sharply with the tribal religion; his own tribe depended heavily for its survival on the revenue from the Ka'bah, and they did not want this financial security undermined by a call to abandon pilgrimages to worship the tribal idols. Muhammad's ﷺ message also included a call to recognise the brotherhood of *ummah*, a community spirit binding all Muslims, and this, too, was perceived as threatening the family loyalties and tribal ties that had held Arabian society together. The leadership of the tribes had always been something which was agreed amongst its members, according to the seniority and standing of the family elders, but now Muhammad ﷺ was claiming a special status for himself and attempting to take on a leadership role.

Muhammad ﷺ continued to preach in Makkah for nearly ten years, facing public opposition but gaining a steady band of followers at the same time. However, in 619 CE, his wife Khadijah died, and so also did the uncle who had introduced him to trading and supported him into adulthood. Muhammad ﷺ was left without the protection he had once enjoyed, and opposition to him began to become more sinister. Some of the followers went to Abyssinia for safety, and Muhammad ﷺ himself started to look for a new place to live where he could continue his preaching in safety.

In 620 CE, Yathrib, the city that was later to become known as al-Madinah, decided that it was in need of a figure who could act as an impartial judge, or arbitrator, between two powerful tribes who had become locked in a bitter dispute. Muhammad ﷺ was given an invitation to act in this role. He decided that he would do so, but he made certain conditions before he would agree to the move. His family should be allowed to move with him, and also his new converts; and they should be supported by the citizens of Medina, financially until they could settle and find their own means of income, and also politically. If the citizens of Makkah decided to continue their persecution of the Muslims and attack Muhammad ﷺ in Yathrib, the citizens had to agree in advance that they would take Muhammad's ﷺ side. With these conditions agreed, two hundred converts secretly emigrated. Muhammad ﷺ stayed behind until they had safely arrived, with his close friend Abu Bakr, and his cousin Ali, who was also his son-in-law. He heard that his opponents had made an agreement to kill him. Ali slept in Muhammad's ﷺ bed, as a decoy, while Muhammad ﷺ himself and Abu Bakr made their escape, hiding in a cave while a search party looked for them. According to legend, by a miracle a spider made a web across the entrance to the cave, making it look as though no-one had entered for a long time, and so the search party missed their opportunity to kill Muhammad ﷺ and his friend, leaving them to finish making their way to Yathrib in safety; they arrived on September 24, 622 CE. This emigration, or **Hijrah**, marked a new stage in Muhammad's ﷺ career, and is considered so significant that the Muslim calendar (the Islamic Era, Anno Hegirae) is dated from this time, as the origin of the umma or Muslim community. Ali, the cousin, stayed in Makkah for long enough to settle any debts and obligations, and then he too joined the Muslims in their new home. These Muslims who emigrated are known as **Muhajirs**, and the people who helped them to escape their persecutors are called **Ansar**. Both groups are treated with great honour by Muslims, and whenever during the course of history Muslims have been persecuted and forced to leave their homes for their own safety, parallels have been drawn with the Great Hijrah.

d) Muhammad ﷺ in Yathrib

In Makkah, Muhammad ﷺ had been under attack, a prophet giving warnings of the dangers of immoral behaviour, and preaching the existence of one God in the face of fierce opposition. In Yathrib, however, the situation was very different. He was no longer the leader of a persecuted minority, but was an important figure, the invited and appointed judge of the whole population, with the power to make decisions which would affect many. The Jewish population might even have been expecting him to be the messianic figure for whom they were hoping. He was also the leader of his own community of Muslims, those who had emigrated with him from Mecca (**Muhajirs**) and also those who had converted to Islam since his arrival in Yathrib (**Ansar**). Muhammad ﷺ had risen rapidly in status from a persecuted prophet to being the political and religious leader of a settled community. His renown was such that the city was given a new name: Madinat an-nabi, 'City of the Prophet', usually called al-Madinah. Islam began to acquire the characteristics of a formal social religion, with rules about proper conduct for daily life. Muhammad's ﷺ house became a centre for prayer, and later it was to be the mosque for al-Madinah.

The Muhajirs had at first lived as guests of other Muslims resident in al-Madinah, but it was obvious that this situation could not carry on indefinitely. They had to find themselves homes and some way of making their own living rather than depending on the generosity of other people. Some set up market stalls alongside the Jews; others set out to continue with the accepted custom of making raids on caravans. Muhammad ﷺ led some of these raids himself. They were usually failures, probably because the targets were tipped off in advance, but eventually in 624 CE a caravan from Yemen was successfully attacked and the Muslims gained the confidence to continue with this way of supporting themselves.

Muhammad ﷺ made a constitution for the city, setting out the responsibilities and duties of the citizens; he also made legislation to ensure peaceful relations with non-Muslim groups such as the Jews, who were recognised as belonging to the same tradition as Islam but who were, at the same time, outside the boundaries of Muslim community, *umma*. This document has been preserved, and is known as the 'Constitution of al-Madinah'; although the document we have in existence today is most probably a combination of earlier documents, nevertheless the main rules and statements are almost certainly those agreed between the citizens of al-Madinah and Muhammad ﷺ himself. Muhammad ﷺ had no immediate authority over groups other than the Muslims, and the Jews did not recognise him as a prophet, but as time went on his successes in battle elevated him to a position of great power. Muhammad ﷺ was determined to establish Islam as the guiding principle in Arabia.

Once the citizens of al-Madinah had become more settled and orderly, Muhammad ﷺ was able to concentrate once again on the city of Makkah. It was the most important city in Arabia for many reasons, including an economic centre, but significantly for Islam, Muhammad ﷺ had received further revelations which showed to him that Makkah was to become the focus of Islam, as a centre of pilgrimage and as the point to which all prayers should be directed. But although Muhammad ﷺ had been told this, the people of Makkah were still very hostile to him and his preaching, seeing him as someone who had turned his back on his tribal loyalties and undermined centuries of social customs. Hostilities between the Muslim ummah and the Makkans was exacerbated as the Muslim community from al-Madinah made raids on Makkan caravans. As the raids became more successful, more support grew for Muhammad ﷺ as a leader, while at the same time, the Quraysh felt more threatened by Muhammad ﷺ and by Islam.

e) The Battle of Badr

The Battle of Badr is of significance for Muslims, because it is seen as the first major military victory won by Muhammad ﷺ against his Makkan enemies. In 624 CE, Muhammad ﷺ led about 315 men on a raid, to attack a wealthy Makkan caravan, which was led by the head of the Umayyah clan of Makkah. The caravan was aware of the danger, and took an unusual route in the hope of avoiding the raiders, but Muhammad ﷺ had organised his followers to fill the wells with sand, and so the caravan was forced to go to Badr where Muhammad's ﷺ men were ready to do battle with them. Although heavily outnumbered, Muhammad's forces were victorious, losing only 14 men in comparison with their opponents' 45 casualties, including many people who were prominent in Makkan public life. Muhammad ﷺ and his followers saw this battle as proof that Allah was on their side and that Muhammad ﷺ was truly his Prophet. The Qur'an tells of how the soldiers had been driven by Allah, and how the battle was a test of faith.

After the battle of Badr, Muhammad's ﷺ newly-found support strengthened his position in al-Madinah and weakened his opponents. One group, known as the 'hypocrites' (**munafiq**) called themselves Muslims but appeared to have little real commitment to its beliefs and practices. The status of the leader of the munafiq was damaged after the battle of Badr, because Muhammad ﷺ took his new popularity as an opportunity to clamp down on the Jewish people who held power in the market places, and the munafiq had allied themselves with the Jews for economic reasons. Muhammad ﷺ, then, was able to capitalize on his success. He also decided to use the marriages of his daughters to strengthen useful relationships.

However, the Makkans inevitably wanted revenge for Badr, and in 625 CE, the Battle of Uhud was fought and was a failure for the Muslims. Their disorganisation was no match for the 3,000 strong Makkan army, and Muhammad ﷺ was wounded. The combined battles of Badr and Uhud meant that the Makkans were roughly even – they had lost men, but they had killed about the same number of Muslims – but this was not enough for them. They wanted to be avenged many times over for their losses at Badr, and so in 627 CE, led by Abu Sufyan, they persuaded some Bedouin tribes to join them, and assembled an army of 10,000 to mount a seige against al-Madinah. The Makkans were used to short and aggressive raids, but Muhammad ﷺ introduced a new tactic for which they were unprepared. He organised the digging of a trench all around al-Madinah, which stopped the attackers in their tracks. The Bedouin did not know what they were supposed to do, and the Makkans seemed unable to tell them, so the mercenaries dispersed and the Makkan forces were so much reduced that they withdrew. This 'Battle of the Ditch' is seen as a turning point for Muhammad ﷺ . His opponents realised that they were spending time and money that they could not afford on battles with the Muslims, and so they began making concessions and forming treaties instead. Muhammad ﷺ had achieved the upper hand.

f) Muhammad's ﷺ return to Makkah

Muhammad ﷺ did not want to overthrow or ruin the Makkans; he hoped that they would eventually become willing Muslims themselves, and join the ummah. The Makkans made concessions, in 628 CE, to allow Muhammad ﷺ and his followers to make the pilgrimage to Makkah that had been revealed as a requirement of Allah. Some of Muhammad's ﷺ enemies, however, broke this agreement two years later, and attacked, so Muhammad ﷺ organised the Muslims into a march on Makkah. The Makkans, weakened by a change of leadership and the conversion of some of their rulers to Islam, made a formal surrender, and Muhammad ﷺ was able to enter Makkah with hardly any resistance. Muhammad ﷺ could have plundered the city and killed his enemies, but instead he chose to act mercifully. He walked symbolically around the Ka'bah seven times, and touched the Black Stone, as a sign that Islam with the help of Allah had been victorious. Many Makkans changed their allegiance and became Muslims.

Muhammad ﷺ , then, had left Makkah as a persecuted prophet with many enemies, but he re-entered it victoriously. He and his followers spent the first days destroying pagan idols and shrines in the Ka'bah and devoting it to the worship of Allah. The next years enabled him to establish himself as the most powerful figure in Arabia. There were raids and battles with neighbouring tribes, but most recognised that it was in their best interests to try and form an allegiance with the Muslims, and many but not all converted to Islam in return for having Muhammad's ﷺ protection and the benefits of belonging to the Ummah. 631CE is known as the 'Year of Deputations', because of the way in which tribes sent deputations to Muhammad ﷺ offering their submission to him and their adoption of Islam.

In March 632 CE, Muhammad ﷺ led a pilgrimage to Makkah, although his health was beginning to fail. He preached his last sermon, of the brotherhood of all Muslims, and died three months later in June 632 CE. No arrangements had been made for his successor, and because he had been such a skilful and charismatic leader, his followers were left with a series of crises about who should have authority. The next years in the development of Islam were to be plagued with arguments and divisions.

Muhammad ﷺ had been a remarkable character, both as a religious leader and as a political figure. He is believed to be the best role model for Muslim life, not only as the person through whom Allah chose to reveal the Qur'an, but in his own life and behaviour he provided a pattern for others to follow. Some have argued that Muhammad's ﷺ polygynous marriages (he had several wives in later life) show that he was not a pure example to follow, but was keen on sensuality and more worldly than he appeared. However, in his defence, it has been pointed out by writers such as **Geoffrey Parrinder** that Muhammad ﷺ lived in a monogamous relationship with his first wife until she died when he was nearly fifty; his subsequent marriages happened for political reasons, to strengthen ties with the Ummah, rather than for Muhammad's ﷺ own benefit. Other men of a similar time and culture, including men of the Bible, have had similar marriages, which often happened as much for the protection of the women as for other reasons.

Muhammad's ﷺ combination of skills as a prophet and as a statesman has been the subject of much comment. Because of his political talents, he was able to win many converts to Islam, people who might otherwise have been content to stay with the customs and beliefs of their families rather than being prepared to listen to the message of the Qur'an. The combination of religious fervour and political astuteness meant that Muhammad ﷺ was able to establish not only a faith as a system of beliefs, but a faith community, with the strength and mutual support that this brings. The rapid spread of Islam after his death has been attributed to Muhammad's ﷺ own personal qualities.

Muhammad ﷺ reformed the religion of the people, encouraging them to return to the monotheism of their ancestor Abraham (known as Ibrahim to Muslims), to live a life of submission (Islam) to the will of Allah, and to have nothing to do with idol worship or superstition. The Jews and the Christians were believed to have corrupted the truth which they had been given, and had introduced their own ideas and woven them into the revelation that God had given them. The Jews, according to Islam, had convinced themselves that they were the chosen people, set apart from everyone else, and believed that they had the right to special privileges with God because of their birth – it was as though they were judging themselves, rather than recognising God as the judge of everything. The Christians had been sent a prophet, Jesus, but they had corrupted what they were told by making Jesus himself into a God, and not realising that there is only one true God who has no equal. Muhammad ﷺ saw his role as one of returning people to the law of Allah, as had been revealed to him. Although Islam has become a major world faith, separate and distinct from the other Semitic traditions of Judaism and Christianity, Muhammad ﷺ did not set out to start a new religion, but tried to reform and return people to the 'straight path' which they should have been following all the time, ever since Ibrahim.

Practice examination questions

1. **a)** Describe how, according to Muslims, the Qur'an was revealed to the prophet Muhammad ﷺ . (33 marks)
   b) 'Muhammad ﷺ was more important as a statesman than as a prophet.' Discuss. (17 marks)

Guide

In part (a), you need to demonstrate a thorough knowledge of the event. You might want to give some background information to set the story into context, but remember that your time in the examination is limited, so concentrate on the revelation of the Qur'an itself. In part (b), you need to evaluate, by looking at different possible approaches to the issue. You might want to give examples of Muhammad's ﷺ success as a statesman, and compare this with his role as a prophet; perhaps you might want to argue that the importance is different for different people, depending on whether their own interests are political or religious.

2. **a)** Describe the religious background of the area in which Islam began. (33 marks)
   b) 'Muhammad's ﷺ aim was to begin a new religion.' Discuss. (17 marks)

Guide

For part (a), notice that you are asked about the religious background, so, although the geographical context is important, you should concentrate on outlining the other belief systems that were prevalent in Muhammad's ﷺ lifetime, rather than explaining where different countries lie. In part (b), you need to assess whether this was really Muhammad's ﷺ aim, or whether he was trying to reform existing religion in some ways. Aim to give different possible opinions about this, and try to give reasons to support your own view.

Suggestions for further reading

Encyclopaedia Britannica – Muhammad, life and works
John Esposito, *Islam, the Straight Path* (Oxford University Press, 1998), chapter 1
W. Montgomery Watt, *Muhammad, Prophet and Statesman* (Oxford University Press, 1961)

8 Judaism

KEYWORDS

covenant – an agreement or bond made between two parties. In the Bible, it refers to the agreements made between G-d and his people.

halakhah – walking with G-d; putting Jewish beliefs into practice, living a Jewish life

kosher/kashrut – fit, or proper, acceptable to G-d

monotheism – the belief that only one true G-d exists

Orthodox – 'right belief'; Orthodox Jews are those who believe that there are no aspects of G-d's Law that can be changed or abandoned.

Shabbat – the Sabbath, 'to cease' or 'to rest', the day set apart from the remainder of the week to be a holy day, when no work is done

Talmud – the written collection of commentaries on the Torah

Tenakh – the name given to the Jewish scriptures, Torah, Nevi'im and Ketuvin

Torah – word meaning 'direction' or 'teaching', often translated as 'Law'. The centre of Jewish life.

1 Sacred writings in Judaism

Judaism is often described as a 'religion of the book'; it depends heavily on its sacred writings as a source of authority. According to Judaism, something of G-d is revealed in these holy books, because they contain a record of the words of G-d spoken to Moses, through the prophets and to other people who received direct religious experience. The holy books can be used to learn new information, to settle disputes, and to give an insight into the mind of G-d; they also give a focus of unity for Jews, because they provide a central, fixed point of reference.

Judaism has a vast collection of sacred writings. Some of them go back for thousands of years, and some have been composed in the fairly recent past. The oldest texts are considered to have the most authority, because they are believed to be the closest to the actual words that the founders of Judaism received directly from G-d. Later writings have interpreted the original texts, adding explanations and examples of how the teachings are to be put into practice; these, too, have great importance for Jews because they contain the collected wisdom of people who have devoted their lives to studying sacred literature.

Traditionally, Jewish sacred texts are divided into two: the written teaching and the oral teaching. The word 'Torah' can be translated as 'teaching', which could cause confusion, because it is used to refer to the Pentateuch (the first five books of the Bible), or to the whole of the Hebrew Bible, and even to the whole Jewish tradition of teaching, both written and oral. Torah is often said to mean 'law', but this translation does not do it justice, because the Torah contains much more than just laws. There is myth, history, poetry, and perhaps most importantly, stories which convey important messages about morality and about the nature of faith.

The Jewish Bible is given many names, including 'The Hebrew Scriptures,' 'The Hebrew Bible,' and 'The Old Testament'. 'The Old Testament' is a term used by Christians, but is not accepted by Jews, because it implies that there is other writing that stands alongside it in holiness and importance, an idea which the Jews reject. Jews call their scriptures Tenakh, which is a Hebrew acronym (i.e. using the initial letters) of the three sections it contains: Torah (Pentateuch), Nevi'im (Prophets), and Ketuvim (Writings).

a) Torah

The Torah, or Pentateuch, contains the first five books: Genesis – Bereishis, Exodus – Shemos, Leviticus – Vayikra, Numbers – Bamidbar and Deuteronomy – Devarim. It is the most important text in the Hebrew Bible; it is believed to have been revealed directly by G-d to Moses, the greatest of all the prophets. Moses is believed to have been given this teaching face to face, at Mount Sinai, in an awe-inspiring scene of thunder and lightning:

> All of Mount Sinai was smoking, because HASHEM had descended upon it in the fire; its smoke ascended like the smoke of the furnace, and the entire mountain shuddered exceedingly. The sound of the shofar grew continually much stronger; Moses would speak and G-d would respond to him with a voice. HASHEM descended upon Mount Sinai to the top of the mountain; HASHEM summoned Moses to the top of the mountain, and Moses ascended.

Exodus 19:18–20

Moses is traditionally believed to have written the five books of the Pentateuch, copying the words exactly as they were given to him. Many Jews reject the suggestion that the writings in the Pentateuch were influenced in any way by human culture; according to the traditions of the rabbis, the words existed with G-d from the beginning of time, and are perfect:

The Rock! — perfect is His work, for all His paths are justice.

Deuteronomy 32:4a

For many Jews, attempts to consider the different possible sources of the Torah literature are unacceptable, because the only source of these words is G-d. The words of the Torah cannot be altered in any way. When scrolls are written for use in the synagogue (Sefer Torah) meticulous care must be taken to ensure that there are no mistakes made.

The Pentateuch tells the story of the relationship between G-d and humanity, from the creation of the universe at the beginning of time until the death of Moses. The first human couple, Adam and Eve, are formed, fall into disobedience by eating the forbidden fruit from the Garden of Eden, and are made to leave into a world of hard work and pain. Noah stands out from his contemporaries as a solitary righteous man, and he builds an Ark to escape the flood which G-d sends to devastate the earth; he makes a covenant with G-d, and G-d promises with a rainbow never again to destroy the world. Abraham, the father of the Jews, is called by G-d and a covenant is formed with him; he is promised many descendants and a land in which they can live. The Israelites go to Egypt in a time of famine, and later are enslaved. G-d sees how the people are suffering in slavery, and appears to Moses in the form of a bush which burns but is not consumed by fire. Moses is commissioned to confront Pharaoh, and after the tenth plague, when the angel of death 'passed over' the homes of the Israelites and spared their first-born sons, the Red Sea is crossed. Moses represents the people and ascends Mount Sinai to meet with G-d. He is given the Ten Commandments. The people turn away from G-d and are ungrateful for their escape; they turn and worship a golden calf. As a punishment, they spend forty years wandering in the wilderness without a homeland. During these years, they are given the rest of the law, explaining to them how to keep the Sabbath and other festivals, how to maintain ritual purity, what to eat, and most importantly, how to love G-d and one another. Moses leads the people to the borders of the Promised Land, and then he dies.

The Torah contains 613 mitzvot (commandments), 248 of which are positive, telling the Jews what they must do, and 365 negative ('You shall not...'). The rules in the Torah are often divided between **ethical** and **ritual**.

Ethical laws – these are concerned with the ways in which Jews behave, particularly towards one another. For example, they are told how to deal honestly in business, how to treat employees, and how to avoid exploitation of the weak. They are told of their obligations to their parents and to the poor.

Ritual laws – these are concerned with the ceremonies and customs of leading a holy life, and include rules about worship, about observance of the Sabbath (Shabbat), about the right ways to keep the festivals, and about the kinds of food which Jews are permitted to eat and the ways in which this should be prepared. The ritual laws are not regarded by Orthodox Jews as less important than the moral laws, but are believed to bring an order and a rhythm to ordinary life, giving holiness to everyday tasks and to the passing of the seasons.

Many of the 613 laws cannot be observed, because they detail the duties of the priests in the Temple, which was twice destroyed. But Jews live in the hope that one day, the Temple will be restored and they will be able to fulfil all of their obligations.

The Torah is read in the synagogue in its entirety during a calendar year, in portions week by week on Shabbat mornings, and also on Mondays and Thursdays, because these were traditionally market days in Jerusalem where people could combine going to market with an opportunity to hear the Torah being read. The Torah is read in sequence throughout the year, except when there are festivals when a special reading might interrupt. The reading of the Torah begins with the first portion (parshah) on Simchat Torah, and ends on Simchat Torah the following year, where it is immediately begun again to show that the word of G-d is eternal. Some synagogues read the Torah on a three-yearly cycle, following a custom which began in Palestine, reading only the first section of each portion in the first year, the second section in the second year, and completing the third in the third year before beginning the cycle again.

The scrolls which are used for the reading of the Torah in the synagogue are written in a Hebrew text which does not give the reader any musical notes or vowels ('unpointed' text), and so the ability to read aloud from it is a very much valued skill, which takes a great deal of study and commitment to perfect.

b) Prophets

The Prophets contains the books of Joshua, Judges, I and II Samuel and I and II Kings (known together as the Early Prophets), as well as Isaiah, Jeremiah, Ezekiel, and the Twelve Minor Prophets (known together as the Later Prophets). These are called minor because the amount of surviving writing attributed to them is less in quantity than that of the major prophets, not because their work is considered to be any less valuable. Jews believe that prophecy is a gift from G-d. In common usage, the word 'prophet' often means someone who can tell the future, but this was not the primary purpose of the prophets of the Jewish scriptures. The prophets were called to deliver messages to the people; they acted as spokesmen. Sometimes this was about the future, explaining what would happen if the listeners did not change their ways, but often, the message was a comment on the present rather than a prediction of the future. In the Tenakh, the message was often ethical; the prophets were sent to warn that unless the people repented and turned back to following G-d, they would be punished.

The books of the *nevi'im* continue the story of the Israelites after they entered the Promised Land. At first, the people were ruled by judges, and then Samuel was called when he was still a child to be a prophet. When he grew up, he anointed the first king of Israel, who was Saul; Saul was succeeded by David, who in spite of his obvious imperfections was considered to be one of the greatest leaders in Jewish history. David was a warrior, and his greatest achievement was the capture of Jerusalem as his capital city. He in turn was succeeded by his son Solomon, in whose reign the first Temple of Jerusalem was built, as a focus for Jewish worship, festivals and pilgrimages. Solomon's death was followed by a series of corrupt leaders; the kingdom was divided into the Northern and Southern Kingdoms of Israel and Judah respectively, with ten tribes in the north and two in the south.

These two kingdoms were eventually invaded and conquered. The Northern Kingdom was the first to fall, to the Assyrians in 721 BCE, when the inhabitants were taken into exile, and the Southern Kingdom fell to the Babylonians in 586 BCE. The Temple was destroyed, and the people of Judaea were also taken into exile, in Babylon.

The prophets interpreted these events of history as being the work of G-d. Some people had tried during this time to keep to the word of G-d, to turn their backs on the idol-worship and fertility religions of the cultures around them, and to deal fairly with the poor. However, many other Jews failed to keep either the moral or the religious commandments, and the prophets warned them of the inevitable destruction of the kingdoms as a result of their behaviour. The prophets interpreted current affairs, showing the people that G-d was in control of everything that happened, steering his people in his own ways, and rewarding and punishing according to his righteous judgement.

In the synagogue on Shabbat, and on other festivals and holy days, a passage from the Prophets is read, following the Torah reading. This is called the **Haftarah** portion, and the Haftarah portion is believed to 'complete' or 'finish' the reading of the Torah. These passages are related in some way to the Torah portion designated for the week. Unlike the Torah reading, which progresses through the Torah in a systematic way to ensure that the whole Torah is read during a calendar year, only a small section of the Prophets is read, each passage chosen because of its thematic relationship to the Torah reading.

Sometimes Jewish scriptures are bound into books called **chumash**, with the weekly parshah and appropriate Haftarah portions set out in the order in which they are read, to make it simpler for people to follow.

c) Writings

The Writings contain Psalms, Proverbs, Job, the 'five scrolls' or 'megillot' (the Song of Songs, Ruth, Lamentations, Ecclesiastes, and Esther), Daniel and Ezra – Nehemiah, and I and II Chronicles. They are believed to be inspired by the Holy Spirit; this is a lesser degree of inspiration than prophecy, which itself is less than the complete revelation of the Torah to Moses. Within the *ketuvim* are different forms of writings:

● Devotional works, such as the book of Psalms, used in later Jewish liturgy
● Historical writings, such as the books of Chronicles, and Ezra – Nehemiah
● Wisdom literature, such as the book of Ecclesiastes, written as a reflection on the puzzles of life
● Poetry, such as the Song of Songs, celebrating the gift of human love.

The writings, like the Prophets, are read not in a sequential way, but at times when the message or theme is in some way connected with the prescribed passage from the Torah.

Some passages are prescribed for particular festivals; for example, the Song of Solomon is read on the Shabbat of Passover week, the Book of Ruth on Shavuot because of its agricultural theme, and the book of Esther on Purim because of the narrative of the story.

2 Ethical monotheism

People are monotheists if they believe that there is only one G-d, who is distinct from the world and from everything else. The word 'holy' means separate, special, different and set apart; and for monotheists, G-d is absolutely distinct from everything else and is therefore holy. G-d does not inhabit natural objects, and is not a part of the universe in any way, but transcends it, and the world is his creation and subservient to him. The world is changeable and finite, whereas G-d is perfect and infinite. G-d is 'supranatural', rather than just supernatural, which means that he exists not only outside the natural world but also above it in the sense of being superior to it.

This belief is central and fundamental to Judaism. It is reaffirmed every day by Jews around the world when they recite the Shema:

Shema yisrael adonai eloheinu adonai ehad
Hear, O Israel, HASHEM is our G-d, Hashem is the One and Only.

Deuteronomy 6:4

It is not clear where this belief originated. In the Bible, according to some scholars, there are references which suggest that at one stage there may have been a belief in many G-ds, with the G-d of the Jews as a kind of tribal, national deity alongside other supernatural beings. In the Hebrew, G-d is often referred to as 'elohim', which is plural; and there are references to the G-ds of other nations:

> They journeyed from Rameses in the first month, on the fifteenth day of the first month — on the day after the pesach-offering — the Children of Israel went forth with an upraised hand, before the eyes of all Egypt. And the Egyptians were burying those among them whom HASHEM had struck, every firstborn; and on their gods HASHEM had inflicted punishments.
>
> *Numbers 33:3–4*

Whether these were believed to be real deities, or just the false beliefs of neighbouring people, is not always clear. Perhaps the people came only gradually to their monotheism, believing at first in a national deity and only later arriving at the realisation that the G-d of Israel was also the creator of the universe; but certainly the Jewish conviction of the unity of G-d was well established by the time of Deuteronomy:

> You shall know this day and take to your heart that HASHEM, He is G-d — in heaven above and on the earth below — there is none other.
>
> *Deuteronomy 4:39*

Ethical monotheism is the term used to indicate belief in one G-d, who is concerned with people's moral behaviour. The belief is that G-d sets the moral rules by which people should live, and judges them according to the ways in which they behave. G-d is the highest standard by which to measure what is good; something is good because G-d says so, there is no higher standard by which G-d might be judged to be wrong. G-d is perfectly good, the source of goodness itself. The correct response of people towards G-d is to find out the right ways to behave in different circumstances, and then to put the rules into practice. Moral behaviour is a form of worship, and to behave badly towards other people is indistinguishable from behaving badly towards G-d. It is also pointed out that, given that there is only one G-d and that all people are made 'in the image of G-d' (Genesis 1:27), then people are, in a sense, all united too as they reflect the unity of G-d. Loving G-d and loving one's neighbour are not two different commandments, but the second follows on automatically from the first.

In some systems of ethics, the individual is free to decide what is the right way to behave, and sometimes there is the view that the morality of an action depends on the circumstances and the society; something that is right for some people, some of the time, might be wrong at other times. In Judaism, the ethics are more absolute. There are rules for behaviour, laid down in the Torah, and the task of the Jew is to make sure that the rules are known and applied as well as they can be in everyday life. Of course there is the freedom to choose whether or not to obey the Law; but the Law remains the same, it does not change with circumstances or apply only to some situations and not to others.

The notion of a G-d who is the creator of the whole universe, who transcends nature and is utterly distinct from it, and yet who is interested in the behaviour of every individual, seems to create a paradox. Jewish mystics, rabbis and poets through the centuries have tried to find different ways of expressing their belief in a G-d who is at the same time holy and personal, while never abandoning the central principle of the unity of G-d. Many different metaphors have been used in attempts to express aspects of the nature of G-d: Creator, Rock, Friend, King of the Universe, the Eternal, the Unique. But Judaism always stresses that, even though people have to break down the concept of G-d into small parts so that their finite minds can cope with it, this does not mean that G-d himself is complex or made up of components. The perfection and simplicity of G-d's nature reveals itself in his unity.

a) A chosen people

In many places in the Jewish scriptures, the Jews are referred to as having a special and unique relationship with G-d, as the nation that has been chosen out of all the nations of the world to have unique responsibilities. In Exodus 19, for example, the Hebrews had been released from slavery in Egypt, and had travelled, under the leadership of Moses, through the wilderness until they reached Sinai. At Sinai, Moses had a direct encounter with G-d. Moses was told that the people were about to enter in a covenant relationship with G-d, and that they were to enter a special and exclusive relationship:

> Moses ascended to G-d, and HASHEM called to him from the mountain, saying, "So shall you say to the House of Jacob and relate to the Children of Israel. 'You have seen what I did to Egypt, and that I have borne you on the wings of eagles and brought you to Me. And now, if you hearken well to Me and observe My covenant, you shall be to Me the most beloved treasure of all peoples, for Mine is the entire world. You shall be to Me a kingdom of ministers and a holy nation.' These are the words that you shall speak to the Children of Israel."
>
> *Exodus 19:3–6*

The reason for the covenant relationship, then, is rooted in history. G-d has released his people from slavery, and this is something which they should remember. For Jews, this does not mean simply reading about the events leading up to the Exodus, as they happened to people long ago. It involves thinking and acting as though they themselves were actually there at the time. When the events of the

Exodus are remembered each year at Passover, Jews refer to how 'we' were brought out of slavery, including themselves in the group with their ancestors. They do not only retell stories of past events, but 'remember' them, using the word 'remember' as the opposite of 'dismember' – the events are put back together, reassembled, with each generation taking part. The chosen people were not just the individuals who were there at Sinai, but are also the Jewish community today. The phrase 'a chosen people' is a free translation of two Hebrew terms: *am segullah*, which means 'a treasured possession', and *am nahallah*, which means 'a heritage people'.

The people are promised that, on the condition that they obey G-d's voice and keep his covenant, they will become a 'treasured possession'. The Hebrew phrase here is *am segullah*, which is difficult to translate into English. If a child has a teddy bear to which it is extremely attached, and that teddy bear is taken everywhere, even when it has almost entirely disintegrated, then that teddy bear could be described as the child's *segullah*. It is more than something important; the relationship between the owner and the *segullah* is unique. In the Ancient Near East, the expression referred to the treasured possessions of the king, and was used in other cultures too, to include not only treasure in terms of gold and silver but also subservient nations of which the king was particularly proud.

The passage in Exodus points out that G-d is G-d of all the peoples of the world. He is not just the tribal G-d of the Jews, alongside other G-ds of other peoples, but the whole world belongs to him. Nevertheless he has chosen to single out one nation. They are to be a 'kingdom of priests'; the role of a priest is to mediate between G-d and the people, offering the sacrifices and making the prayers on behalf of everyone else, and the Jews as a nation are to have this role. They are to behave as priests; they will set an example for everyone else to follow. They have the responsibility of living out G-d's revelation to the rest of the world. They will be more pure in their conduct, because they will be allowed closer to G-d than others, just as the priest is allowed to go into holier places than the rest of a congregation. The standards set for them are more demanding than for other nations; they are to be a 'holy' nation – set apart, like G-d, and different from other people.

> See, I have taught you decrees and ordinances, as HASHEM, my G-d, has commanded me, to do so in the midst of the Land to which you come, to possess it. You shall safeguard and perform them, for it is your wisdom and discernment in the eyes of the peoples, who shall hear all these decrees and who shall say, "Surely a wise and discerning people is this great nation!" For which is a great nation that has a G-d Who is so close to it, as is Hashem, our G-d, whenever we call to Him? And which is a great nation that has righteous decrees and ordinances, such as this entire Torah that I place before you this day?
>
> *Deuteronomy 4:5–8*

The covenant relationship between G-d and his people meant that the people were to be faithful to G-d's commandments, and in return G-d would take special care of them and bless them. This has been a difficult concept for Jews; even in Biblical times, the 'chosen nation' were taken away into exile, and throughout history, they have been persecuted and pushed to the edge of destruction. Why, in view of their special status, were the Jews not protected by G-d against all enemies? The writings of the Exilic prophets, and of many others since, have struggled to come to an understanding of how keeping firm to the laws of G-d in the face of suffering is an essential aspect of the role of the chosen people. Suffering and persecution have come to be seen as a necessary consequence of the covenant, and even as evidence for it. Some of the explanations given for Jewish suffering point to the failures of the people to keep faithfully to the laws of G-d; because of his particular love for them, G-d has punished them, and if they succeed, like Job, in facing their sufferings with patience and faithfulness, then they will be worthy of G-d's special blessing. Because of their covenant relationship, they have been destined to be purified by suffering until the coming of the Messiah; and this belief has been one of the keys to Jewish morale and self-consciousness across the centuries.

b) Halakhah

Central to the whole idea of ethical monotheism is the concept of **halakhah**, or 'walking with G-d'. In the words of the prophet Micah:

> He has told you, O man, what is good! What does HASHEM require of you but to do justice, to love kindness and to walk humbly with your G-d.
>
> *Micah 6:8*

Jews seek to live a **halakhic** life, walking with G-d, following the route that G-d has prepared for them and keeping G-d with them as a travelling companion. But although devout Jews try to keep the commandments and follow the prescribed way of behaviour according to the Torah, there can be difficulties. What should they do if they encounter a circumstance where the Torah does not tell them what to do? What should they do if they follow the demands of the Torah, but their consciences tell them that they have only done the minimum and they want to do more? How can they know the right way to behave when questions arise in the context of modern culture, rather than the culture of Biblical times; for example, how can families ensure that their dishwashers are kosher?

These questions have given rise to an enormous amount of debate within Judaism. Ever since the beginning, rabbis have studied the Torah and discussed at length the different ways of interpreting the rules and principles found within it. The 'Oral Torah' which has resulted is a vast collection of interpretations of the written Torah, showing Jews how to understand the written laws and how to apply them in different situations. Orthodox Jews believe that G-d gave the Oral Law to Moses at the same time as he gave the written law, and that Moses taught it to others, who handed it on faithfully to subsequent generations as **rabbis** (teachers). Schools were founded for the study and transmission of the oral law, but there were often disagreements. Two of the most famous of the early rabbis were Hillel and Shammai, who lived and taught during the first century CE; they often disagreed about the interpretation of the Torah, and stories of their responses to difficult questions are a valued part of Jewish tradition.

c) Talmud

According to tradition, at Sinai, as well as receiving the written Pentateuch, Moses also received the **Mishnah** and the **Gemara**, which together form what is known as the **Talmud**. The oral tradition of interpreting the written law was kept as a word of mouth transmission until about the second century CE, when it was felt that there was a need to keep a written record of the discussions. The lives of Jewish people were changing; in particular, there was contact with Hellenism (Greek influence) and the Roman Empire, which presented the Jews with a completely different way of understanding the world and morality. The people had been used to living an agricultural existence, but now they were moving towards city living, and new situations and difficulties arose which the Torah did not address.

The oral tradition was growing all the time, and it was difficult for people to remember which opinions had been given, by whom, and what the outcome of different discussions had been. With the growth of the oral tradition, there was a corresponding drop in the number of Jews knowledgeable enough to pass it on reliably, because the Jewish Revolt of 69/70 CE and the later Bar Kochba Rebellion in 135 CE had resulted in many deaths, especially among the Jews who took their religion particularly seriously. Rabbi Judah Hanasi (135–217 CE) a leading scholar and figure of religious authority, decided that the time had come to commit the oral teachings to writing, and the Mishnah (the name meaning 'repetition') was formed. It was a record of most of the oral traditions that had been repeated by word of mouth up until this point, collected together and edited by Hanasi.

The Mishnah is divided into six sections, called **sedarim**, which are further subdivided, and which give rules for every aspect of life at the time of the second century, so that Jews could use it as a reference and look up anything that they wanted to know:

1. **Zera'im** (seeds) – this section contains the agricultural rules of Palestine, explaining the laws about produce brought to the Temple in Jerusalem, appropriate blessings to use, and the proportions of crops which should be left for the poor to glean.
2. **Mo'ed** (holy days) – this tells Jews how to celebrate Passover, Purim, Rosh Hashanah, Yom Kippur, Sukkot and Shavuot.
3. **Nashim** (women) – this section deals with laws related to marriage, for example who may marry whom, and the rules relating to widows and to divorce.
4. **Nezikin** (damages) – this covers Jewish civil and criminal law, for example how to conduct a case in court, and how to decide on appropriate methods of dealing with offenders.
5. **Kodashim** (holy things) – this section contains the rules connected with sacrifices and ritual slaughter.
6. **Taharot** (purities) – this explains the things that can cause a person to be ritually impure, and the ways of becoming pure again.

However, even after the completion of the Mishnah, people still found that they needed a commentary in order to apply the principles of halakhah to their own circumstances. The rabbis discussed the Torah and the Mishnah, studying them carefully in an attempt to make sure that if complicated situations arose, they could still advise people to do the right thing. Eventually, the discussion of the rabbis was also written down, and is known as the **Gemara**, which means 'completion'. The Gemara is not a separate document but is written alongside the Mishnah, as an annotation of it, so that when people are studying it they can see the point that was raised and the reasons for differences of opinion. This combination of Mishnah and Gemara is known as the Talmud, from the Hebrew verb l-m-d, 'to study' or 'to teach'. In fact, two Talmuds were formed, one in Palestine in around 400 CE and one in Babylon a hundred years later; the Babylonian Talmud came to be regarded as the more authoritative. It is sometimes known as the 'second Scripture' of Judaism, a body of literature which Jewish parents hope their children will one day want to study as a career, in a **yeshiva** or Jewish academy. The Talmud is an extraordinary piece of literature, a vast collection of discussions and opinions; although the final decision on an issue is given, the fact that the minority view is also preserved in writing leaves the way open for further discussion and future debate should the need arise.

Most of the contents of the Talmud provide a commentary on the ways in which to keep the Law, how to walk with G-d; and this type of writing is referred to as Halakhah. The rest of the Talmud relates to the parts of the Torah which were not law but which told the story: of creation, Noah, Abraham, Joseph and so on. The story-line, as well as the Law, also has its commentary and points of discussion, and is known as Agadah. The narrative and its commentary illustrate for

Jews how keeping or disobeying the Law works out in practice, by looking at examples of Biblical figures.

Other books, too, apart from the Talmud, contain Agadah, and these are known as **Midrash** or 'searching out', because they scrutinise the stories of the Torah in an effort to uncover every message and illustration that has a bearing on Jewish life.

Study of the Torah, the Talmud, the Midrash and other forms of Jewish literature have always played an important and valued part in Jewish life. Academies of Jewish learning, known as **yeshivot**, have discussed and regulated Jewish life for centuries. Rabbis and scholars gather to search the scriptures, to memorise, and to work out the meanings and application of Jewish traditions for everyday life.

3 Ethical monotheism and modern Judaism

Jews in the modern world have a wide range of beliefs about how ethical monotheism should affect their lives and behaviour. For some Jews, the demands and temptations of modern living are incompatible with the teachings of the Torah. This can mean that they choose to have as little contact as they can with modern life; the Torah is perfect, and therefore if society moves away from its demands, it is the society which has to be rejected. Some ultra-Orthodox Jews keep themselves very separate from the world and the trappings of modern living, keeping to the letter of the Torah and its surrounding traditions. They believe that it is impossible to separate the ethical and the ritual laws; all are commanded by G-d, and it is not for people to decide that some are more important than others. Being obedient to G-d as the chosen people involves keeping all the laws unquestioningly, not abandoning some and only observing a few.

Other Jews find that, because they live in modern times, they should try to do so, and they aim to find a way of accommodating their Jewish beliefs with the pressures of everyday secular society. Some, perhaps, feel that the detailed laws of ritual food and dress are inappropriate to modern life, and they believe that the main ethical principles of Judaism should be the focus for behaviour. Belief in one G-d, and concern for other people, should for some Jews take priority over keeping a kosher kitchen or reciting the prescribed blessings.

Applying Jewish rules in modern Western society can be very difficult. What opinions should a Jew hold about GM foods, or surrogate motherhood? Are the new medicines the doctor has prescribed kosher? Do the things forbidden on the Sabbath because they are 'work' still have to be avoided even now that people have machines to do these tasks for them?

The need for a constant updating of the application of the Torah has existed even since Biblical times. Ezra, who was a leader of the Jewish community who returned to the Promised Land after the

Babylonian Exile, found himself having to interpret the law for changed circumstances:

> For Ezra set his heart to expound the Torah of HASHEM and to fulfil and to teach [its] statute and law in Israel.
>
> *Ezra 7:10*

The tradition of **responsa** began about a thousand years ago, which has given rise to another form of Jewish literature: *she'elot uteshuvot*, or 'questions and answers'. Questions were, and still are, addressed to rabbis who are believed to have expertise in Jewish legal matters, and some of these have been recorded in writings which give a fascinating insight into the ways in which Jews have conducted their daily lives over the years.

In modern societies, where there is a Jewish population large enough to support it, there is a **Bet Din**, or rabbinic court, where three rabbis of suitable character and experience make decisions about matters arising in modern Jewish life, for those Jews who want to take it seriously. Difficult questions about whether non-Jews should be allowed to convert to Judaism and whether divorces should proceed are debated and decisions are taken, and rulings are made about kosher food and practices. If someone wishes to introduce a new flavour of ice-cream suitable for Jewish consumers, or wants to open a hotel that will attract observant Jews, the Bet Din will be called upon to carry out the necessary checks and give the seal of approval.

Practice examination questions

1. a) Explain what is meant by 'ethical monotheism'. (33 marks)
   b) 'The Talmud is essential for an understanding of Jewish Law.' Discuss. (17 marks)

Guide

In part (a), you need to be able to explain Jewish beliefs in one G-d, and the relation between this belief and human moral behaviour. You might be able to use some short quotations from the Bible in order to illustrate your answer. You could contrast monotheism with other forms of belief, and explain how morality and belief are intertwined in Judaism. In part (b), you should assess the importance of the Talmud for Jews. You might look at the ways in which the Talmud is used and studied; you could also consider the extent to which people were able to understand the Jewish Law before the Talmud came into existence.

2. a) Explain why the first five books of the Bible have more importance for Jews than any other literature. (33 marks)
   b) 'Believing that they are a chosen nation has more advantages than disadvantages for the Jews.' Discuss. (17 marks)

Guide

In part (a) you should show that you understand the nature of the Torah, and its centrality to Jewish life. You will probably want to explain the origins of the Torah as coming directly from G-d, in contrast with other forms of literature, and you could consider the implications of this for Judaism. In part (b), you are asked to evaluate the role of the 'chosen nation'. As well as showing that you know what this means, you are asked for advantages and disadvantages, and so you need to think about what these might be. Remember that you are asked to weigh the advantages against the disadvantages, and not just list some without comment.

Suggestions for further reading

C. M. Pilkington, *Teach Yourself Judaism* (Hodder & Stoughton, 2000)
Jonathan Magonet, *The Explorer's Guide to Judaism* (Hodder & Stoughton, 1998)

CHESTER COLLEGE LIBRARY

Index